Other recent books by Clive Bloom

CULT FICTION: Popular Reading and Pulp Theory

GOTHIC HORROR: A Reader's Guide from Poe to King and Beyond (*editor*)

LITERATURE, POLITICS AND INTELLECTUAL CRISIS IN BRITAIN TODAY

Bestsellers: Popular Fiction Since 1900

Clive Bloom

First published 2002 by
PALGRAVE MACMILLAN
Houndmills, Basingstoke, Hampshire RG21 6XS and
175 Fifth Avenue, New York, NY 10010
Companies and representatives throughout the world

PALGRAVE MACMILLAN is the global academic imprint of the Palgrave Macmillan division of St. Martin's Press, LLC and of Palgrave Macmillan Ltd. Macmillan® is a registered trademark in the United States, United Kingdom and other countries. Palgrave is a registered trademark in the European Union and other countries.

ISBN 0–333–68742–6 hardcover
ISBN 0–333–68743–4 paperback

This book is printed on paper suitable for recycling and made from fully managed and sustained forest sources.

A catalogue record for this book is available from the British Library.

Library of Congress Cataloging-in-Publication Data

Bloom, Clive.
    Bestsellers : popular fiction since 1900 / Clive Bloom.
        p.   cm.
    Includes bibliographical references (p.) and index.
    ISBN 0–333–68742–6 (hardcover)
    1. English fiction – 20th century – History and criticism.   2. Popular literature – Great Britain – History and criticism.   3. Books and reading – Great Britain – History – 20th century.   4. Best sellers – Great Britain – Bibliography.   I. Title.
    PR888.P68 B58 2002
    823'.9109 – dc21

2002020886

10   9   8   7   6   5   4   3   2   1
11   10   09   08   07   06   05   04   03   02

Printed and bound in Great Britain by
Antony Rowe Ltd, Chippenham and Eastbourne

Contents

Preface

Across the first seventy years of the twentieth century few records were kept of best-selling fiction, its authors, its readers, its production or its distribution. Those records that were kept were tidied away into box files and ledgers and left to gather dust until Hitler's bombs or American university bulk buying reduced them to an ashy or archival destiny. Only in the last quarter of the century did proper records, centrally available, make sense of the jumble of information that made up the bestseller market, and those were somewhat contradictory at best, given the guarded nature of accounting.

Many hours of research often brought to light problems to which there was no immediate solution – the record remaining fragmentary. Research into the history of publishing is now a thriving, if slightly esoteric, branch of literary history, but the literary history of the bestseller is in fact embryonic. Yet to undertake such a work is to gain an insight into one of the popular arts of an entire nation over a hundred years. To achieve this one cannot work alone and I am happily obliged to acknowledge a veritable army of researchers, helpers and well-wishers without whom this book would not have appeared. They are, in no particular order: Lynette Grypp; Ron Sutsko; Alison Main; Theresa Urbanic; Scott Eden; Meagen Ryan; Amy Crawford; Margaret Walsh; Courtney K. Sosnowski; Renée Ireton; Kimberley K. McGhay; Colleen Crowley; Kelly G. Puzio; Alexandra Matthews; Christina Grace; Laura Haden; Kristina Zurcher; Adam Manella; Denise M. Krotzer; Edward Dawson; Karen Lorenz; Annie Thompson; Anne Anderson; Allyson Luck; Meggan Newland; Kristina Peterson; Colleen Conway; Erin Kappler; Ed Dawson; Melissa Radey; Kathleen Scheibel; Kristen Doyle; Laura Anne Weiler; Courtney McDonough; Frank Chetalo; Katie Caspersen; Meghan Fitzgerald; Ryan Furmick; Tom Moran; Janine Bemasere; Sheryl Hahn; Tonya Lentzo; Marty Moran; Kathleen Sclef; Lindsey Hamilton; Lesley Belden; Beth Wladyka; Shaye Loughlin; Tara Lynn Jewett; Nora Mahoney; Malin Stearns; Sara Jost; Corinne Mahoney; Andrea Allocco; Allison Fashek; Jeffrey J. Harrington; Beth A. Burau; Anna Kosse; Colin Langan; Kristin Lutz; James Pastore; Jennifer Wellman; Jaime Ullinger; Jessica Fries; Annie Moses; Sarah Balzli; Heather Waigand; Kathryn A. Koch; Megan Griffin; Katherine Breitenbach; Laura Bastedo; Sarah Seidel; Claire Dampeer; Lori Delaney.

Particular thanks are due to Maxim Jakubowski of Murder One; author Tim Hardy; Bill Edwards at Labour Force; Amanda Campbell at Sheffield Central Library; Julia Strong at the National Library Trust; Louis Jardon at the DfEE Standard and Effectiveness Unit; Susan Ridge at the Registrar of Public Lending Right; John Nicholson of the Small Press Group. I am especially grateful to Helena Blakemore who helped compile some of the author information in the middle section of this volume. Helena wrote Appendix 10. Further thanks must go to Tony Kenley, Yasmin Kenley, Lesley Bloom, Farah Mendlesohn and my editors Eleanor Birne and Emily Rosser at Palgrave Macmillan; also to Steve Holland, Mike Ashley and John Clute. As always my thanks to Valery Rose and Jocelyn Stockley. I am grateful to the Arts and Humanities Research Board, which helped fund part of this research.

A number of booksellers gave time and information, including: Books Etc.; Blackwell's; Foyles; Silver Moon Women's Bookshop (now sadly closed); Waterstone's; W. H. Smith. Publishers also gave time to be interviewed, including: Harlequin Mills and Boon Ltd; Pan-Macmillan Publishing; Robinson Ltd; and Virgin. Boots the Chemists and Harrods were kind enough to supply information about their lending libraries.

Like all research this book remains provisional, a partial guide to the popular literary taste of a nation. It is a map of reading and as such may guide others to answers that I have missed, for which I hope it will prove helpful. It has been compiled from a number of sources: publishers' records; booksellers' accounts; library records; the pages of the *Bookseller*; Mass Observation; advertising notices; miscellaneous ephemeral sources; scholarly studies; market research conducted commercially as well as by academics; personal interviews. It is, nevertheless, intended as more than the sum of its parts. What is intended is not only to provide the most complete record so far of best-selling fiction in Britain but also to offer the sense of a cultural, sociological and aesthetic context, a landscape of one type of curiously specific phenomenon of recent times: the bestseller.

Acknowledgements

The author is grateful to the Curtis Brown Group Ltd, London, on behalf of the Trustees of the Mass Observation Archive, University of Sussex, for permission to quote from 'Mass Observation Report: Reading in Tottenham, Nov. 1947' (FR 2537); to Philip Jones and the *Bookseller* (www.theBookseller.com) for permission to quote from its web page (20 December 1999); to Brian Stableford for permission to quote from his article 'Robert Hichens and *The Garden of Allah*', *Million*, no. 3 (May–June 1992); to Wendy Bradley for permission to quote from her article 'Judith Krantz', *Million*, no. 2 (March–April 1991); and to David Pringle of *Million* for general permission to quote from the journal. The information regarding Joan Collins was originally published in Clive Bloom, *Literature, Politics and Intellectual Crisis in Britain Today* (Basingstoke: Palgrave Macmillan, 2000).

For Jonathan, James and Sasha

1
Origins, Problems and Philosophy of the Bestseller

'Why then,' said the Tinker, 'it's true I mends kettles, sharpens scissors and such, but I likewise peddles books an' nov-els, an' what's more I reads 'em – so, if you must put me in your book, you might call me a literary cove.'

(Jeffrey Farnol, *The Broad Highway*, ch. 1)

In the mid-nineteenth century it caused surprise and slight consternation, like being caught doing something a little embarrassing. So it was when a visitor to one of London's political clubs saw the Prime Minister, W. E. Gladstone, sitting quietly in a corner engrossed, not in some work of political or philosophical importance but in a romantic novel, *Red as a Rose is She*. By the early twentieth century the whole business of fiction was almost respectable, its authors the latest in celebrities: interviewed, photographed and fêted by critics and readers alike. The *Strand Magazine* in search of amusing anecdotes for its August edition of 1906 could not resist a paragraph or two on the relative stature of some of the great lights in fiction-writing over the previous quarter of a century. There, as expected, were Dickens and Thackeray, not quite as popular as in previous years but still pre-eminent. Behind them, however, was Thomas Hall Caine, a writer whose popularity between the 1890s and 1920 made him fabulously rich and gained him a knighthood. Looking back over their friendship Bram Stoker, himself the author of *Dracula* (1897), recalled of Caine,

The man exhausts himself in narrative as I have never seen with anyone else. Indeed when he had finished a novel he used to seem as exhausted as a woman after childbirth. At such times he would be

1

in a terrible state of nerves – trembling and sleepless. At that very time he had not quite got through the nervous crisis after completion of *The Bondman*. At such times everything seemed to worry him; things that he would shortly after laugh at.[1]

Caine's *The Bondman*, issued in three volumes (from January 1890) and circulated through the subscription lending libraries, ensured his fame and fortune for thirty years and made him Heinemann's best-selling author with sales of over a million. Yet, bestsellerdom was also a curse and in less than a decade of his death his books were dust, along with his reputation.

So it was with the most popular female author, Marie Corelli, whose origins as plain Mary Mackay did not stop her claiming an exotic Italian pedigree. If she disparaged the 'twaddle' of her plots, Corelli nevertheless knew that her fame stood on the firm foundations of that exoticism, eroticism, spiritualism and anti-materialism beloved of ordinary shop girls (as critical snobs correctly but snidely suggested).

From the early twentieth century onwards the author was an authority – on healthy, spiritual wellbeing and moral uprightness; someone whose views on life would be as important as her words on the page. Writing of her success in 1894, Corelli would emphasise her sincerity and her genuine desire to speak to her readers 'heart to heart' and on their own terms:

> I have had no difficulty in making my career or winning my public. And I attribute my good fortune to the simple fact that I have always tried to write straight from my own heart to the hearts of others, regardless of opinions and indifferent to results. My object in writing has never been, and will never be, to concoct a mere story which shall bring me a certain amount of cash or notoriety, but solely because I wish to say something which, be it ill or well said, is the candid and independent expression of a thought which I . . . have uttered. . . . *A Romance of Two Worlds* . . . was the simply-worded narration of a singular psychological experience, and included certain theories on religion which I, personally speaking, accept and believe. I had no sort of literary pride in my work whatsoever; there was nothing of self in the wish I had, that my ideas, such as they were, should reach the public, for I had no particular need of money, and certainly no hankering after fame.[2]

Such thoughts would echo through women's fiction throughout the next century whether the author was Florence Barclay, Ethel Dell or

Barbara Cartland, and as with all three of Corelli's followers it would be the complete identification of author's life with writer's fiction that would hold readers' attention in enraptured fascination. The cult of the author had arrived and Corelli's portrait, doctored and flatteringly retouched as she aged, adorned her works, which, since the extraordinary success of *The Sorrows of Satan* (1895), sold around 100,000 copies each year before World War One (approximately twice as many as Hall Caine). After her death in 1924 Corelli too was abandoned by her 'fans', and was remembered, if at all, by later generations as little more than a late Victorian curiosity.

If Marie Corelli and Hall Caine were all but forgotten (and certainly unread) by the end of the twentieth century they had nevertheless laid the foundation for the modern bestseller. Phenomenally successful sales could still be generated by authors whose interests were sentimental, sensational and supernatural, authors such as Stephen King, the biggest selling American writer of all time.

King's career had begun in the mid-1970s with the publication of *Carrie* (1974), a work that revisited and revised the horror genre. By the 1980s, King's work dominated the genre and, indeed, dominated bestseller lists. An extraordinary work rate included novels, short stories and film scripts, and, during 1999, an excursion into the Internet. The possibilities offered by the Internet had certainly not been lost on the publishing world or on its authors. King issued his first self-published 'e-book', *The Plant*, late in 1999. In the first week 152,000 fans downloaded the first section. Previously, working with publisher Simon and Schuster, King had earned nearly half a million dollars (in five days) for his e-book *Riding the Bullet*, although collecting the fees proved more difficult. Such authors provide the basis for our subject.

This book is about the history of bestsellers since 1900. It is confined to best-selling fiction rather than covering all literary production – which would have had to include the extraordinary popularity of cookery books, self-help manuals, gardening advice, books on the occult and a whole range of ephemeral production. As it is, a study of best-selling *fiction* of the last hundred years is still a daunting task and it has had to be further restricted by not including children's fiction.

The proposal then is to look at best-selling *adult* fiction, an apparently simple task requiring a basic command of sales figures and story outlines. I am conscious, however, that the division between adult and children's fiction has recently been under sustained assault by authors and publishers whose readership is usually considered too young for certain forms of content such as pornography or violence, for instance. An increase in 'mature' content has suggested that hard and fast divisions may lack credibility and indeed it is quite obvious that works of classic literature may be read by children prior to their acquaintance with contemporary works written explicitly for a younger readership. The award of the 2002 Whitbread Prize to Philip Pullman for his children's book *The Amber Spyglass* muddied divisions even further, a situation reinforced by novelist Anne Fine's 'definition of a children's book as one that is ideally met for the first time in childhood' (*The Times*, 23 January 2002). Such comments remain, despite media hype, and despite the repackaging of such authors as J. K. Rowling or Pullman for a dual readership, merely disingenuous as it is quite obvious that most fiction aimed at children (or younger people) is *not* intended for any other market.

The works of Philip Pullman, Anne Fine or J. K. Rowling appeal across age ranges because young people and adults now share a simultaneously experienced popular culture – a multi-channelled and complex space where hierarchic experiential priorities no longer apply. Children have become more knowing and aware (not necessarily less naïve) while adults have struggled to 'know' less, nostalgic for their own lost innocence, destroyed too soon in an age of information overload. What unites such groups is the search for a new cosmology (without God) which will offer certainty (as well as adventure) and a new morality based on a 'one world' philosophy.

These developments are a recent phenomenon, in which children's literature suddenly appeals to those searching for 'real' literary qualities and to panels of expert judges desperate to award headline-winning trophies. Meanwhile, popular genre writers have *always* appealed to young readers and were always considered 'immature' by readers who were antagonistic towards popular culture. Until very recently children's fiction was different *in kind* from adult fiction (J. R. R. Tolkien's *Lord of the Rings* trilogy was itself aimed at adults) and this division I have retained as historically valid. Such an obvious approach proves, ironically, to offer limited interest or enlightenment unless it is contextualised within the sociology of reading, the production history of print and the aesthetic ideology of fiction itself. In providing meaningful contexts for fiction in the last hundred years we lend depth to our story but also create extraordinary problems for our investigations in attempting to bridge interpretative gaps and statistical confusions. Best-selling fiction gives us an insight into the modes and methods of literary production (both as aesthetic object and as commodity) and perceptual history (the needs and interests of readers); it provides a unique insight into the imaginative history of a nation over a one-hundred-year period.

This book takes as its rough starting date the year 1900 although it is clear that many writers of the nineteenth century continued to enjoy popularity long into the twentieth. The end of World War One also suggests a starting point as tensions inside the book trade and readers' demands brought younger and more daring writers to the fore; this, for instance, is the era when the women's romance, which dominated much of the publishing industry, came into its own – codified and organised into a self-contained world by the 1930s.

Dates do not coincide with attitudes or habits and so our start date remains but a guide to those changes in publishing, authorship, genre and reading that come to dominate the modern era. By the same token, a date such as 2002 hardly accounts in any significant way for genres and reading demands that may continue many years into the twenty-first century. Thus the twentieth century may be 'longer' at both its opening and its end. Nevertheless, the opening date of 1900 and the terminal date of 'the present' are not just a convenient short-hand, because they do frame the significant and specific changes in fictional bestsellerdom that this book takes as its subject.

And the last hundred years are not just any of a number of periods that could have been chosen. They form *the* century of literary production and consumption, the supremely *literate* century, in which, despite radio, film, television, computers, videos, CDs, tapes, and the rise of interactive technology, more books (i.e. more printed material) are consumed by a greater number of people who speak and read English than at any other time in history. We live, despite fears about illiteracy, in *the* age of reading when books are more freely available and far cheaper than at any other time, and where their disposability has only increased their proliferation, in schools, in homes, and in libraries. We may no longer treasure books, we may no longer live in an age where print is the supreme expressive form (for information and for entertainment), but we do live in an age where print is more pervasive than ever and where authorship is very big business. An archaeology of best-selling fiction is ironically, for an age supposedly dominated by the visual image, an archaeology of a deeply literate age.

Even in the twenty-first century books remain the most reliable, efficient, accessible and easily disposable sources of information available, reliant neither on electrical nor chemical sources of energy. Moreover, their contents are enhanced rather than diminished by other media, which support rather than detract from the power of books to enthral the imagination. Whatever the next century holds for print it is certain that in the last century fictional *literary* imagination pervaded every corner of social life: central to entertainment as well as to ideas. Literary fiction continues to be plundered for theatre, film, radio, television and computer games and each, in turn, modifies and renews literary fiction for the insatiable appetite of a literate public. Film versions of *Harry Potter and the Philosopher's Stone* and *Lord of the Rings* dominated the box office during 2001 and, alongside sales of all sorts of associated merchandise, renewed interest in the authors and their books in a continuous loop of production.

How then might we define a bestseller? In theory the answer is simple: the work of fiction sold in the most units (books in a given price range) to the most people over a set period of time. In practice the answer is extremely complex, running into difficulties as to the definition of units (hardback; paperback; serialisation) and period of time (month of publication; a year; the twentieth century), the importance of the price at which it is sold (significance of cost of hardback or paperback) and the definition of fiction itself (whether the work is literary, popular, pulp).

All this is compounded by an extraordinary lack of evidence. Paper records of sales did not get collated for statistical and comparative purposes until the late 1970s, leaving over seventy years of company records all of which were kept without regard to posterity, were destroyed in company changes or the destruction of the Blitz, or were shipped out to lie uncatalogued in American universities. Still others are left to us incomplete or without commentary or explanation, the clerks long since dead. And, of course, I refer here to only the main publishing houses, rather than the myriad smaller publishers whose output often outshone (in terms of sales) their major rivals but whose commercial life was brief, usually provincial, and ended abruptly by bankruptcy or censorship and often with the destruction of stock and records: 'husband and wife' concerns catering for working-class entertainment or juvenile thrills. What is left is an archaeology of a recent *industrial* and *commercial* past without care for future enquiry. Where contemporary records are complete they remain secrets locked within the publishing company for fear of competition, or, if a bookseller is approached, either the records reflect a paranoiac distrust of scholarly enquiry or, if an answer is provided, it gives only a vague 'sense' of what sells best at any particular location. Publishers, book-selling managers and local librarians seem still to act upon personal instinct rather than relying on marketing (and therefore statistical and particular) studies, or, where such studies are available, they remain limited to a particular campaign or local need. Most often records remain secret and unavailable.

Until very recently (the last twenty years of the twentieth century) little could be proved with certainty about what sold best, which authors were most popular or who read what or why. That this is the case does not allow us to abdicate our responsibility to try to gather what evidence exists, for this evidence is the best we will be able to gather if we wish to put together a picture of the British literary imagination.

What types of books, authors, and genres must we then include? As already stated, this study specifically excludes works aimed at children, but it certainly includes authors who, some would argue, were initially juvenile in content and read by juveniles in practice. I have included discussion of this where appropriate. I have also excluded 'classic' writers who died before the twentieth century began. In one sense this is arbitrary in terms of bestsellerdom. It is clear that Jane Austen's works sold many more copies in the twentieth century than in the whole of the nineteenth and certainly in her own lifetime; Dickens sells as many books now as during his own lifetime and George Eliot still has a readership even if it might be largely academic. These writers remain bestsellers, often outselling modern authors, either because of their popularity (boosted by films, television serialisations, etc.) or because of special circumstances (being required school or college reading). Whether such books are still read in the same way as in the century in which the authors lived is another matter entirely. Equally, schoolbooks may be sold in large numbers but never read.

By all accounts the classic authors, the authors of the English canon, remain bestsellers with no real threat of diminishment. On the threshold of the twenty-first century Jane Austen remains a bestseller. More finely put, only *now* is she a bestseller, with all that that entails, and only in this century does it make sense to talk of her and her works as such (she is both celebrity and writer). With all that, and notwithstanding what I have just said, pre-twentieth-century writers who died before 1900 have been *excluded* from the current study.

The problem repeats itself in an acute and problematic sense at the other end of the literary spectrum – the 'pulp' end, of anonymous and multiple authorship and 'mushroom' publishing. It is in this area that the most frantic and urgent scholarly and amateur investigations have occurred, especially into the censorship and suppression of the presses and authors involved. Pseudonymous authorship, especially at this level of literary production, was and is almost *de rigueur*, the opposite of the cult of the author in 'serious' fiction. Here more than anywhere else, hearsay, rumour and memory often stand in for production records and printed testimony. Authors even forget which books they wrote and under what name! Libraries banned their work wholesale from establishments, and shop libraries, lending at 2d a book, have all vanished as if they never existed. What remained, at least until recently, was nostalgic anecdote, now bolstered in part by amateur scholarship into particular 'lost' authors and publishing houses (usually family printer/distributors). Even this work (this archaeology by metal detector) has relied on anecdote and unreliable claims. Much of the output of this process has long gone unnoticed except by collectors of cult material, and has been considered (even by most of its readers) as a subliterature unworthy of serious attention. So much of this material is now yellowing and crumbling, unworthy of the library shelf, but once it was read to death by numerous readers considered illiterate by their betters.

As for its authors, they might be part-timers or journeyman workers who never felt themselves 'authors' in the literary sense, but wrote nevertheless for a living or part of a living and abandoned writing when things got better, or they went on to literary work and quickly forgot their past. Others simply died forgotten. Yet even though much of this output outsold conventional books in numbers large enough to register as bestsellers they sold through methods and to readers which together guaranteed obscurity; best forgotten as an embarrassment. These books too, however, must be recorded amongst the world of bestsellers if justice is to be done to the myriad authors who never made a legitimate bestseller list and who never appeared in a literary review except to be condemned, but who nevertheless, through paperback and magazine, created a subcultural bestsellerdom of ideologically and morally unsound imaginative fiction, created by and for a literary underclass.

And thus the problem of literacy becomes cultural. The question of who could read and at what level of skill provides both a general and a specific context for the study of best-selling (i.e. mass) fiction. The general context requires some knowledge of reading skills among different groups and reading trends in the population across regions and historical time. It will also tell us about changes in competence since the reform of education after 1870. Literacy competence and literary

competence are also two different things regulated by hierarchical relationships of class and gender played out in the English lessons of
schools across Britain. Illiteracy then ceases to be merely a *technical*
question but is rather one determined by a moral–medical ethic which
covers everything from simple incompetence or mental laziness, to a
biological dysfunction (dyslexia), to a general dislike of another group's
reading matter (romance, adventure, comic books). These questions are
often hierarchic in nature and moral in character. This is especially true
in the change of attitude towards illiteracy.

The main beneficiaries of the growing literacy, especially as it related
to fiction, were women. Professional attitudes to authorship had long
been a feature amongst middle-class female writers and novel reading
(as a frivolous pastime) was seen by commentators as typically 'female',
readership actually being largely made up of middle- and upper-class
women anyway. As the twentieth century began, working-class women
and newer groups of middle-class housewives or female office workers
needed books to read at home and while commuting, whilst seaside
breaks would be accompanied by a romantic novelette (of roughly
15,000 to 20,000 words, priced at 2d ['tuppence'] and presented in
paperback form). From the 1920s onwards there were specialised
women's journals and papers (aimed at different classes and ages), specialised forms of fiction (novelettes) and specialised genres (romance,
family saga), all directly appealing to women unattracted by the
sportspapers and hobbybooks of their male companions. It is still the
case that many more women consume fiction than men and that
women buy and borrow more of it and read it more frequently, and that
this seems a permanent tendency already almost two hundred years old!
At the end of the twentieth century women had also finally risen to
positions of importance in the editorial side of publishing, even if men
still dominated the industry in senior management. It goes without
saying that many of the top-selling fiction authors of the twentieth
century were women, writing in almost all genres, that their success was
and remains due to a female readership, and that women authors will
continue to maintain this position.

The general context of gender interests and literacy (the ability to read
sequentially with understanding) had a direct and specific influence on
aesthetic change in literary production between the late 1880s and the
beginning of the First World War. The vast new pool of readers created
by elementary education produced a huge new market for literary entertainment and printed information. These new readers from the working
and lower middle classes wanted entertainment and escape above all.

For their social 'betters' the literacy of these new readers was little more than a new illiteracy and thus the conceptual framework of literacy (technical and social) subtly shifted to separate the classes. It made illegitimate much of mass public taste. Illiterates were now not only people without reading and writing skills but also those whose reading habits and tastes did not match those of a more educated class. Illiteracy was to become both a metaphor for cultural degeneracy and a 'technical' term for incompetence. The very subject matter of popular reading was denigrated as trivia for the half-educated – 'bread and circuses' for those who still could not be trusted with the vote, the greatest number of whom were women.

The publishing world had been modernising before the beginning of compulsory elementary education. By the 1860s publishers were able to take advantage of modern financing arrangements and long-term investments, new forms of rapid distribution (railways) and new opportunities for marketing (library purchase, serialisation, part works, cheap editions). By the 1880s the publishing world had become a publishing industry, still run, to be sure, as a quasi-gentleman's club, but nevertheless run on determinedly *commercial* lines (morality happily coincided with the market). Mudie's, Boots and other commercial libraries fed the appetite of the middle-class reader whilst penny and sixpenny 'paperbacks' and 'chapbooks' kept workers happy. There was a publishing mode for all classes and both genders. From the 1880s, and fixed by the time of the First World War, there was a mass literacy both general and regulated, divided and subdivided into markets and specialised groups. These markets demanded fictions both diverse and plentiful with consequences that were far reaching for both authorship and subject matter.

The middle nineteenth century saw the role of writer turn into the modern concept of professional author. Heralded by Charles Dickens, Wilkie Collins and Mrs Braddon, the nature of authorship became intricately entwined with that of commercial enterprise: the author as entrepreneur. For all intents and purposes, and despite the appearance of authors who were celebrities (see below), authorship before the last quarter of the nineteenth century fell mainly into two categories – either one was an anonymous hack producing broadsheets and chapbooks or one was an anonymous 'lady' or 'gentleman' whose interest in fiction might be serious but was essentially that of a dedicated amateur (this was no reflection on artistic competence). Notwithstanding Jane Austen's famous defence of the novel in *Northanger Abbey*, it took until mid-century for a concept of authorship to become common amongst practitioners in which the production of contemporary vernacular fiction could be viewed as more than a rather unwholesome living. For aristocratic and upper middle-class authors in the nineteenth century, fiction-writing was little less than trade and little more than a diversion with a possible hint of immoral earnings to boot.

Such writers would never put a name to a work, leaving publishers no option but to advertise by association: 'by the author of' taking the place of the author's true identity. Readers soon understood and waited for the next book 'by the author of'. It was to be the end of the nineteenth century before such authors would allow their names to appear and even then, long into the twentieth century, upper-class writers might hide their name behind a pseudonym. 'Q', for instance, hid the real name of the Edward VII Professor of English at Cambridge, Sir Arthur Quiller-Couch, and Eric Blair adopted an alter ego from a Suffolk River – the Orwell; 'Ouida' hid the real identity of Louise Ramée (d. 1908).

Pseudonymous names were also adopted by middle-class or working-class authors either to create glamour or to offer the opportunity to write different genres under different names. Thus we find writers who adopt exotic or tough-guy nomenclature, writers who adopt a single name (a favourite during the 1930s and 1940s amongst military writers) or use initials to hide either their gender or their usual profession (as a disguise for a vicar or social reformer). At the 'novelette' end of the market, a small publisher might use a house name under which numerous writers would produce work, or a series of house names for their different lists. Even in the late 1990s, this practice, in various degrees and guises, still existed – especially in the appearance of best-selling female pornography written by 'a lady' or 'anon', or when an author was known for working under two names in two distinct (or sometimes similar) genres. In all cases, the author's name took on the potency of a commercial product – a matter of copyright law and property ownership and one key to ultimate (or any) success. The author need not be a real person, rather the name must designate a brand, a genre and a style.

If the author was not quite a Carlylean hero he or she was certainly a *professional*. In 1884 the social reformer Walter Besant formed the first guild/union, the Society of Authors. Even before, with Dickens in the lead, the author had become a *celebrity* as interesting as the books produced – and writers were sought out in their own right for opinions, interviews and later portrait photographs to fill the new mass-production magazines. Celebrity authors frequently travelled the Atlantic – as well known in Kansas as in Kensington.

For some, this new authorial freedom and power, which lacked any apparent responsibility to fiction except to entertain and provide escapism, was deeply troublesome. By the end of the nineteenth century all professionally minded authors who wrote for money were, therefore, implicated in the world of trade and commerce. The spectre of the hack still haunted those who wanted to create serious novels – Joseph Conrad's work hovered between juvenile adventure and symbolist art, Henry James could never reconcile his need to work for money with his artistic aspiration, whilst others like Virginia Woolf happily separated journalism from their art, or, like Arnold Bennett or H. G. Wells, attempted to reconcile the two. For a number of writers such considerations took second place to their desire to drum up moral reform as entertaining fiction. The novel soon displaced the tract in popularity, and Christian evangelical and missionary groups soon realised the power of fiction to disguise their religious, moral and social agenda – temperance, fidelity, family, loyalty, manliness, femininity, stalwartness in adversity, and the defence of the spiritual and moral status quo. It is extraordinary how many vicars and vicars' wives took up fiction before World War One and how many became best-selling authors. Others combined family sagas or women's romance with spirituality or theosophical issues. By 1918, the novel had learned not to be an excuse for a moral or spiritual tract and had become fully *secularised*. By the 1930s the common terms 'highbrow', 'lowbrow' and 'middlebrow' created a convenient aesthetic and psychological equivalent to the British class system, labelling authors and readers in one epigrammatic blow.

The creation of professional authorship had other effects. It offered escape to working-class boys and girls talented enough to write a nippy yarn or romance – a tradition that linked Edgar Wallace to James Herbert and Ethel M. Dell to Jackie Collins. It also led to specialised authorship in terms of both genre and medium. The unprecedented rise in mass literacy that had clearly become permanent by the late 1880s also created an unprecedented form: truly *popular* literature, marketed on a mass-commercial and modern basis. Such literature offered regular work to working-class writers who took up popular fiction to subsidise their serious work, or fame to upper-class authors who took to popular fiction as the result of an amateur challenge (John Buchan) or as a *jeu d'esprit* (M. R. James).

The changes in authorship that occurred in the late nineteenth and early twentieth centuries were anticipated by the growing professionalisation that took root in the 1840s among writers, especially in the growing trade of journalism. What these changes anticipated and helped to create, but could not have predicted, was the extraordinary rise in print and the immense increase of fictional work. Popular fiction required 'new' fictional specialisation both in content and in style.

By the early 1900s, Britain was essentially a literate country with newspapers, sportspapers and 'magazines' (story and interest 'papers') selling in huge numbers. From the 1880s many working-class readers could afford to purchase books produced at sixpence and the work of such authors was voraciously collected. New areas had continually to be developed or redeveloped: detective fiction, country romance, town romance, imperial adventure, literary thriller, spy romance, science fiction, ghost tales and tales of the supernatural, western adventure; from the 1930s, American-style crime fiction; from the 1960s, juvenile romance, and gang life and sex and adventure thrillers from America (soon copied by British writers); from the 1970s, a revival in horror; from the 1980s, the sex and shopping novel and the rise of the 'Aga saga' – and so on.

Whilst different genres have flourished at different times, almost all have the capacity to be recycled, providing they are sufficiently modernised. Thus the Edwardian romantic morality tale found new life in the family sagas, historical romances and costume romances that have flourished since the 1950s, whilst the gothic has been constantly plundered and reinvented to fit in with and renew other genres. The repertory of the modern popular canon had been created by the 1920s on elements that could be mixed and matched with relative impunity. Serious fiction, with one eye on art and the other on sales, could plunder this pool of artistic components for its own best-selling and prize-winning expressions.

The fifty years of modern class consolidation between the late 1880s and the 1930s brought a corresponding solidification of literary genres, a solidification that (with variation) still exists on the brink of the twenty-first century. This stratification of the system also created a corresponding internal set of divisions and hierarchy of genres. At the end of the twentieth century the two leading popular genres were the same as at its beginning and still commanded the greatest sales: detective fiction and women's romance. The former now includes everything from Agatha Christie to Elmore Leonard (or subgenre writers like John Grisham) and the latter has spread from Ethel Dell to Mills and Boon, Barbara Cartland and Joanna Trollope, but both genres still retain recognisable elements from their origins, providing continuity within creative traditions, based on a knowledge of possible variations (such as the Black Lace style of women's erotic romance). Among all this the traditional format holds good, as witnessed by Colin Dexter's Inspector Morse books, or Catherine Cookson's 'historical' romances.

Genre specialisation often led to authorship being divided on gender lines but this should not be overestimated. It is, of course, true that many more women write women's romances, Aga sagas, and family sagas and that more men write of war, crime and horror, but this specialisation, which certainly runs on gender lines, did not and does not stop men and women crossing genre boundaries – a number of women have written westerns (using initials or pseudonyms) and men (using pseudonyms) have written women's romance. What counts is the ability to write in accordance with the artistic restraints of the genre and the imaginative sensibilities of the reader. The use of initials or pseudonyms would allow, as it still does, a certain freedom to writers to cross such boundaries.

Popular genres do not, however, have equal status. Some are considered more serious than others (which often means less 'female' or less 'juvenile'). This becomes obvious when one compares the two leading genres that account for almost all the annual fictional output: detective fiction and women's romance. Detective fiction always had *cachet*.

By the late nineteenth century new genres were supported by a well-organised, market-driven, commercially minded publishing and book-selling *industry* with a constant eye to fashion and fancy (mixed with a quaint and gentlemanly olde worlde disdain for the whole process). By the time of the First World War almost all the techniques of modern book production and bookselling were in place, from methods of production and marketing to packaging and point of sale. Each book was, and is, more than just its narrative content: the sixpence Chatto and Windus paperback anticipated the Allen Lane 'Penguin' revolution by forty years; the Hodder yellowback looked towards the New English Library by as many years; cheap ha'penny and tuppenny women's novelettes anticipated Mills and Boon by fifty, and so on. The very shape, look, design, and inside-cover information reflected, as it still reflects, a symbiosis of advertising, artistic creativity, pricing and customer awareness.

But times also change and publishing, like all else, had to reinvent itself to sell essentially the same product (even if the individual authors become forgotten). Thus Chatto and Windus's sixpenny series had collapsed by the end of the First World War, despite including such huge best-selling authors as 'Ouida' and Hall Caine. Works that had sold in the tens and sometimes hundreds of thousands could not be sold in hundreds by the 1920s and had to be pulped. Readers' sensibilities shifted in ways that often anticipated a publisher's faith in an individual author or series but rarely disturbed the established nature of a market for a series. Genres were, and still are, rapidly modernised or 'reinvented' whilst authors once central to such genres are forgotten. What vanished somewhere between 1914 and 1919 was Victorian sentimental morality and it vanished first amongst proletarian readers of sixpenny series, never to return. A writer remains contemporary because his or her back catalogues can be continuously updated and remarketed for new readerships. If this cannot occur, the writer vanishes.

Fiction is, much as any other writing, a victim of changing times and changing morality. Writers are both sustained and condemned by their peculiarities of style and interest – the semi-eternality of writing no guarantor of the permanence of receptive reading. All art is subject to the vicissitudes of history, and literature (because the vernacular changes) more so than most. The bestseller is the one style of book that both succeeds and is destroyed by its own appeal to a singular and momentary contemporaneity. It is the fiction that most becomes its period and which is most caught in its own age. Such a comment requires a careful qualification: best-selling fiction is not simply a barometer of contemporary imagination, a type of acute pathological and sociological exemplary instance which sums up all that is interesting culturally (usually pessimistically) and all that is ephemeral artistically. Rather, such art is part and parcel of a sociological climate that includes an aesthetic dimension and in which the sociological and aesthetic are symbiotically joined, but where neither is reducible to the other. The bestseller is not a mere sociological slice of contemporary life, and its use by historians in search of cultural values needs careful handling if it's not to be reduced simply to a correspondence with the most morbid, sentimental or foolish perceptions of an age.

Such work, then, suffers one of a number of fates. It may simply be quickly and irrevocably forgotten; it may be transformed into another medium (usually film or television) and be read, if at all, as an adjunct to people's visual imagination; it may slowly grow across a decade or century until it becomes a type of commentary on a whole age or sensibility or it may become a cult or nostalgia item kept alive by enthusiasts and conventions. If it is lucky, it may (along with its author) become a popular classic – an almost oxymoronic concept – a work still read as a type of superior entertainment, alongside the canon of serious literature when a superior reading 'holiday' is required. Such is the fate of Robert Louis Stevenson's adventures, John Buchan's thrillers, and

Arthur Conan Doyle's tales of Sherlock Holmes. This is the work of classic middle-brow taste.

It may, on the other hand, become the exemplary instance of a genre and the author, the pivot around which the genre revolves, and this is especially true of pulp fiction and its creators, such as Edgar Rice Burroughs' tales of Tarzan of the Apes, R. E. Howard's Conan the Barbarian, or H. P. Lovecraft's tales of Cthulhu. Curiously, because popular authors are equivalent to a brand name (and their work a branded product), an author's name may stand in for any one particular title, becoming, as it were, a label for a self-contained œuvre. Such is the case with Agatha Christie, Ian Fleming, Harold Robbins, Jackie Collins, Stephen King or Catherine Cookson.

Interestingly, the attempts to revive a writer because of perceived historical interest, intrinsic worth or mere nostalgia always end in modest or poor sales. Literary appeal must be immediate and contain contemporary interest, otherwise interest remains antiquarian at best and academic at worst. Decay may occasionally affect a whole genre. The western, as presented in film, enjoys both popular interest and critical acclaim, but as a literary genre it has always been considered the province of semi-literate working men and juveniles, the dwindling stocks of such books read, if at all, by a slowly ageing readership, the genre dying a slow death by inattention. Or oblivion may come instantaneously to a whole group of books, such as the village tales of moral decline or family virtue that flourished before the 1920s and vanished thereafter (until stripped of their Christian and temperance virtue and reincarnated as the modern 'Aga saga' tales of immoral doings in middle England).

Popular fiction (all fiction) vanishes because it has a limited shelf life. It *must* be constantly reinvented (transferred to new media) if it is to retain freshness and this is as true for content as it is for things as central and yet 'invisible' as typographic setting. Dickens's work presented in its original form would be, to modern eyes, quite unreadable because the typography would be sight destroying. Any collector of books cannot help but notice the revolution in typographic spacing and lettering between the late nineteenth century and the 1920s.

This revolution is, in itself, a remarkable reinvention of the literary imagination, freed from the cramped and minuscule double-column typography of the previous century. Here, in mute form, is the visual corollary to a remarkable change in sensibility. The book itself is an ever renewed space for the sequentiality of literary narrative, a space in which imagination must be *designed* for contemporary tastes.

Any study of best-selling fiction is also a study of popular literature in its broadest sense, but a study of popular literature is a broader concept than the more narrow one of the bestseller and covers a wide range of ideological (especially sociological, political, and aesthetic) areas of which the bestseller is only one acute example. Popular literature and the analogous area, popular fiction, need therefore *no* necessary relationship to mass sales; rather they act as a focus for the intermixture of sociological and political questions, expressed through aesthetic means, found in the mass consumption of culture. The bestseller, appropriately, reaches the most readers and is therefore, almost by accident, *popular* in the sense given above. 'Popular' literature defines a perceptual arena, a field out of which the bestseller emerges. This field includes fiction that may not sell well at all, but aspires to the level of bestsellerdom by imitation, and is always already implicated in the aesthetics of popular culture, especially in the attempt to copy successful genre prototypes. In some ways, such poor-selling books may actually tell us more about popular reading, because of their unsuccessful exaggerations or writing formulas and often crude or bizarre imitative style. A bestseller can never be clearly predicted (and is therefore a type of necessary but reassuring 'sport' of popular literary production). The vast mass of failures tell us much about popular tastes and perceptions, but cannot be charted in the same way as the bestseller.

Because of their relative ephemerality (in terms of sales), best-selling authors are always faced with the possibility of falling back into the morass of unsuccessful popular fiction: imitative of their own work and therefore of the successful authors they once were. It is the publisher's job to prevent such a catastrophe – a falling into the popular as self pastiche, the author thus becoming too 'popular' for success!

Popular fiction is the expression of mass, industrial and consumer society. It is organised into aesthetic categories that often correspond to sociological, political and economic categories, cross-divided themselves by gender considerations. Popular fiction is always commercially oriented and its production and marketing is essentially corporate and industrial, aimed at the maximum distribution and sales of units (books) and the capitalisation on past successes for potential future sales. This is especially true when elongating the life of a series or author.

All literature works, on one level or another, on precedent (tradition); and popular fiction is the area where it is necessary to reinvent the precedents that were most successful. T. S. Eliot's famously ironic view that poor artists imitate and great artists steal is, in one sense, only a type of aphoristic half truth as the popular artist must steal even more successfully if the work produced is to replace a previous product to which it has an uncanny resemblance (this is especially true in science fiction, horror, women's romance and detective fiction). The new author's work is a type of sleight of hand, making what they produce appear momentarily new and fresh, until inevitably it falls back into the mass of titles on a similar theme, written in similar narrative style and set in a similar place. Absolute theft, with the allowance of plagiarism and the absolute necessity of not simply copying (a guarantee of failure), is the psychological predisposition of the successful popular author and his most potent aesthetic tool, allowing incorporation to enhance his own work whilst also acknowledging the genre tradition which is being followed. As T. S. Eliot said of great artists, what is needed is talent (craft) not genius but it must be talent which itself is a type of genius (for organisation) if it is to create a best-selling formula. Nowhere is this more evident than in the organisational aesthetic of the detective story or family saga.

The concept of tradition is tinged with the sort of ironic posture so beloved of serious artists and supposedly lacking in popular fictionalists. It folds within itself the nature of *legitimacy*, hence:

> The notion of legitimacy blends the two fundamental operations of the mind: analogy and convention (that is, the process of establishing arbitrary equivalences). They are branches that fork from a single trunk, namely substitution. In the case of analogy, the only legitimacy is that of holy investiture, which through a play of resonances and sympathies descends through all the gradations of being. Where that resonance dies out, no legitimacy can be granted. In the case of convention, legitimacy is a prime example of the arbitrary agreement that makes possible the functioning of all sorts of mechanisms, ranging from language to society.[3]

Popular fiction works through infinite analogous and substitutional modes directed by convention.

> As always, convention is concerned not with essences or substances, but with function – and it is ready to barter one form or another (for it is the very soul of substitution).[4]

The great and legitimate work demands for itself an *origin* from whence it *must* have sprung but to which it cannot attach a connective thread. The thread is the fiction of *genealogy*, rising out of a distant pool, a hazy origin.[5] That origin, *of necessity*, had to be something *other* than popular literature but tradition no longer enables one to claim an origin, but rather conceals it.[6] What is concealed is the origin in the substitutive pool of popular fiction. All *vernacular* literature was *ipso facto* popular (common, coarse – vulgate – vulgar), opposed to classicism's purity and aristocracy of descent. Yet classicism could offer no *living* tradition, only a renewable contemporary vulgate could offer that.

Popular fiction pre-dates serious fiction and serious fiction is cursed to act as popular fiction's antidote and nemesis. Out of popular fiction, serious fiction separates and congeals: the substitutive mode *par excellence* trapped by the ideology of authorship that claims:

> [If] one could fill the gap of that missing origin, one could at least make one's way without deception all the way to the present. Then they discovered origin as deception, thus choosing the form of deception into which they wanted to fall – and which would bedevil them to the last.[7]

Popular fiction is never other than itself, never less than the totality of all the possibilities of the contemporary vernacular. It can never really 'fall away' from itself; its standards cannot drop, be dumbed down, or be less than they once were; it is as it is, the possibility of all its many guises – protean, yet ordered. There was never a better time or a golden age from which things declined, but rather better books and worse books, remembered or forgotten books, against which incomplete and nostalgic judgements are haphazardly entertained.

The language of popular literature cannot decline from a standard because it does not have a standard, cannot 'fall' because it had no golden age. Serious literature, on the other hand, by setting itself an arbitrary genealogy and in believing its own myth of moral ascendancy and aristocratic (aesthetic) *hauteur*, can decline, for it *alone* can fall into popular idiom, be tainted by what it attempts to refuse or to ignore and thus become *illegitimate*, become popular – a bestseller. Only a serious artist can become a literary prostitute, too closely associated with disguise, convention, titillation and commercial reward. The arbitrary attempts to differentiate common English once it enters print, in order to create a superior language, are themselves doomed to reproduce the *indeterminable* differences of convention, mode and intention whose origins are concealed in the analogy and substitution of bastard genealogies. And thus, finally, the empty mantle of aristocracy passes to the (morally superior) author of *art* fiction.

The absolute rule of the nobility, hierarchic distance, detached now from any contact with the land, any exchange of feudal obligations, any immediate function, and abandoned only to the cruel game of Court favours, was rediscovered, revived – even to the point of tacit fanaticism – in the refinement of taste, in the pursuit of delicacies, in the gradual discovery of a unique style.[8]

For nearly two hundred years popular culture (mass culture from the 1880s and consumer culture from the 1950s) has been under the twin scrutiny of the magistrate and the scholar. Whilst the democratic project remained incomplete this scrutiny was carried out in the name of political will and moral appropriateness. With the democratic political project completed by the 1920s the debate became more 'secularised' and the policing gaze of court official and educational expert turned to the problem of literacy in an age of mass populations. Censorship and academic opprobrium have been the usual response to the rise of popular culture, and popular fiction in particular.

The problem of style irradiates every line and energises every argument. The art style and the popular style supposedly glare at each other from opposing sides but the most execrable style survives next to the most sublime. Narrative does not need style, it needs panache – a gamble deriving from a passion: the convolution of dramatic crisis. And this can cut two ways; so that style (the constructive vitality of word and grammar) can work to be all in all (the art novel) or work towards its own neutrality (the popular), which always acknowledges its inability *to express quite enough*. Only in its translation into another medium can popular fiction find itself again returned in a continuous loop of renewal because it is never complete in itself. In seeking its own absolute limit the art novel enwraps itself within itself: untranslatable, irrascible, and sublime. Popular fiction always seeks other partners.

Style is the central problem of any particular author and irrelevant to any general history of literature. What survives is beyond style and beyond literature's adequacy to itself. What survives is the inability to push style to the point of closing off literature into a hermetically sealed space. Popular fiction carries this inadequacy in order to reinvent itself elsewhere (on film, television, etc.), feeding from this space to reinvent itself over again. Style is therefore a peculiar and potent chimera, bereft of power when corroded by history. Only style that neutralises itself, which sees itself vanishing into the corner of a page or the corner of an eye, can reinvent itself. The self-conscious novel, determined by an introspective eye (as with Virginia Woolf), becomes popular (as Woolf has become) because it *narrates* introspection and *acts it out*.

A literature whose elegance of style closes it within its own gemlike facets can only ever have a minority audience. Its tendency moves towards the minimalism of *belle lettres*, the essay or the *bon mot* turning it into an anecdote for masonic recognition amongst an elite group, whose gaze is marked by a type of refusal of historical movement. The great popular work opens out into a need for translation into other media – a symbiosis immediately recognised by dramatists and film-makers in search of a narrative correlative to their visual dreams. Art fiction highlights its style, delights in it and makes of style a fetish. Popular fiction neutralises style, seems only interested in narrative, content and convention, and delights in making language invisible in order to tell a tale. Yet popular fiction may still make a fetish of one aspect of its style.

The fetish of popular fiction will be unlike the fetish of the art novel (which can only be itself alone) but will make of its language *a form of lifestyle*, foregrounding objects and events rather than psychological characterisation. As such, characters become symbiotically associated with the things they own, which then act as substitutes for inner characterisation. Paradoxical though it may seem, popular fiction is always striving to find linguistic (aesthetic) equivalence to its narrative power but only if that equivalence spills over beyond language. This is exactly what art novels strive to avoid even when their theme is lifestyle (of the bourgeoisie for instance or the artist). Popular fiction releases a desire in language to become the very life that is being portrayed by it. Here language looks beyond itself and into the world, but a world already distributed and arranged according to the geometry of its own trajectory, its own abstract needs, now striving for materialisation: fiction as lifestyle.

> Breakfast was Bond's favourite meal of the day. When he was stationed in London it was always the same. It consisted of very strong coffee, from De Bry in New Oxford Street, brewed in an American Chemex, of which he drank two large cups, black and without sugar. The single egg, in the dark blue egg-cup with a gold ring round the top, was boiled for three and a third minutes.
>
> It was a very fresh, speckled brown egg from French Marans hens. . . . (Bond disliked white eggs and, faddish as he was in many small things, it amused him to maintain that there was such a thing as the

perfect boiled egg.) Then there were two thick slices of wholewheat toast, a large pat of deep yellow Jersey butter and three squat glass jars containing Tiptree 'Little Scarlet' strawberry jam, Cooper's Vintage Oxford marmalade and Norwegian Heather Honey from Fortnum's. The coffee pot and the silver on the tray were Queen Anne, and the china was Minton, of the same dark blue and gold and white as the egg-cup.

(Ian Fleming, From Russia with Love, ch. 11)

Or

Fontaine Khaled woke alone in her New York apartment. She removed her black lace sleep-mask, and reached for the orange juice in her bedside fridge.

Gulping the deliciously cold liquid she groaned aloud. A mammoth hangover was threatening to engulf her entirely. Christ! Studio 54. Two fags. One black. One white. What an entertainment.

She attempted to step out of bed, but felt too weak, and collapsed back amongst her Porthault pillows.

She reached over to her bedside table and picked a bottle of vitamin pills. E was washed down with the orange juice, then C, then a multivitamin, and lastly two massive yeast tablets.

(Jackie Collins, The Bitch, ch. 2)

The transposition of lifestyle into fiction and fiction into lifestyle is nowhere more apparent than at the centre of the popular romantic imagination. Here both lifestyle and fiction meet within the very style of the romance genre.

'Is Honey really magic?' Serena asked. She is a very attractive young married friend of mine, who is keenly interested in health.

'I think it is,' I replied, 'and I believe that everyone who has ever studied the history of Honey is convinced that it has in it a magic ingredient. Although Honey has been analysed for hundreds of years by scientists of every generation, there remains a mysterious 4 per cent they have never been able to break down.'

'How exciting,' Serena exclaimed.

'They know that Honey contains vitamins and minerals,' I went on, 'in fact five very important vitamins which are absolutely necessary to life. These, of course, are found also in other products, but in Honey there is contained, I am convinced, the Elixir of Life. This

is the reason why Honey is stimulating to sex, and it is also responsible for its fantastic healing properties.'

'Tell me more about Honey,' Serena begged. 'I really know very
little about it.'

(Barbara Cartland, *The Magic of Honey*, p. 7)

Lifestyle in fiction demands narratives of experiential pleasure.

It is for this reason that character so dominates popular fiction, and
it is for this reason that the neutralisation of language (to the point of
invisibility) paradoxically enlarges the content of that language: characterisation. The greatest literary characters of the late nineteenth and
twentieth centuries are the 'monsters' released by the neutralisation of
language and the subsequent materialisation of 'personalities': here
dwell Dracula, Sherlock Holmes and James Bond. Each manifestation is
available to us all, regardless of ethnic origin or gender, because each is
the ephemeral child of style and therefore totally malleable and yet they
are also already beyond their original authors' control. No wonder each
such monstrous character escapes the control of the author and, in their
turn, each has had to 'die'. No wonder authors want nothing to do with
them, no wonder they rid themselves of them because of insatiable
public demand (a demand they grow to hate) and no wonder these creatures are still the fertile breeders of even more of their kind, each their
own œuvre, a world giving birth to worlds (more vampires, more blood,
more detectives, more corpses, more spies, more martinis).

And the creature that outlives its literary origin is the one least
indebted to literary form, stepping most easily into myth. Thus the
status of Superman and Batman goes quite beyond a set of storylines
into a mythic mode, captured and *retold* in endless variation. What
counts is convention repeated as ritual and lived as 'life style' in the
neutralisation of language barriers and literary limits. The perfect state
of popular literature is to become popular myth and hence to form
literary language into secular liturgy. Contemporary fiction becomes
sacred when words and sentences are no longer held merely to a page
of prose or the surface of a page, but resurface as the realisation of that
surface, *as* surface (in film, television or electronic games) – an unalter-
able present where nothing can be changed.

Popular fiction is constantly trying to *reinvent* itself as popular, already
finding itself trapped in the history of its own conventions, already too
late to make good. Popular fiction, in its apotheosis, the bestseller, seems
to look always backwards for its own perfect style, its own adequacy to
its material. And this is what readers demand. The grail is the discov-

ery of the analogous link, an author who can rewrite the conventions of revered predecessors. For instance, in women's romantic fiction, the search for the link between Jane Austen and Mrs Radcliffe animates much of the genre because of convention and the demands of convention.

Thus popular women's fiction becomes a séance, reviving not merely the shadows and ventriloquistic voices of long-dead authors but also their conventions: domesticity, marriage, money and gothic terrors. Such conventions cannot be 'improved' or psychologised, rather they can be recycled as 'different' and therefore as always *contemporaneous*. The conventions are determined by history but work as if they weren't. The search for an origin is therefore really a search for a perfect convention, an appropriate device. Such conventions paradoxically 'progress' in order to defeat the history that produced them and thereby make each successive stage of the convention's style resonate with an inherent modernity. Thus popular modernity becomes the art of literary repetition, homage and pastiche. This is Sir Arthur Conan Doyle's parody of his own creation:

> Mr Sherlock Holmes, who was usually very late in the mornings, save upon those not infrequent occasions when he was up all night, was seated at the breakfast table. I stood upon the hearth-rug and picked up the stick which our visitor had left behind him the night before. It was a fine, thick piece of wood, bulbous-headed, of the sort which is known as a 'Penang lawyer.' Just under the head was a broad silver band, nearly an inch across. 'To James Mortimer, M.R.C.S., from his friends of the C.C.H.,' was engraved upon it, with the date '1884.' It was just such a stick as the old-fashioned family practitioner used to carry – dignified, solid, and reassuring.
>
> 'Well, Watson, what do you make of it?'
>
> Holmes was sitting with his back to me, and I had given him no sign of my occupation.
>
> 'How did you know what I was doing? I believe you have eyes in the back of your head.'
>
> 'I have, at least, a well-polished, silver-plated coffee-pot in front of me,' said he. 'But, tell me, Watson, what do you make of our visitor's stick? Since we have been so unfortunate as to miss him and have no notion of his errand, this accidental souvenir becomes of importance. Let me hear you reconstruct the man by an examination of it.'
>
> (Arthur Conan Doyle, *The Hound of the Baskervilles*, ch. 1)

This is A. A. Milne's pastiche homage almost twenty years later:

> Anthony smoked thoughtfully for a little. Then he took his pipe out of his mouth and turned to his friend.
> 'Are you prepared to be the complete Watson?' he asked.
> 'Watson?'
> 'Do-you-follow-me-Watson; that one. Are you prepared to have quite obvious things explained to you, to ask futile questions, to give me chances of scoring off you, to make brilliant discoveries of your own two or three days after I have made them myself – all that kind of thing? Because it all helps.'
>
> (A. A. Milne, *The Red House Mystery*, ch. 11)

The writer whose popularity is gained through the bestseller list but who pursues a private vision or is, as Eliot pointed out, pursuing a private obsession (erotic violence, empire, the glory of war, spiritual regeneration) will almost always produce perverse emotionality, captured by history and captured in a time warp not even useful for nostalgia. Such writing quickly becomes quaint, or ridiculous. Though it uses a convention, it fails to renew it and thus make it contemporary.

The special worlds of P. G. Wodehouse (and even Agatha Christie) remain alive because they are essentially *pastiche* and therefore contemporary even if the pastiche is sometimes unconscious. On the other hand a writer may be unlucky and lose a popular readership only to gain a cult or antiquarian one in the glow of imperial nostalgia. Thus the aficionado cannot resist:

> I had closed the window to exclude the yellow mist, but subconsciously I was aware of its encircling presence, walling me in, and now I found myself in such a silence as I had known in deserts but could scarce have deemed possible in fog-bound London, in the heart of the world's metropolis.
> . . . my nervous system was somewhat overwrought as a result of my hurried return from Cairo – from Cairo where I had left behind many a fondly cherished hope. . . .
> Nayland Smith stood before me, muffled up in a heavy travelling coat, and with his hat pulled down over his brows. . . .
> 'God knows what *is* afoot this time Petrie!' he replied . . . 'You and I have lived no commonplace lives, Dr Fu-Manchu has seen to that; but if I am to believe what the Chief has told me to-day, even stranger things are ahead of us!'
>
> (Sax Rohmer, *The Hand of Fu Manchu*, ch. 1)

In an extreme case the aficionado may revive popular fiction as a type of avant-gardism. Such is the case with the affectionate obsessions of Stewart Home with bestseller Richard Allen, or the ironic plagiarism of Harold Robbins by Kathy Acker.

Writers may even choose to fill the gap left by the death of a best-selling author by taking on his or her mantle or stealing from the *pool* of characters for their own work, as if, by a magical turn, characters had broken free from their creators and left their origin without right of ownership or need of permission. Thus evolve the literary universes of Baker Street, Transylvania, Arkham and Middle Earth. It is not necessary to honour predecessor authors here, but to acknowledge their conventions, both be true to them and move them into the contemporary. By so doing the original creators are themselves honoured.

In some cases, the original author's work may be largely forgotten, but a loved character may survive until a later author realises the potential use of a narrative still available and somehow encapsulated in this figure from the past. This is the case with George MacDonald Fraser who borrowed 'Flashman' from Thomas Hughes's now virtually unread *Tom Brown's Schooldays*. What was rejected was all that was not contemporary (that about the original which made *Tom Brown* a supposed 'classic' even if unread!) and what has been saved is the core of our interest: the character of Flashman. In the same way Lionel Bart in his musical *Oliver!* shifted interest from the insipid Oliver to the true centre of the story: Fagin. In the case of both Flashman and Fagin, neither are punished in modern revised narratives which no longer pander to long abandoned morality, but both live on (realistically) to cheat, steal and entertain us. What is significant in the case of both Dickens's *Oliver Twist* and Hughes's *Tom Brown's Schooldays* is that both texts have been saved from themselves by the extraction of a subordinate character. The 'modern' elements of the two tales reside not in their central characters but in peripheral or secondary figures. Both books have been rescued by popular culture not only on behalf of contemporaneity but also on behalf of their own unresolved aesthetic trajectories. The 'art' of both *Tom Brown* and *Oliver Twist* was distorted to accommodate a moral whose imposition 'warped' the stories. Rewriting them addresses that imposition, 'corrects' it and so offers the original tales a way to return to a contemporary readership.

> I had read *Tom Brown's Schooldays* as a child [comments George Mac-Donald Fraser] and I remember being very disappointed when Flashman was expelled because that was the most interesting character

gone. Now I don't know if Hughes based him on anyone in particular, but I wouldn't mind betting that he discovered that Flashman was becoming a more dominant character than he wanted him to be. Flashman wasn't the sort of character Hughes wanted, so he axed him . . . something went out of the book after that. There was nothing to challenge Brown any longer; his struggles become entirely moral rather than physical.[9]

No use of literary language can claim, *ab initio*, an aesthetic principle that is superior *per se* and no such claim can avoid the acrid whiff of moral, class and personal superiority. What emerges is a test of psychic health and moral eugenics rather than literary judgement. What is left is condemnation dressed as artistic judgement, and in each condemnation the unwashed smell of the popular creeps through. Can popular literature (one supposedly without self-awareness) be the only cynical literature? Is the 'unthinking' sentimentalism of popular fiction the only site of literary kitsch? Is it possible that the thinking person's literary cynicism reproduced in retroism and nihilism (empty stylistics, the devotion to an amused detachment denoting wit), a type of intellectual kitsch born as a response to, and a perverse indulgence in, the popular (here taken up ironically and emptied of its original sentiment – its *living* connection to main culture), can also form a type of kitsch sensibility?

The very nature of popular culture is determined by its relationship to mass populations, but this does not mean it is simply determined by a crude and dumbed down anti-aesthetic kitsch or that the popular mentality is one manipulated (by the media, advertising, etc.) into a congealed monolith. *All* contemporary literature has *some* relationship to mass culture, after attempting to detach itself from it or more successfully define itself within it. The consumer culture of capitalism, far from being in a steady state (the liberal position) or living from crisis to crisis (the Marxist position), is always anarchic, diffused, irregular and regionally specific. Popular culture, and therefore popular fiction, reflects this. Bestsellers *incorporate* the largest number of perceptual constituencies and temporarily unite disparate or contradictory ideological concerns in an aesthetic form. Of its nature, the bestseller is a temporary phenomenon and its power to unite readers soon collapses. The popular 'classic' becomes so by uniting and holding the varied ideological positions of one class or group whilst appealing to other groups through other media (film or television series).

Mass literature has nothing *per se* to do with merely working-class readers, and mass culture has nothing *per se* to tell us about working-class life in any clear sense. Rather, popular fiction when it reaches bestseller level tells us about a condition of reading which has been *proletarianised*, whoever reads such work and from whatever background. Yet such proletarianisation does not turn us into mindless slaves of consumerism nor into the hedonistic clones of *Brave New World*. It always includes imagination, negotiation and *refusal* and allows minority groups (with differing degrees of success) to negotiate their space in contradiction to the *vox populi*: a voice within a voice. Print itself reflects the complex and anarchic nature of literary production, and the haphazard nature of any formula for predicting literary success shows how *little* manipulative power the media (and publishing in particular) often has. Print is a vast and anarchic field of competing interests.

2
How the British Read

Literacy

Assessing literacy levels

In 1911 *The New Dictionary of Statistics* informed its enquirers that just over 3 per cent of men and a little under 4 per cent of women were recorded as illiterate between 1896 and 1900, and that this had gradually fallen to around 2 per cent for either sex by 1907.[1] The literacy test was simple and negative, for if you could not sign your name on a marriage register you were deemed illiterate. By 1914 this figure was reduced to 1 per cent.[2] By such determinants Britain became almost a fully literate country by the beginning of World War One. Sir Cyril Burt's investigations refined such statistics into the categories 'illiterate' and 'semi-literate' (with reading ages between 6 and 8 years old) and thereby inflated the semi-literate population (barely able to comprehend a single newspaper paragraph) to 3 million. Burt was not only incautious with his figures, he also took his samples from poor rural and slum areas, suggesting general results from a specialised constituency.[3] Burt's work did nothing to resolve the question of *capacity* among literate readers – a question simply left in abeyance by other investigators, all of whose methods differed![4]

Documentation remained sketchy throughout the twentieth century and in 1990 UNESCO reported that Britain lagged behind other advanced industrial countries in its investigations into literacy rates and levels. The Adult Literacy Campaign which began in 1973 found it had to start almost afresh in its enquiries. In 1974 the British Association of Settlements (BAS) published figures based upon 'the best related evidence, and on the firm opinions of acknowledged experts in the field', using six previous surveys carried out by the National Foundation for

Educational Research (NFER) from 1948 onwards.[5] On the basis of these mixed sources and the 'opinion' of 'experts', BAS estimated that approximately 6 per cent or 2 million adults were functionally illiterate, with reading levels below that of a 9-year-old. Other organisations suggested a basic age of 13 as representing a functional reading level and so the BAS figures appeared conservative. Whilst the BAS results were improvements upon Burt's, they too were flawed by the methods used to gather the evidence, and again they told nothing of reading levels amongst those who could read and write at reasonable levels of fluency.

With haphazard research, no real gains in insight were available for almost ninety years. One researcher for NFER working in 1996 came to the conclusion that literacy rates had not changed significantly since 1948.[6] The conclusion was that literacy levels (despite or because of education change and experiment) had remained stable since 1900. Nevertheless, by the late 1990s a flurry of activity, accompanied by fears over falling educational standards, resulted in a number of new surveys of a more detailed kind.

> In 1997, the Organisation for Economic Co-operation and Development (OECD) and the UK Office for National Statistics both published the results from the International Adult Literacy Survey (IALS), which surveyed the literacy standards of several different countries. Within this survey, literacy standards were tested in relation to several different factors, including gender, class, and level of education; and furthermore (and with particular significance to cultural studies of literature) literacy was divided not just into levels but into categories according to type. Distinctions were made between ability to read and understand quantitative material (material related to arithmetic operations), document material (material contained in various documents such as formats, job applications, maps, and train timetables), and prose material (material from texts such as editorials, news stories, poems, and fiction).[7]

Thus literacy standards were being tested for the first time with specific reference to the ability to read literature.

> The majority of the British population between the ages of sixteen and sixty-five displayed either a level 3 (31.3 per cent) or a level 2 (30.3 per cent) reading ability, 21.8 per cent displayed level 1 abilities while 16.6 per cent displayed abilities which qualified them for levels 4 or 5. Within the UK the three most important factors

determining literacy levels were, in order of importance: highest level of educational attainment, social class, and age. Not surprisingly, those who reached a higher level of education statistically reached a higher level of literacy. Furthermore, there was also a correlation between the highest level of education reached and the amount of reading an individual did, with the amount of individuals reading in each group increasing with rising levels of education. In terms of social class, Social Classes I and II possessed the highest percentage of individuals at reading levels 3 and 4/5, while Social Classes IV and V possessed the highest percentage of individuals at reading level 1. Individuals between the ages of sixteen and twenty-five on the whole displayed a higher level of reading ability than individuals from the same social background between the ages of forty-six and fifty-five.[8]

The methods and measurements used for the IALS, although different from those of Burt or his predecessors, did confirm the obvious: the highest reading attainments belonged to the wealthiest class and the poorest attainments to the very poor (Burt's slum dwellers and poorer, country people). The almost negligible difference in men's and women's reading abilities (with men slightly ahead) had vanished for all practical purposes by the end of the twentieth century, although this masked the fact that the vast majority of people who read regularly were overwhelmingly female. Other statistical surveys confirmed that literate women consumed large amounts of fiction, but that:

> Much of the fiction which is read is chosen because it is 'light' and 'accessible.' Many want a book which grabs their attention in the first few pages, is easily understood, and which they can 'lose themselves' in. The Classics are very seldom read, with Catherine Cookson and Danielle Steel as the most popular authors.[9]

Yet something else could be proved by the consistency of literacy levels from the opening to the end of the century – not only did economic position and educational opportunity continue to affect levels of attainment but they also provided evidence of consistency in the subject matter of reading material, the conservation of genres being determined by the conservative nature of social change, educational opportunity and economic position.

Illiteracy is a mirror to literacy but this also indicates that education and economics alone cannot account for changes in taste amongst the literate, which must be explained also in terms of gender and generational change and historical crises. Thus reading dramatically increased during the First World War and the economic slump leading up to World War Two. In both cases changes in taste could be accounted for not only by crises in the social imagination but also by generational change, some authors declining during the two periods as their readership aged and died. By the end of the twentieth century, MORI surveys had confirmed previous findings going back a century.[10]

Literacy in practice

The problem of accounting for literacy levels has remained a matter of controversy and debate, framed as it often is by the question of *writing* ability rather than reading level. The ability to sign one's name on official documents is not any real test of literacy, and figures gathered by researchers tend to drift toward numerical inflation at either end of the scale. By the 1860s, it was certainly true that in many areas of Britain literacy rates, meaning the ability to read and write at a functional level, were near enough universal. The educational reforms of 1870 formalised an already thriving elementary system and consolidated gains in literacy levels determined by informal and semi-formal processes in education that had existed a good half-century previously. By the 1880s as few as 3 per cent of the population were illiterate and by the 1890s the solidly literate base produced by the 1870 reforms meant that a vast potential market lay ready to be exploited. Led by London, literacy throughout the country reached at least 90 per cent for both sexes in all areas at the beginning of the twentieth century. The market amongst lower middle-class and working-class readers was effectively created when rising incomes, increasing leisure and greater national cohesion aligned with reasonable levels of reading ability.

The British working class might not be able to write as well as their betters but they could certainly read, and for most people in the nineteenth as well as the twentieth century *reading* was the decisive measure of literacy. Writing was a *skill*, reserved for others, rarely needed formally and usually practised informally and haphazardly (diaries, letters, postcards, etc.). This was clearly attested to throughout the nineteenth century by the growth of ephemeral printed material, ranging from fly posters to newspapers and recorded in the extraordinary rise in postal correspondence. The readership and appetite for newspapers was a clear indication of the new reading habits, creating a reading *public* (educated to take information second hand and deliberate upon it to create a mass opinion) rather than an active mob (acting on impulse through local, visual stimuli). By the 1870s, train carriages were littered with abandoned newspapers and although no newspaper had yet become national (except *The Times*) there existed a public of perhaps 5.5 million to 6 million readers. The appetite for newspaper print was insatiable and newspapers were consumed on trains, on the omnibus, in public houses and in the newly created 'newsrooms' of public libraries. Newspapers were read out loud to the family, to work colleagues and to servants as well as being consumed in silence in public or in the library reading room.

If in the 1860s most papers catered for middle-class readers, by the 1870s there was the half-penny *Echo*, the *News of the World*, the *Weekly Dispatch*, *Reynold's News*, *Morning Post*, or *Daily Telegraph* to cater for the lower middle classes, working classes, and servant classes. The *Illustrated London News* (launched 1842) combined words and pictures and found a large readership in the 1880s and 1890s. The *Strand Magazine* combined articles and pictures in a 'pot pouri' style, reaching a general readership of between 300,000 and 500,000, especially so when a new Conan Doyle story appeared. At the turn of the twentieth century, the penny dailies catered for the lower middle-class 'respectable' reader with family and responsibilities whilst manual labourers found interest in the ha'penny press. Such newspapers reached into slum homes as well as cottages.

By the end of the nineteenth century things had already changed regarding the *raison d'être* behind newspaper production and this was directly linked to readership demand. Previously newspapers had been largely political in nature, local in kind and educational in requirement, and agitation throughout the country for the removal of governmental taxes (stamp duties) on print and paper had focused on the fact that cheaper print created a better educated population which would have earned the right to participate in democracy. In the mid-1800s the newspaper was seen as a moral force but by the end of the century the literacy/democracy campaign had largely been won and newspapers turned increasingly to entertainment. Thus the notion of 'cheap' in the 1830s and 1840s became a byword for 'nasty' by the 1900s.

The 'new journalism' as it was dubbed, relied on sport, sensation and personality, much of which it took from the style and content of working-class Sunday newspapers, which were voraciously consumed in preference, or as an accompaniment, to going to church. Thus the British Sunday of church, sex, scandal and gossip took its peculiar shape, led by papers such as the *News of the World*.

Family-oriented papers and magazines as well as temperance journals were also read. In the 1870s another innovation was added to Sunday and weekday reading habits – the serialised novel – Mrs Braddon's output of 1873 being syndicated across the country. By 1889, novels and short stories were important components of newspaper and magazine publishing, channelling new and rising authors into hitherto unexplored formats (the requirements of a new popular aesthetics both of style and of content). Fiction 'bureaux' appeared, to exploit this new market for ephemeral fiction, and it was into this market that almost the entire output of many popular writers first went, especially those engaged in tales of adventure, of affairs of the heart and of the supernatural. The sporting thrillers of Nat Gould were advertised and sold through the *News of the World*, cheap editions bearing the impressed slogan on their back cover 'News of the World for thrilling serials by the best authors'. Published by the 'Modern Publishing Company' such books also carried advertisements promising to banish 'nerves', relieve influenza (Collis Browne's chlorodyne) and reveal the secrets of one's personality.

Alongside national newspapers and Sundays there were specialist publications produced on a weekly or monthly basis, offering advice on hobbies, gardening, electronics and fashion. Women's magazines were foremost in this area, including not only *Vogue* (1916) and *Harper's Bazaar* (1929) for richer readers but also *Good Housekeeping* (1929) aimed at the middle-class housewife who had been used previously to the help of servants and now was 'abandoned' in the suburbs unable to cook or clean. For poorer female readers were the likes of *Woman's Weekly* (1911), *Woman's Own* (1932) and *Woman*, with romantic stories, hints and tips on beauty, fashion and cookery and readers' queries.

One consequence of this was the boom in spin-off fiction produced in novelette form for reading at the seaside or in snatched leisure hours. Such work was hugely popular and immediately disposable (after lending to friends) and included an unbroken line of works, from those with titles such as *Joy Grantham* (a novelette by Joseph Nelson: no. 33, *Sunday Companion* Library) priced at 3d and produced around the time of World War One, to the 2d 'London Novels' and 'Smart Novels' of the 1930s, right through to the Women's World Library of the late 1940s and 1950s with its romantic tales and advertisements for engagement rings from Bravington's Jewellers. Popular women's fiction constellated around such publications, produced in the millions and numbered (in their editions) in the hundreds. This was the readership that might also turn to substantial novels by Elinor Glyn (selling in a cheap 6d edition by the 1920s) or Charles Garvice whose covers for the 'Hutchinson Famous Novels' series (also at 6d) were emblazoned with the slogan 'the

most popular writer of love stories in the world' – and all of it produced in *paperback*, wood-pulp editions. It was this reading with its 'less
Christian', more 'liberated' sense of women's role that finally put paid
to the work of Ouida and Mari Corelli and opened the way for Ethel M.
Dell and later Mills and Boon.

Children had their own publications, which would exploit imperial
adventure, sporting, scientific and educational themes. *Gem* and *Magnet*
were joined by *Hotspur* and *Wizard*, whilst a newer concept of the
children's paper was to appear with cartoon strips under the *Dandy*
(1937) and *Magic Beano* (1938: *Beano*) labels. Combining education and
entertainment, and with an emphasis on science and the future, the
Eagle followed in 1950. During the twentieth century the importance
of children's papers (dominated by two-column printed pages) diminished; they were finally to be replaced by comics using an almost exclu-
sive 'cartoon' strip formula. None the less, many of these more modern
comics retained genres and settings that had been 'abandoned' by adult
fiction or that had previously been popular only in printed form. As
late as the middle 1960s, *Wizard* retained a print format that empha-
sized stories from both World Wars, but which also included tales of
soccer, cricket and the 'Wild West'. Illustration was reserved for the front
and back covers. *Hotspur* and *Hornet* abandoned printed tales almost
altogether as did the later, derivative, *Valiant*. War, soccer, detective,
and imperial adventure stories dominated the *Hornet* in the 1960s as
they did the *Hotspur* during the same period, although by this time
Hotspur included a British copy of the Batman character called 'The
Black Hawk' (with wings like a bat!) and a tale about a public school
(Johnny Jones of Kingsleigh Public School). By the 1970s such tales were
too easily pastiched, and *Valiant's Captain Hurricane* reduced the Second
World War to violent farce. *Valiant* also included a Star Trek strip, and
colour. Tales such as 'Janus Stark' (a Victorian escapologist), 'Yellowknife
of the Yard' (a Sioux chief become Scotland Yard detective!) and 'The
Claw' (an invisible man with one steel hand) recalled the literary sensibility of an earlier age, mixing H. G. Wells with Edgar Wallace and
Sidney Horler.

Reading and the influences of cinema, television and radio

By the time of the First World War, the desire for newspapers and magazines to provide entertainment had been augmented by the advent of
cinema. It soon became clear that newspapers, fiction and cinema had
a symbiotic relationship. Of all entertainment, cinema was the most

popular (followed by the dance hall) and was *American*. In most major cities cinemas began to occupy or replace the old music halls until in the 1930s large cinemas, with balconies for the better off, could seat audiences of 4,000. Throughout the early part of the century audiences grew, until by the mid-1930s at least 40 per cent of the population went at least once a week and a quarter at least twice a week to the 5,000 cinemas across the country. Programmes were changed frequently and individual cinema turnover per week could be many thousands. By 1946 total charges for admission per year had risen to 1.6 billion pounds. Cinema and radio stars soon featured regularly in papers and magazines, the cult of celebrity dominating much reading. Instead of threatening the book trade these new stories actually created new niches and possibilities, not the least of which was 'novelisation' of a popular film complete with stills from the movie, such as Guy Thorne's *Butterfly on a Wheel*, available in an edition of the Reader's Library in the mid-1920s. An editorial note added to the book was quite clear about the new interrelationship between best-selling fiction and successful plays and films, hence:

> In the very modern world, an enjoyable story is frequently presented to the public in three different forms: as a novel, as a stage play, and as a motion picture. Sometimes the original form in which the tale achieves fame is as a film, and the publishers and theatrical producers then exploit its popularity for their own advantage. Sometimes the story is seen first as an attractive production on the stage; and at other times it is a novel which originally is so impressive that playwrights and writers of the screen set to work to adapt its story to their own forms of entertainment.

Like the cinema, fiction series such as the Reader's Library were designed for a new mass public, using the technology of mass production to service 'a real modern demand'.

> The Reader's Library Film Edition has been instituted to meet a real modern demand. Interest in a film is by no means exhausted merely by seeing it. The two arts, or forms of expression, the picture and the written word in book form, react one on the other. Imagination, stimulated by the film, is yet not satisfied until its story is wholly absorbed. In a word, the film-goer wishes also to read the book of the film, and the reader to see the picture.
> To meet this undeniable call for literature associated with the film,

it would not be enough to produce books of inferior quality. The Publishers' aim, therefore, has been to present them in clear type, on excellent paper, and with beautiful and durable bindings. Publication will coincide with the appearance of each new and important film.

Nothing of the kind has ever before been possible, even in the days when book production has been the least expensive. To render it possible now it will be necessary that each volume should have a sale of hundreds of thousands of copies, and that many volumes of the series should in due course find their way into nearly every home, however humble, in the British Empire.

The publishers have the utmost confidence that this end will be achieved, for during the four years that these books have been on the market forty million copies have been sold in Great Britain.

(Guy Thorne, *Butterfly on a Wheel*, inside cover)

The reading public grew as cinema grew, ever eager not only for information about the latest stars but also for stories that echoed, or fed, the world of movies.

A new public, a cinema-going public, wants to read nothing but novels, and only those which are 'hot huddles of sensation'. The huddle that is hottest and most sensational, providing that such qualities are effective but decently draped, will be this or that Book of the Month or 'recommendation'; and this mass public without traditions of book-buying or book-owning will at once swarm into the libraries in search of it.[11]

The popularity of the western novel (for instance) grew alongside westerns at the cinema and the television series that followed in the 1960s and diminished with the diminishment of the popularity of the genre on the wide screen and on the small screen as the century progressed. Between 1919 and 1939 reading became a popular and regular form of mass leisure entertainment to be enjoyed at home, at work or on the 'prom'. The number of books published between 1914 and 1939 almost doubled from nearly 9,000 titles to 14,000 titles and sales climbed from 7.2 million in 1928 to 26.8 million by 1939. In 1911 public libraries owned just over 54 million books, by 1939 that figure was over 247 million.

By the 1930s, newspapers were the most important single literary medium in Britain with over two-thirds of the population reading a daily paper and three-quarters reading a Sunday paper; sales went steadily up from a readership of around 4.5 million to approximately 10.5 million. Popular papers like the *Daily Express* grew to 2.5 million readers per day and Sundays like the *News of the World* reached nearly 4 million people. By 1947 well over 29 million people read a Sunday paper with the *News of the World* reaching a staggering 8 million readers by the mid-1950s. Such huge circulation figures made Alfred Harmsworth (Lord Northcliffe), Lord Rothermere and Lord Beaverbrook significant public figures as well as rich ones, but it also made them cagey and competitive, instantly wanting to know 'the way the public thinks'.

> Tom Clarke records of Northcliffe how one night at dinner, he asked if any of us had read *If Winter Comes* and added, 'I cannot understand why people are reading it. It sends me to sleep. I am bored to death with the silly creature with the bicycle.' 'Why do you read it then, Chief?' I asked. 'Because,' he replied, 'it is important for me to know why 500,000 people have bought or read that book. My business is to know what the public wants to read.'[12]

Yet belief that you could judge the public's mind (especially women's minds – and *modern* women at that) by reading a best-selling novel led almost always and inevitably to a dismissal of such readers (and their class) as illiterates (and moral derelicts). The *Bookseller* pompously intoned in 1919,

> Surely the kind of people who are content to accept 'the pictures' as a substitute for books are so unsophisticated, and the sort of novels they would otherwise read are of such a quality, that there is nothing at all to worry about.[13]

And even T. Fisher Unwin, who was sympathetic to the cinema-influenced reader, believed that a large reading public would be of a 'lower grade'. It was not too long before popular reading was seen as not only debased but immoral and corrupting. The *Daily News* (13 Dec. 22) noted of Edith Thompson[14] at her trial that,

> Here was Mrs Thompson, child . . . of a favoured age; one of those well-fed, well-dressed young women that the suburbs have produced in the last twenty years; educated up to a point; given an opportunity to realise what a wonder she is . . . by being allowed to hold a

responsible post in commerce, and being paid a salary for it that would have made her grandmother swoon. She was now at the stage when she developed an imagination.

Then, when what she needed was God and William Shakespeare, she was given cheap sweets and Gloria de Vere.

The Thompson case is a symbol of what happens to a State which attains to a certain degree of material prosperity, but lacks a general passion for art and religion.[15]

Modern woman was illiterate and immoral because of her *ability* to read (the wrong novels!) rather than despite it. Literacy was not a matter of technical ability but one of *moral choice* beyond the reach of statistics. When everybody could and did read then all that was left to researchers was a certain conservative ethics of reading which sociological investigations confirmed rather than dismissed.

The advent of television and more particularly the appearance of commercial television signalled to those of the 'establishment' that illiteracy was now the norm. When commercial television began in 1955, Norman Collins, then Deputy Chairman of Associated Television, complained,

> that the overwhelming mass of viewers' letters which Associated Television received were illiterate. 'They are ungrammatical and execrably written,' he said. 'And what is more distressing, they evidence an attitude of mind that I do not think can be regarded as very admirable.' All the writers wanted, he said, were pictures of film stars, television stars, or reasons why there were not more jazz programmes, or why there could not be more programmes of a musical kind. 'I hold teachers very largely responsible if that is the attitude of people in their teens and early twenties,' he said. 'If we provided simply that it would be deplorable.'[16]

The appearance of television, nevertheless, meant a new source of reading matter for a new public – a source only strengthened with the revival of cinema during the 1980s and 1990s.

> There was a yet more radical effect on newspapers, however, in that what had been presumed to be their *raison d'être* was undermined: the twenty-four-hour cycle of a newspaper tended to lose its point as a news medium, in face of the recurring instalments of news on television. Broadsheet newspapers could try to adjust to the situation

by supplying detailed background to news headlines, perhaps seasoned by an investigative twist. For the popular press, the problem might have seemed to be more intractable. The *Daily Mirror* and *Daily Sketch* began by pretending that television did not exist, despite the evidence that it was a major component in their readers' lives. An innovation of the *Sun*, as transformed under Rupert Murdoch's ownership for 1969, was to assume that it was a mistake to treat television as a rival medium: on the contrary, television, or especially its more down-home productions, would be treated in great depth. Crises in the plots of soap-operas, but also the actors' true-life romances and tribulations, were to be voraciously analysed, with characters and thespians, fact and fiction, becoming sumptuously confused. This betokened what was to become a favourite strategy in the face of the new medium, and one by no means restricted to the popular press: displaced as the primary emissary of news, newspapers would increasingly focus on providing entertainment, with fiction enjoying a doughty reputation as liable to be more entertaining than fact.[17]

The advent of television (and more especially commercial television) divided literary opinion right from the start.

The year of 1951 started out well: a study in *The Bookseller* reported that TV had no effect on the amount of books sold. Despite this confidence, the question came under discussion again during a March lunch of the National Book League. Mr Cecil Madden of the BBC TV service related that, in his job, he had been told to entertain children, not to educate them. Mr W. W. Robson of Oxford said that passivity in children would result from such TV watching. However, Ms C. A. Lejeun, a film and TV critic, disagreed and said that no effect on the book trade would be seen. Later in that year, the PEB Broadsheet reported that by May of 1951, there were 869,200 TV licences, and that since 1948, there had been only a 6% rise in spending on books, but a 45% rise in spending on magazines – a form of communication with a shorter attention span similar to that for TV.[18]

Such fears reflected earlier concern over popular fiction and its debilitating effects, especially upon young women.

Dr Bernard Holland, the well known specialist, interviewed by the *Daily Express* gives it as his opinion that one reason of the increasing popularity of novels is to be found in the fact that people are too lazy to study serious literature. Owing perhaps to this cause, many novelists seem to write down to the level of their audience, and if by doing so gain in sales they certainly lose in the faculty of doing really good work. Women, according to Dr Holland, are most inclined to reading second class novels; some indeed, read romances because they like to imagine what they themselves would do if they were the heroines.[19]

In 1953 there was even a Simplified Spelling Bill introduced to Parliament by MP Mont Follick, and in the same year the Archbishop of Canterbury remarked that the use of television for educational purposes was 'nothing less than a perfect disaster'.[20]

Yet it soon became clear that television posed less of a threat than an opportunity despite the fact that reading habits may have been lessened amongst poorer and less well educated people (the very people Dr Holland accused of lowering the standard of fiction).

By 1952, however, the book industry either stopped deluding itself or TV became so popular that it could not help but notice. A BBC inquiry into the income and educational levels of 3,137 'TV families' found that seven viewers out of ten had obtained no full-time education, 30 per cent had ended their education at the ages of 16–19, and 67 per cent had finished school at 14 or 15. Furthermore, a family of a lower income was more likely to get a TV than a family of a higher income, who would rely upon books. In the survey, 42 per cent of viewers said that their reading time had diminished with the purchase of their TV set, and people also cut back on radio and cinema time if they had TVs.[21]

Despite some decline, therefore, publishers soon realised the power of television promotion. During 1956, ITV ran a programme called *The Living Page*, sponsored by four publishers, who joined together as Television Books Ltd to promote their titles. Books were also regular features of television factual programming and, of course, fiction could be dramatised for television audiences. The downturn of reading reported by libraries in 1954 because of television was already reversed by 1957. In 1995 alone, television directly accounted for the sale of 177,000 copies of Jane Austen's *Pride and Prejudice*:

Libraries in London report that watching television has no adverse effects on reading habits. In fact, since television debuted at the end

of 1956, Carlisle Library has had adult lending library records including 2,642 titles lent on one day and 34,749 titles lent in one month.
They claim that, 'the good feature programs of television undoubtedly stimulate interest, and an eager desire for books of a more pur-
posive kind covering a wider range and scope has been noticed.'[22]

During 1961 the debate flared again when portable transistor radios
became available.

> Current controversy on the social effects of television are very rem-
> iniscent of public debate in the 1920s on the consequences of radio
> in the home. . . . Broadcasting, it was then said, would not only keep
> people away from the concert halls; it would stop them from reading
> books. But in fact the sale of books increased and more than one
> local librarian referred to wireless communication as a new ally . . .
> creating and deepening the interest of the public in higher forms of
> literature.[23]

By the 1960s television was a complementary medium, not a rival,
and a shop window which bore the message 'Buy a book, help STAMP
out TV' appeared positively antediluvian.[24] The success of television and
the crossover from television series to paperback book could also aid
publishers in their search for things which could not appear on the
'box'. This could be used to boost titles associated with a television series
where a book series could act as a continuation of the programmes.
During the successful television series hosted by Alfred Hitchcock
during 1957, a book series was published by Pan called 'Stories They
Wouldn't Let Me Do on TV', a rather cheeky (and successful) attempt
to cash in on the success of the programme and yet suggest thrills not
permissible on television.

The library system

Another important guide to literacy and reading habits has been the
growth of lending libraries and their central importance to communal
life throughout the twentieth century. Circulating libraries have, of
course, existed since the nineteenth century, but these had been mostly
commercial enterprises. The most significant of these was Mudie's.

> Serialisation by no means threatened the three-decker in which the
> majority of lesser novelists continued to appear. The *Publishers'*

Circular listed six times as many in 1887 (184) as in 1837 (31). A prime factor in its survival, and increased prosperity, in the mid-century period was the dramatic growth in the circulating library business. In the 1840s and 50s Mudie's library in particular expanded to control a major section of the metropolitan market and a sizeable portion of that in the country and overseas. At his zenith, in the 1860s, he earned up to £40,000 a year in subscriptions. . . . Mudie's triumph was the outcome not of cautious whittling down of costs but of slashing them dramatically, so short circuiting the gap that existed between high book prices and low income. . . . One reason that fiction tends to gravitate towards the cheapest form of publishing is that in most cases it is read once only, and then quickly. In America this economic logic led to books of incredible cheapness, designed to be thrown away after use. In Britain it was not the book which was cheapened but the reading of it.[25]

Mudie's not only lent out books, it also, by its methods of business, determined the shape of fiction – its packaging *as fiction* and therefore ultimately its content and style. Other commercial circulating libraries continued long into the twentieth century, Boots and Harrods both lending books on subscription. Smaller enterprises, such as local newsagents and tobacconists, lent out mainly paperbacks to local working-class or lower middle-class readers, as a lucrative sideline and communal service, almost to the end of the century. Whilst most had vanished by the 1980s, at least one London suburban newsagent in Highams Park continued lending books into 1984. Such paperbacks were usually romances from Mills and Boon and were lent to an exclusively older female readership. Nevertheless, Harrods also did a good trade in romance, delivered to your door rather than collected from a corner-shop counter. The days of the commercial circulating library were, however, numbered. Harrods closed its facilities quite late in the century, during 1989, Boots earlier in 1961, whilst Day's Circulating Library which had opened in 1776, closed in 1957. It was Britain's oldest circulating library. By the 1990s, such libraries had vanished to be replaced by their modern equivalent – the video-hire store.

Whilst companies such as Boots concentrated on their pharmaceutical and cosmetic departments and closed their lending facilities, things went somewhat differently for W. H. Smith and Son. The House of W. H. Smith began life as a 'newsagent', located at 4 Grosvenor Street around the year 1792. It was there that Henry Walton Smith and his wife Anna brought up their two sons, Henry Edward and William Henry.

With the death of their father but under the eye of their astute mother, the two brothers opened a reading room at 192 Strand, concentrating their business upon the fast delivery of newspapers and the production of stationery. By beating competition from the mail coaches, Smith's red-painted carts and coaches took up-to-date news across country in record time.

In 1846, a second William was born and W. H. Smith and Son was created, specialising in the use of mail express trains to deliver the news, whilst also creating railway station bookstalls (Euston being the first). Although the bookstalls sold current popular fiction, the elder W. H. Smith always considered that side of the business as 'rubbish' and it was not until his death that bookselling was considered a respectable part of the family firm. It was then that the lending library was begun.

> The creation of the lending library gave fresh emphasis to the need for more novels in a popular form, and the Firm bought up the copyright of Charles Lever's books and issued them in the yellow covers which were to become so famous. . . . [s]oon the 'yellow-backs' had arrived.
>
> (Anon., *The Story of W. H. Smith and Son*, p. 71)

The company, however, withdrew from book publishing (mainly because of costs) and concentrated instead on lending, distribution and stationery. By 1906 W. H. Smith had withdrawn many of its bookstalls and replaced them with town shops packed with the fiction that Smith Senior had so disliked. The Book Department (begun 1849) had by 1952 risen from fifty staff to over six hundred, dealing in not only books but also magazines and overseas accounts. Meanwhile, the library prospered.

> Everything about the Library [was] planned on a very grand scale. . . . Nearly four hundred of the Firm's shops and bookstalls [were] library branches, and there [were] many customers who receive[d] their library books direct, either by post or – in London – by van.
>
> (Ibid., p. 72)

All this had considerable consequences for publishers.

> For a new novel by a popular author there [was] naturally a tremendous demand, and the Library [had] to order in thousands if there [were] to be enough at the branches on the day of publication. But

even then the order may have [had] to be increased to meet further demands. Sometimes a very large order [was] placed for a book by a comparatively unknown author because it [was] believed to be outstanding.

(Ibid., p. 74)

By the early 1950s, W. H. Smith employed over 17,000 staff in numerous bookshops, bookstalls, warehouses and distribution centres. At the end of the twentieth century the library had finally been closed (in 1961) and the company had lost its family connections after a takeover, yet it remained as it had begun, a stationers and newsagent specialising in a broad range of new and classic fiction.

Commercial libraries were augmented by those created by philanthropists such as Andrew Carnegie. Born poor in 1835 in Dunfermline, Scotland, he emigrated to the United States and having made a vast fortune gave much of it back, as was the fashion of the day, in grants for libraries, museums and art galleries. Carnegie's sense of social justice, though hardly present in his business dealings, returned in the endowment of public libraries that bear his name. In 1919 there were 3,000 Carnegie libraries in the world at an estimated foundation cost of $60 million. Such largesse was not without its critics. The eccentric MP Sir Frederick Banbury commented in the same year, 'I do not believe that public libraries have done any good because the books read . . . are chiefly sensational works.' He had never been to a public library. The examples of self-improvement and morality were central to this democratising creed and the public library system funded by local government long continued this zealous path. When in the 1930s the vast industrial 'garden' estate of Becontree Heath in Essex had reached completion, with the workers housed in the newest cottage-style homes with modern facilities and small garden plots, it was a municipal library rather than a church that finished the work and gave the community focus. Throughout the early part of the century the local public library system grew. At the end of the twentieth century, councils such as Redbridge, maintaining a large area of the eastern suburbs of London, could boast neither a communal museum (until 2000) nor an art gallery but could take pride in exceptional library facilities.

Libraries still remain a focus for much communal activity and users of libraries are more socially mixed than those who buy books regularly. In October 1999, the National Library Trust reported that 22 per cent of library users are professional or managerial (classes A and B); 28 per cent are white-collar men (class C); 24 per cent are skilled manual workers (classes D and E). A visit to any local library during the working hours of the working week will certainly offer evidence of high use by the retired, housewives, and schoolchildren.[26] Nowadays, libraries are more than just book lenders.

The Public Lending Right has also tracked library use since 1982 and in October 1999 it reported that between 1988–9 and 1997–8 percentages of adult fiction books loaned out had fallen from 53.9 per cent to 52 per cent, light romance was down from 14.1 per cent to 10.6 per cent, humorous fiction from 7 per cent to only 2 per cent and short stories to a negligible 0.2 per cent. War fiction also declined from 1.8 per cent to 1.3 per cent. Such a decline becomes more significant when 'best-selling' loans are considered (a bestseller being considered a book loaned out throughout the system over one million times). Hence, for instance, in 1990–1, 64.29 per cent of bestsellers consisted of adult fiction, but this steadily declined over the last years of the century to only 43.75 per cent. In contrast children's fiction has soared from a mere 28 per cent of bestseller loans to 50 per cent of all such borrowings.[27]

Such changes and especially the diminution of book borrowing reflect the place and significance of the library in the community. Since the 1980s libraries have actively sought to diversify their provision by putting records, videos, CDs, DVDs, and audio-tapes on their shelves as well as providing 'information' centres and computer facilities. Marked amongst such changes is the extraordinary increase in audio 'talking books', and in areas with a multi-ethnic component, shelves given over to books in Urdu, Gudjerati, and Hindi. Technical innovation has simply followed market trends, where in the ten-year period 1989–99 the market for videos, CDs and tapes had increased by 60 per cent. It remains a curious fact, however, that the 'decline' in adult bestseller borrowing cannot be totally explained by library organisation changes or market-led decisions. Such a decline was also recorded between 1915 and 1949. Such changes remain unclear and are likely to have social rather than commercial origins.

Bare statistics are long and dull without any sense of why actual people want to go to a library and borrow a book. Although unlikely to yield very scientific results it was nevertheless this question that was in the mind of Mass Observation's determined researchers when they took up the challenge to interview members of the library-using public in 1947. This is how they went about their work.

To find out more about how people select books five men and five women, selected at random, were followed and closely observed from the time they entered the lending library to the time they left. The fiction shelves at the Metrop library [*sic*] extend all round the walls, and the non-fiction books are in the middle. Next to the sociology shelf and opposite some fiction shelves, are a few shelves where the fiction that has just been brought back is placed temporarily by the librarians before it is put back in its proper place on the fiction shelves. It is customary for many people to crowd round this shelf, since the books that have been just taken out may be supposed to be the most popular. Five of the people followed (4 men and 1 woman) went straight to this shelf on coming into the library. A further three people (2 men, 1 woman) looked first at the books on the librarian's counter which had just been brought back. Thus eight out of the ten went for 'popular' books first.[28]

A random questioning of borrowers as to their habits brought mixed answers. On being asked 'Why did [readers] choose that book?' researchers were told,

'Well, I've read John Buchan's books before. That's the reason.' (Man 30)

'I'm getting on in age. I want light reading. You understand that, don't you? I don't want to study anything at my time of life. Perhaps I come here two or three times a week. I'm a great reader.' (Man 65)

'I used to like Ethel M. Dell . . . but they don't seem to have any of those now. You just have to [take a] chance I look, and I think if they are promising.' (Woman 50)

'Well, I took it because it's a thriller. That's the reason. I like thrillers, you see. I always read thrillers.' (Man 16)

'Well, because I do like Ernest Raymond's books and I read all of them as far as I can.'[29]

And on a further question about how books were selected, readers told their interviewers,

'Sometimes by the author and sometimes I have to look inside to see if there's anything worthwhile to pick on you know.' (Man 70)

'Well, I've just got a list of authors that I'm keen on and I just go round the different authors and see if I can find one of those.' (Woman 30)

'Well, I generally go for mystery books, and I look for them especially.'   (Man 45)

'Well, it's a job to say. I tell you the type of books I like to get hold of – similar to Jules Verne, like that. And air stories.'   (Man 25)

'I like – what shall I say? A good, clean, decent novel, that's got some sense in it. I like something that's really worthwhile.'   (Woman 45)[30]

Researchers then secretly followed borrowers to document their movements. One woman's movements were recorded in such detail that they suggest counter-surveillance, rather than mere people-watching. (Interestingly, this account does bring out the *tactile* quality of book selection.)

Saturday, January 10th
2.40 enters library bringing back two books. Walks past sociology shelf, gazing up at the ceiling, and on to a 'just-in' fiction shelf. Crowds round this with other people bending forward to see. Takes out a book and keeps it without opening it. Coughs. Stoops down and touches shelf. Takes down book called *Michael*, opens it and looks at it 2 seconds and keeps. Then she opens the first one she took down and looks at it and shuts it almost immediately. Then she bends again towards the shelf looking at the titles short-sightedly. She opens the first book she took out again and looks at it for 10 seconds. Then she puts it back on the shelf. Touches the backs of the books looking at them. Takes down another book, *Without Motive*, by Winston Graham, and looks at this for 6 seconds and puts it back.

Then she moves over to the fiction shelves (authors beginning with G) opposite, moves along to authors F, shuffling her feet, looking at these shelves. Then she opens the book she has already taken again and looks at it 6 seconds, and shuts it and looks back at shelf.

She goes over to the other side of the library where the authors beginning with W are. Blows her nose. Looks at the top shelf with her mouth hanging open. Takes down a book and looks at the middle of it, then at the page where the library's stamp is, then at the back, and puts it back on the shelf after 11 seconds. She fingers the backs of the books and bends forward to read the titles better. She has settled opposite Hugh Walpole's books. She takes down *The Park Forest*, looks and puts it back at once. Then she takes down *The Silver Thorn* by the same author, and looks at the end of it for 7 seconds. Puts it back on an empty shelf at the bottom. She takes down the next Walpole to this and looks at it 8 seconds and slams it back on the shelf. She has been working along the Walpoles from left to right one after the other, and goes on doing this, taking the next books out and looking at them respectively 7 seconds, 2 seconds, 24 seconds (*John Cornelius*), and 34 seconds. Observer notices that in nearly every case she looks mostly at the end of the book, especially the last page. Then she takes down another book (still Walpole), looks at the end and then at the middle, in all 14 seconds, and keeps this. She takes out the last Walpole on the shelf and looks at this for 11 seconds and puts it back again.

At 2.53 she goes out with the two books (both fiction) that she has chosen, having spent 13 minutes in the library.[31]

Light fiction proved more popular amongst such library users than serious works and both proved more popular than the 'classics'. One male borrower looked for 'snappy . . . quick reading' whilst another read Nicholas Blake because it did not require 'a lot of concentration'.[32] Comparing public libraries with the commercial libraries brought the following conclusion.

Public libraries have a rather more serious-minded clientele than the 2d. libraries. Asked how the war had affected people's taste in reading some librarians at 2d. libraries said:

'I still notice that they are reading light stuff mostly, although there are some people that want something with a little more in it. It seems to me that the average person wants something to distract.'

'Fiction. Blood and murder, love and blood, all of them just the same.'

'Reading is lighter. More interesting, sophisticated novels. Nothing heavy or dull. And no political books are ever wanted. I think they get too much of that in the newspapers.'

'Well, it's just ordinary like – romance and mystery.'[33]

The male interviewee concluded mournfully that whilst men wanted something 'blood and thunderish', women only borrowed 'a lot of slop'.[34]

The British public library system, maintained on the rates (now council tax) and providing a service to the local ratepayers, has remained a bulwark of local life since its inception. Expanding in its provision, the service has lost much of its old moral guardianship, something it maintained into the 1970s. The debate over the function of library provision ('socially useful reading' or 'everything that the public requested' as one librarian put it in 1952) has been part of an evolution in the library service with its willingness to integrate literature and the printed word into a wider, media-based provision. No longer the guardians of local morality (as to which books could be borrowed by whom), the local librarian is not a mere purveyor of cheap (fictional) entertainment and despite archaic fears that literature on demand meant cheap novelettes and pornography (a worry in 1951–2 from a correspondent from Harrods to the *Bookseller*), libraries remain centres of excellence in most British communities. If it is true that the phenomenal building rate of new libraries during 1946 to 1951 has not been topped, closures have been relatively carefully guarded against despite bad times in the 1970s.

The financial difficulties which led many councils in 1999 to consider shutting some local branches brought vigorous denunciation from local pressure groups, the *Evening Standard* (in London) and the Secretary of State. The ministerial verdict on 54 'good' authorities, 85 'satisfactory' authorities and 10 'poor' authorities (in that year) was that closures were not to be tolerated. Libraries were still central to the cultural (and social) wellbeing of a community. In the words of the Secretary of State, Chris Smith, local 'libraries [were] street corner universities'.[35]

Librarians, sales, and the female reader

By the end of the twentieth century the changing needs of library borrowers had begun to cause anxiety amongst librarians eager to understand the new circumstances within which they were required to provide their service. The model soon adopted for their investigations was none other than the same model for book purchase – the book borrower was now to be treated as a customer. Such market-led considerations provided a close analogy between borrowers and purchasers and from it emerged the first real evidence for the 'identity' of book purchasers.

Dividing their customers between heavy, medium, and light borrowers, librarians found that heavy borrowers were also multiple purchasers and, as obvious as it may seem, light borrowers rarely bought books. Heavy borrowers kept abreast of new authors and titles, seeking out reviews and searching shelves, whilst others did so in diminishing degrees. Two-thirds or more of heavy borrowers found their love of reading in childhood and encouraged their own children to read, whilst only one-third of light borrowers did the same. Equally, heavy borrowers enjoyed reading whenever possible, at meals, in bed, relaxing in the evening. Light borrowers read much less, preferring television or newspapers. Yet there were subtle similarities. Heavy borrowers tended to read Conservative newspapers: *Daily Mail, Sun, Telegraph* or *Express*; little different from light readers, whose tastes ran exclusively to the more popular tabloids. A high proportion listened to BBC Radio 2 but this, as in other things, tended to reflect age rather than any sense of intellectual division – readers tending to be slightly older, conservative in taste in both books and music. In social habits and attitudes (going to the pub, cinema and for a meal), heavy borrowers differed little from light borrowers. If a third of heavy borrowers bought hardbacks, so did light borrowers; if half bought paperbacks, so did light borrowers with little to differentiate them except in the amounts of books bought or borrowed.

Book buying, even for heavy borrowers, was a luxury, an indulgence and not a necessity whilst book borrowing remained a needed routine. Heavy borrowers were also people who were likely to 'taste' a new author by borrowing the work from a friend or library before going to the bookshop. They were also people whose natural conservatism meant they retained a loyalty to certain favourite names and expected to find these in the library in preference to a bookshop, for most saw no point in purchasing what could be borrowed. And this routine was nothing less than *female* with almost three-quarters of all fiction borrowed or bought by women, a mirror image of the purchase of non-fiction by men. Thus avid book purchasers and borrowers were the same in 1999 as in 1900, mostly women, with traditional tastes and habits, reading in private for leisure and relaxation vast quantities of fiction: crime thrillers and detective novels, romances, family sagas; younger women enjoying fantasy and horror too. There is, in short, a remarkable consistency between women's reading in 1999 and in 1900, genres mutating (rather than absolutely changing) to suit new tastes and situations. Women readers are vital to the book trade. During 1994, publishers spent £100,000 advertising John le Carré's *Night Manager* in order to attract a female readership. Adverts were placed in shopping centres and on radio. Jilly Cooper's *The Man who Made Husbands Jealous* was advertised on television and in *Cosmopolitan*, the *Sunday Express* and the *Mail on Sunday*.

It is instructive, in terms of gender preference, to consider the changes in the reading habits of children as they grew into their teenage years. Here clear genre preferences tended to emerge as children grew up. For instance, three-quarters of all boys and girls aged between four and seven enjoyed 'adventure' books but by the age of eleven to sixteen, four-fifths of boys and only two-fifths of girls still did. Books about sport represented an even greater shift with just under half of all four- to seven-year-old boys enjoying such books compared with under two-fifths for girls of the same age. By teenage years the number of boys reading about sport stayed consistent but girls had almost ceased to be interested. Interest in 'romance' is obviously low in young children but by eleven to sixteen girls were reading four times as much romance as boys and over twice as many 'diary'-style books. The enjoyment of horror books remained evenly split but boys overwhelmingly preferred 'fantasy' adventure and hobby books. Thus, by sixteen, children had formed their adult reading habits, divided almost too neatly on gender lines.

The predominance of women readers (and their concomitant demands on theme and character) meant that by the 1980s, although women represented only about a third of best-selling authors (in any year) and despite the dearth of female critics (see Appendix 10), more and more books used a female as a central character. Being women-led, by the late twentieth century the book market (in fiction) had no choice but to cater for such readers' needs. Oprah Winfrey in the United States could promote a book on her shows (almost exclusively watched by women) and guarantee sales of over a million copies. Such power meant that by the mid-1990s, seven out of ten books on the bestseller lists had female lead characters, of whom Clarice Starling (from Thomas Harris's Hannibal Lecter series) became the most famous. Other works with female main characters included Joanna Trollope's *The Choir* (1992); Maeve Binchy's *The Glass Lake* (1995); Nicholas Evans's *The Horse Whisperer* (1996); Jostein Gaarder's *Sophie's World* (1996); Wilbur Smith's *The Seventh Scroll* (1996); Peter Hoeg's *Miss Smilla's Feeling for Snow* (1996); and Robert James Waller's *The Bridges of Madison County* (1993).* As almost three-quarters of all publishing staff were women, and by the late twentieth century many had commanding jobs, the symbiosis of market demand, publisher response and author commissions put female sensibility at the centre of fictional narrative. To sell to women was commercial common sense. With the appearance in 1997 of the sassy and sexy 'neurotic modern career woman' novel, epitomised by Helen Fielding's *Bridget Jones's Diary*, the market became saturated with Bridget Jones clone novels promoted to exhaustion in supermarket displays, on the shelves of W. H. Smith and in the windows of major

---

* Paperback release dates.

book-selling chains. Of note in this regard was the appearance at the end of the century of a number of women writers whose contemporary themed novels commanded big advances for their authors. Such was the case with Amy Jenkins, Jenny Colgan, Freya North, Louise Bagshaw, Claire Calman, Lauren McCrussan and Tiffanie Darke.

Helen Fielding's comic character seemed to sum up the dilemma of the successful woman of the late twentieth century, a woman who had gained everything her grandmothers had fought for, a hundred years before, and yet who was left with little of value. A member of the 'chattering classes', Bridget Jones is an overweight and on-the-shelf, female, thirty-something, part-time feminist living in London with a group of equally unfocused friends drifting into middle age. Bridget's mother, living the feminist ideal life, is nothing less than a perpetual embarrassment, as Bridget, obsessed with self-help books such as John Gray's *Men are from Mars, Women are from Venus* (1993), tries to make sense of her boyfriend problems. The book sums up a lost 'post'-feminist generation of women, avid readers of both self-help manuals and neurotic comedy novels that satirise them. All in all, 'this confusion, [she guesses], is the price . . . for becoming a modern woman' (p. 19).

Yet, above all, the book is a novel of modern middle-class manners and mores summed up in lists of dinner-party food.

> An unbelievable amount of food and wine was consumed since the generous girls, as well as bringing a bottle of wine each, had all brought a little extra something from M & S.* Therefore, in addition to the three-course meal and two bottles of wine (1 fizzy, 1 white) I had already bought from M & S (I mean prepared by entire day's slaving over hot stove) we had:
>
> > 1 tub hummus & pkt mini-pittas.
> > 12 smoked salmon and cream cheese pinwheels.
> > 12 mini-pizzas.
> > 1 raspberry pavlova.
> > 1 tiramisu (party size).
> > 2 Swiss Mountain Bars.
>
> (p. 125)

And it is a life summed up in diaries obsessed with detailing the results of over-consumption:

* Marks & Spencer Stores.

Saturday 13 May

> *9st 1lb 8oz, cigarettes 7, calories 1145, Instants 5 (won £2 therefore total Instants expenditure only £3, v.g.), Lottery proper £2, number of correct numbers 1 (better).*

How come have put on only 8oz after last night's over-consumption orgy?

(p. 124)

With its knowing self-awareness, *Bridget Jones's Diary* was, nevertheless, finally (if ironically) set within the boundaries of an earlier conservative fiction in which it saw itself reflected. Jane Austen was born again in post-modern *homage* – Bridget Jones has a boyfriend called Mark Darcy and the BBC shows *Pride and Prejudice* (it was actually shown in 1999).

> **8:55 a.m.** Just nipped out for fags prior to getting changed for BBC *Pride and Prejudice*. . . . I would hate to see Darcy and Elizabeth in bed, smoking a cigarette afterwards. That would be unnatural and wrong and I would quickly lose interest. . . . Darcy and Elizabeth. They are my chosen representatives in the field of shagging, or, rather, courtship.

(pp. 246–7)

Unsurprisingly, Candace Bushnell's *4 Blondes* (2001) was puffed by the *Sunday Telegraph* as 'Jane Austen with a martini' (cover blurb).

Nowhere is this conservatism and traditionalism better exemplified than in the work of 'Miss Read' (Dora Saint). Her fictional village of Thrush Green provided a nostalgic setting for her elderly spinsters and clerics, and remained a place where 'chaps' could enjoy a 'reviving cup of tea' and older ladies could look forward to 'jollifications' or return library books to their friends, whilst neighbours drank 'mugs of hot milk and [ate] digestive biscuits' while 'counting stitches [on their] knitting needle' (*Celebrations at Thrush Green*, 1992, ch. 1). Such language enhanced rather than prohibited the popularity of Miss Read's books and she remained in the top fifty authors throughout the last quarter of the twentieth century.

If writing for women might reflect the 'truth' of the heart, men's fiction reflected, in contrast, the truth of technology, with writers such as Jack Higgins, Peter Benchley, Arthur Hailey, John Grisham and James Clavell researching details of the more abstruse realms of World War

Two sabotage, deep sea exploration, the car industry, legal labyrinths or oriental history. Overwhelmingly the information is detailed and technological in order to offer depth and realism to thriller plotlines. Tom Clancy's *The Hunt for Red October* (1984) acknowledges naval experts and a Lieutenant-Commander of the US Navy in its credits and was originally published by the Naval Institute Press. Praised for its 'flawless authenticity' (*Wall Street Journal*) it combines a tense thriller-style with intriguing technical detail.

> Ryan lifted a pointer. 'In addition to being considerably larger than our own *Ohio*-class Trident submarines, *Red October* has a number of technical differences. She carries twenty-six missiles instead of our twenty-four. The earlier *Typhoon*-class vessels, from which she was developed, only have twenty. *October* carried the new SS-N-20 sea-launched ballistic missile, the Seahawk. It's a solid-fuel missile with a range of about six thousand nautical miles, and it carries eight multiple independently targetable re-entry vehicles, MIRVs, each with an estimated yield of five hundred kilotons. It's the same RV carried by their SS-18s, but there are less of them per launcher.'
>
> (Tom Clancy, *The Hunt for Red October*, p. 109)

Publishers

Building on an established market

By the middle of the nineteenth century publishing had become a modern, capital-intense business, the old connection between printing and publishing having been severed in most companies. The industry was set to take on those modern characteristics that were to last into the late twentieth century.

The British book trade in the nineteenth century was a modern industry in every way. It took advantage of mechanised systems of production, developed highly efficient distribution arrangements based on the most up-to-date means of transport, and evolved a division of labour both between and within its various branches. Many firms were still family businesses, but they were large and well-organised, and many of their owners were employers of labour on a substantial scale. Millions of pounds of capital investment poured into the trade, much of it generated directly from profit. It was inevitable that attitudes within the industry also underwent a profound change. The parochialism of the battle for literary property and the restrictive practices of the congers and the trade sales vanished into history; the trade was in the marketplace, and the first consideration was economic success in the face of competition.[36]

With the appearance of the Net Book Agreement in 1900, the book industry would become both a stable and a conservative force for the best part of a century, indeed.

> The British book trade is kept in line by the Publishers' Association, the Society of Authors and the Booksellers' Association, all set up together with the Net Book Agreement in the last two decades of the nineteenth century, after a long period of damaging, Hobbesian war of all against all. On one level the professional institutions have served to maintain a gentlemanly code. On another they serve as dams against a recurrence of potentially suicidal individualism. The British trade has thus founded itself on discipline, self-control and protectionism – sometimes with a fierceness reminiscent of the Catholic Church in its most militant phase.[37]

At least until the early 1970s this 'created stability, prosperity, order and professional dignity', continuity being provided by the consistency of a mainly rising market, which despite occasional depressions, reached a high in the 1960s, with a strong conservative readership base served by both local booksellers and retail chains like W. H. Smith or commercial and borough libraries across the country.[38] Firms such as Macmillan (founded 1843), John Cassell (1846) or Routledge (1836) continued to prosper and develop whilst newer names such as Gollancz (founded 1931), Jonathan Cape (founded 1921) or Penguin (founded 1935) catered for a growing and profitable mass market. The paperback revolution greatly increased sales of all types of book but especially fiction.

The phenomenal rise of fiction, and especially fiction aimed at a mass market, was already noticeable at the beginning of the twentieth century. Publishers could not fail to notice this new 'taste' for 'stories' read for pleasure and diversion even if the trade was alarmed by the trend.

> By 1910, fiction advertisement largely surpassed the advertisements for new editions of classics . . . which had diminished greatly. The advertisements of the 1890 editions were dominated by . . . Victorian classics or other older work. The increase in the popularity of the six-

penny novels and other cheap editions . . . marked the gradual heightening of the popularity of fiction, particularly current fiction.[39]

Notwithstanding the fears of critics and correspondents, publishers soon realised the need for a strong backlist and cheap-edition libraries of old titles. By 1913 the *Bookseller* was overwhelmingly full of adverts for re-issued fiction in cheap editions. Such editions were offered as 'libraries' (a working-class substitute for the private gentleman's collection) in seven-penny, sixpenny, threp'ny or slightly grander one shilling versions. Such editions would keep older writers' work alive and throughout the early century, as backlists were enlarged, there remained an emphasis on reprinting nineteenth-century classics like Austen, Dickens and Kipling in cheaply issued books. Sir Arthur Conan Doyle's work always sold well throughout the twentieth century in cheap reprints or cheaper editions. In 1911 new three-penny and sixpenny versions of his 'Round the Fire Stories' were available, and as late as 1953, Christina Foyle would comment on the continuing popularity of his work.[40] Publishers would also experiment with cheaper 'quality' bindings, ever aware of the possibilities of capturing a market segment not yet catered for; so, for instance, Herbert Jenkins experimented with a half-crown novel in 1920 as did Victor Gollancz in the 1930s.

Uniform cheap editions were not new to publishing (George Routledge had a 'Railway Library', 1848–98) but they quickly became a staple of the industry, making it possible to 'reinvent' old titles for new purposes. John Long published a 'Shilling Series', Cassell produced a 'Sixpenny Novel Series' and a 'Shilling Series', Macmillan had a 'Colonial Library of Copyright Books', Chapman and Hall a 'Two Shilling Net Novel Series', Everett and Co. had a 'seven-penny series of Copyright Fiction' and Hutchinson a 'seven-penny library'; but such series did not always succeed: both Nelson's 'seven-penny series' and 'The Readers Library' failed. Although the possibility of uniform publishing did not become clear until the advent of Penguin, it was nevertheless the case that very long print runs of out-of-copyright material could produce vast profits; if the model was originally German, the profit was British. By 1900 the effect of the Copyright Act of 1842 meant that authors deceased seven or more years previously and books published forty-two years ago now fell into the public domain. All the famous Victorian authors found a new revival between the covers of Nelson's 'classics' (beginning 1905), Grant Richard's 'World's Classics' (1901; taken over by Oxford University Press in 1905), Collins's 'Pocket Classics' (1903) and Dent's 'Everyman's Library' (1906).[41]

The success of the four series was immediate and has been lasting. By the middle of 1955 Nelson had passed 50 million copies; Collins had sold over 25 million copies of about 300 titles, 4.5 million of them since 1945 when only some 130 titles were in print. Dent, with near on 1000 volumes of 'Everyman's Library', have reached a total sale of nearly 41 million, and the 'World's Classics', with 550 titles, about 12.5 million.[42]

Cheap editions, endlessly recycled, kept classics and new authors constantly before the public, and if cheap editions were (and are) a useful staple for educational demand (especially for examined books), they proved even more useful for keeping current authors at high levels of demand. In 1913 Nat Gould's tales of racetracks and colonial life had already sold 7 million copies for John Long and by 1920 this had risen to a claimed 20 million. Such claims were not just publishers' wishful thinking. Florence L. Barclay's best-selling *The Rosary* enjoyed 'phenomenal popularity' during 1912 with the more expensive editions topping sales of 250,000; the promise of continuous cheap reprints guaranteed longevity. By 1920 she was still a bestseller. Charles Garvice, whose famed romantic tales, written for 'the man in the street, and still more for the girl in the garden', appealed to 'the natural instincts of men and women, whatever their rank', died that year, his sales of 7 million copies from world-wide sales augmented by a posthumous cheap reprint of 125,000 copies.[43]

With hardbacks often selling at seven shillings and sixpence most readers had to wait for cheaper reprints or get their books from a library. In 1923 one writer lamented,

> If it were possible for novels to be published at a lower price, say three and sixpence, the sale of those by known writers would very largely increase. As matters now stand seven and sixpence is very often more than the novel reader is prepared to pay for a novel, and he, or she, has to be content with borrowing it from the circulating library.[44]

It was not long before newer novelists (and their backlists) dominated the fiction market to the neglect of classics (and the lamentations of literary critics). 'Cheap' became a synonym for 'nasty' and 'popular' for 'mass-produced'.

With the decline of new fiction and restrictions on print and paper at the start of World War Two, booksellers noted a return to classic literature.

> Messrs J. M. Dent and Sons noticed a very marked increase in the demand for their *Everyman Library*: '. . . demand from the bookseller [for these well-known classics] during the first 5 months of the war had been about 25% greater than during the same period in the preceding year. . . . Tolstoy's *War and Peace* had an exceptional sale.'
>
> '. . . people's ordinary lives have been disturbed by the war and many felt a sense of isolation – it was like when you have the flu. At such times, people turn to classics. They want to read something that takes you back to the golden age, and they settle down to read the books they have always meant to read at some time but never had.'[45]

For a short period writers such as Trollope enjoyed renewed interest, as library borrowing records suggest.[46] Even poetry revived, as Christina Foyle remembered.

> There has been quite a large demand for poetry. Poetry, as I expect you know has not sold at all for the last 20 years, but wars usually do create an interest in poetry. During the last war [World War One] our best was [the] *Rubáiyat of Omar Khayyám*. We must have sold a million copies of that book alone.[47]

This trend was short-lived, although the classic novel (a bestseller in cheap reprints) would survive, as film and television revived stories by Dickens, Austen or Thackeray amidst a market dominated by crime fiction and romance. The shortage of new authors during the war meant that by the late 1940s nineteenth-century authors would still be competing with Edgar Wallace, Sax Rohmer, Warwick Deeping, Ethel M. Dell, Ruby M. Ayres, Naomi Jacob and Agatha Christie, all of whom were proving exceptionally popular. Even the contemporary taste for British authors of American-style pulp fiction was little less than an attempt to keep such stories on the market once war had cut off supplies of the real thing: new thrillers (referred to generically in the United States as mysteries) by genuinely American authors.

The market for hardback books

Despite the temporary setback of the war, with its shortages of paper and new authors and its destruction of bookshops and warehouses, the industry soon recovered, continuing its trend toward innovation and change that had begun in the 1930s. The central feature of twentieth-century publishing was always towards economy of scale in both production and marketing. This had already begun in earnest with the creation of strong backlists, easily recognisable formats, experimentation with book packaging and specialist 'genre' libraries. Strong backlists could be endlessly exploited through cheap reprints but some publishers were looking to enjoy the benefits of scale with regard to new publications. Victor Gollancz, for instance, hoping to exploit the potential sales of his detective list from a tie-in with the *Evening Standard*, declared in the *Bookseller* in November 1950:

> So certain are we of a really colossal sale for this book that, though a completely new book, we are publishing it straight away at what may be called a 'cheap edition' price.

Yet the backlist remained the staple source of mass-produced books, acting both as an insurance policy against bad times and as an investment ready and available for exploitation during good years or under exceptional circumstances. Thus the BBC radio serialisation of Warwick Deeping's *Sorrell and Son* during 1950 created sales of over 600,000 hardbacks for an otherwise moribund title.

The problem of how to fully exploit a new title nevertheless remained relatively unsolved. Indeed, little had changed in the production of new titles since Heinemann had 'levelled off' the library 'three-decker' with the publication of Hall Caine's *The Manxman*, in 1894. Book clubs were one solution.

The Book Club had originated in America where mail order was almost the only way of reaching remote farms and villages. The Book of the Month Club, which had begun in 1926, was soon proving its worth to British publishers who wished to escape control of the booksellers and at the same time expand their potential purchasers. Three years later, in 1929, the Book Society was founded in Britain with books selected by a rather dubious panel of literary 'experts'. Gollancz's Left Book Club followed in 1935 and a little later so did the Reprint Society, a consortium of five publishers including Jonathan Cape. W. H. Smith soon joined in, returning mail order to the retail sector, thence going on to dominate the market. As well as these clubs, specialist groups were catered for by the Right Book Club (thought up by Sir Oswald Mosley to promote fascism), Woman's Book Club, Art Book Club etc., all of them together accounting for 5 per cent of the market. By 1955 approximately 1 million sales were through book clubs, until paperback sales cut this by approximately a third in 1957.

Book clubs continued their success throughout the twentieth century, and mail order for books steadily increased with the appearance of Internet sales through Amazon, Waterstone's and BOL (Books on Line) during the 1990s. Nevertheless, the problem of determining patterns of success for new titles remained obscure and problematic. Nowhere was this more obvious than in the area of bestsellers, whose appeal could not be predicted. With no market research and laughably minuscule levels of advertising the search for the bestseller could never be anything other than a haphazard and serendipitous affair. Success in the market could only ever be pursued after the event or after book clubs had guaranteed purchases, or newspapers had been persuaded to buy serial rights and extract rights. Thor Heyerdahl's *Kon Tiki* (1950), which sold 875,000 hardbacks in its first eleven months, became a 'super bestseller' only after being finally bought on a whim by Philip Unwin in 1948.

If the bestseller aided less marketable titles, it could not be relied upon as a regular staple for publishers until the late 1980s when a small number of very large houses controlled the bestseller lists. Even then, marketing budgets were relatively low and high returns were often offset by the risk of failure elsewhere. Rather than the content of books it was their format in printed form that determined profitability; a successful book could be succinctly sold over a period of many years at diminishing retail costs, thus gaining ever new (yet poorer) retail sectors. At the same time classic hardback publishing was considered the prestige model in a traditional and gentlemanly profession. Thus profitability could still be squared with quality and the various mutations of the hardback still left it recognisable, but simply multiplied in more cheaply produced units. Library purchasing, which accounted for the largest book-buying sector (approximately one-fifth), was, of course, solely based upon hardback purchases, and this was only slightly modified by the 1970s.

The Paperback

Paperback production seemed to threaten traditional publishing methods, seemed indeed to be a revolution not merely in publishing but in culture itself. The paperback revolution put publishing firmly within an industrial and commercial setting, yet 'serious' culture and 'serious' literature, in particular, were seen by many critics and publishers alike as antithetical to mass society. Thus the widening of the book market was not merely a commercial but also a *moral* decision. Critics such as Q. D. Leavis spilt much ink on worrying whether the increase in the market had actually diminished quality – commercial crassness over-taking and overwhelming artistic merit in the search for quick profits. Gentlemen publishers were obliged to take care of business and had no choice but to look for increasing markets. (Their status was always problematic: gentlemen and tradesmen, as Harold Macmillan was considered by his prospective aristocratic parents-in-law.) Geoffrey Faber, for instance, could easily equate the *restriction* of the market with a retention of artistic quality; by 1934 he was arguing that,

> The market is glutted. General publishing is therefore fast degener-ating into a gambling competition for potential bestsellers. This is a profoundly unsatisfactory state of affairs which may have – will have – very evil effects on the future of English letters. . . . But in so far as over-production is a cause of the evil, we have the remedy in our own hands. We have only to agree to reduce our output in order to restore the book trade to a healthy condition.[48]

Such a refrain was repeated throughout the century and especially at times of *falling* sales, as in the 1970s. Could, therefore, a wider *quality* market be found, outside that which already existed and which would not end up 'fast degenerating' but would retain its 'healthy condition' in terms both of sales and of moral quality? The appearance and the marketing of paperbacks would provide important answers.

The paperback revolution is usually credited to Allen Lane whose Penguin imprint was launched through F. W. Woolworth stores on 30 July 1935.

> Penguins needed the most aggressive and Americanised of the mul-tiple stores to break into the market. They needed mass sales, above the bestseller threshold (13,000–17,000 was the initial break-even range); Lane calculated that he would need an annual volume sale of 2 million. And they exploited a new, technologically transformed kind of book, the mass-market paperback, a phenomenon Mrs Leavis does not anticipate in *Fiction and the Reading Public*. No-one would maintain that Penguin Books have aggravated the cultural condition. Yet Penguins could not have succeeded without the vulgar '3d and 6d' store which represented for the Leavises in 1933 some of 'the worst effects of mass-production and standardisation'.[49]

Lane and his brothers had a simple and clear vision: middle-brow titles, produced in clearly designed packaging (which included an innovative logo), colour coded for making choosing easier, paper-bound and mass produced – the list itself dependent upon successful backlist authors augmented with carefully chosen lesser names whose books would be protected and promoted by their place within a recognisable series. As one critic put it, these titles aimed at 'description or expression of knowledge in understandable terms' for a middle-brow readership who would, perhaps, usually borrow books from a library rather than purchase them.[50] By being sold through large general retailers such books 'lost' a certain prestige but gained a wide and paying readership who would now buy on impulse whilst looking for other goods, or actively seek out a good read at a 'reasonable' price. Books by Ernest Hemingway, André Maurois, Compton Mackenzie, Dorothy L. Sayers, and Agatha Christie (July 1935) were followed by those of Liam O'Flaherty, Norman Douglas, Dashiell Hammett, Louise Bromfield, Victoria Sackville West and Samuel Butler (October 1935). Although eclectic, the books reflected a higher seriousness, even in the choice of thrillers. This all harked back to the moral and educational purposes of nineteenth-century publishers who realised that cheaper books did not need to mean diminishment of standards.

The mainstream paperback augmented rather than replaced hardback books and even the most recalcitrant hardback publisher soon understood the possibilities opened up by paperback reprints. Nevertheless, paperback publishing caused a problem for traditional competition. In March 1957 Gollancz attempted an experiment in which certain titles were simultaneously published in cloth and paper cover versions. In March 1957 Macmillan experimented with a paperback series destined for 'the intelligent man's library'. Michael Joseph launched a hybrid, neither hardback nor paperback. Influenced by the 'new spirit' of the Festival of Britain, the Mermaid Series sold at 4s 6d and was meant to bring 'colour' to the book industry.

Yet, from being vilified as the destroyer of the book trade and the enemy of culture, Lane's Penguins were soon acknowledged as the saving grace of bookselling and a vital new innovation in the dissemination of cultural values. The style was soon copied by American publishers such as Dell, and imprints such as Ace, Signet and Gold Medal Books. In Britain, Hodder and Stoughton repackaged their yellow-back popular titles and re-released them in paperback versions, thus creating new readerships for E. Phillips Oppenheim, Sidney Horler, Edgar Wallace and Sax Rohmer. There were obvious copycat publications too, such as the Toucan novel series produced by Stanley Paul during the 1940s. By the mid-1950s Penguin had sold 4 million copies of current titles (including Paul Brickell's *The Dambusters*, 1951; 1954). The 1960s completed this pattern of growth and paperback ascendancy.

Paperbacks and pulp fiction

Outside middle-brow taste, cheap paperback publishing had always existed at the less literate end of the publishing world. The success of the 'pulp' paperback market was independent of mainstream paperback development and had an independent history. Paper-bound novelettes had found special success during the 1920s and 1930s, especially amongst women readers, but the pulp paperback found a new male market when the supply of American pulp magazines dried up during World War Two. British writers armed with maps of Los Angeles and a line of gangster patois were soon filling the gap that had been left, and books with erotically suggestive and scantily clad 'dames' on their gaudy covers were soon selling everything from crime fiction to wartime adventure, westerns, science fiction, horror and soft-core pornography. Such books were sold primarily to middle-class adolescents and working-class youths and represented reading unrestrained by moral or cultural scruples. Taking their cue from the school of hard-boiled fiction that had been a regular feature of American pulp magazines in the 1930s such books were more directly influenced by James Hadley Chase's own homage to the hardboiled, *No Orchids for Miss Blandish* (1939). Available through the Universal Book Club, Chase's book was the link between the new working-class fiction of the 'mushroom publishers' and mainstream paperback production. By the late 1940s the best-selling paperback edition sported its own scantily dressed 'floozy'.

The interest in all things American, and more especially in the opportunities made available by using American characters and situations, was not lost on writers before the advent of cinema. Dickens, Trollope and Stoker all exploited opportunities to visit the United States, included American characters in their works or used American scenarios. Writers as diverse as H. DeVere Stackpoole, F. Tennyson Jesse, John Buchan, Arthur Conan Doyle and Mrs Humphry Ward all included Americans in their novels as did Bram Stoker in *Dracula* (1897). Mrs Humphry Ward's 1911 hit *Daphne* was a study of 'American divorce'.

Reciprocating the compliment, Frances Hodgson Burnett's *Little Lord Fauntleroy* (1886) featured an American heir to British baronial wealth, and Edgar Rice Burroughs found spectacular popularity with the creation of *Tarzan of the Apes*, lost son and heir of Lord and Lady Greystoke.

Lord Greystoke . . . was the type of Englishman that one likes to associate with, the noblest monuments of historic achievement . . . a
strong, virile man.

> (Edgar Rice Burroughs, *Tarzan of the Apes*, ch. 1)

James Hadley Chase's 'notorious' style of bestseller confirmed, nevertheless, the established preference of British readers for American-style
subjects, putting paid to the old imperial adventure at the same time.
The novel contained the violence and eroticism that readers enjoyed
from American gangster movies and newsreels, providing for a taste that
overwhelmingly preferred Hollywood glamour to home-grown good-
ness. The halting of American magazine imports during the war left a
market susceptible to British versions of American pulp fiction and
Chase's book summed this up. In later years Chase toned down passages
of too erotic or violent a nature, thus a line such as 'I'd give a year's
rent to lay that dame' became the much tamer 'I'd give ten years of my
life for a roll in the hay with her.'

Peter Cheyney also saw opportunity in the taste for the street-smart
language of American crime fiction. His character Lemmy Caution, a
wise-cracking, dame-chasing FBI agent, brought humour to the violence
and erotic sensation of Chase's hoodlums.

Life can be goddam wonderful. And how! It can be so beautiful that
every time somethin' swell happens you don't believe it. Some guys
call this cynicism an' other bozos describe it as wishful thinkin' like
the guy who made himself up like Santa Claus so's he could put a
ladder in some babe's stockin' at Christmas.

Me – I am feelin' so depressed that I would cut my throat, only
then I would not have anythin' to worry about – except my throat.
An' the reason for all this depression which is now settlin' over this
piece of Paris in the month of March 1945 can be summed up in one
word . . . dames!

> (Peter Cheyney, *I'll Say She Does*, ch. 1)

Cheyney's books were immensely popular with service men and
prisoners of war.

I have always been rather pleased with inventing Lemmy Caution
who has, during the last ten years, found his way into a large slice
of the world and acquired a popularity with many people; but I can
say without undue sentimentality that the proudest moment in my
life as a writer was when I read this [prisoner of war] letter.

They said that during their years of captivity the Caution books had brought them entertainment and laughter – at times and under circumstances when laughter was not particularly easy. They told me stories of Lemmy Caution in the *Stalags* – one, of the *padre* who, walking about the camp with his nose in a large book of Devotions, was discovered, eventually, to have *Dames Don't Care* inside the covers.

(Peter Cheyney, *I'll Say She Does*, 1945, Author's Note)

By the late 1940s the heyday of the American pulp magazine had passed, some publications barely hanging on into the 1950s, bypassed by television and mainstream popular fiction. (Only in science fiction did the pulp magazine continue to have a healthy existence.) Yet the legacy of the sensationalism of 1930s magazines remained to be exploited by a new generation of popular authors – the war delaying and yet exaggerating the potential for the revival of glamour and escapism. Nowhere is this more apparent than in the work of Harold Robbins. In Robbins, the male-directed pulp fiction of pre-war days was transmogrified into the female leisure reading of the 1960s. In *The Carpetbaggers* (1961), Robbins's use of multiple storylines which follow individual characters allowed him the liberty of exploiting genres otherwise incompatible as well as (historically) redundant. Thus, in an opening scene, Robbins invokes a redundant genre (the western) by displacing it into a novel about wealth and glamour.

I was playing around the corner of the porch and my father was reading the weekly Reno paper on the big rocker near the front door. It was about eight o'clock in the morning and the sun was already high in the sky. I heard the clip-clop of a horse and came around to the front to see.

A man was getting off his horse. He moved with a deceptively slow grace. He threw the reins over the hitching post and walked toward the house. At the foot of the steps, he stopped and looked up.

My father put the paper down and got to his feet. He was a big man. Six two. Beefy. Ruddy face that burned to a crisp in the sun. He looked down.

Nevada squinted up at him. 'Jonas Cord?'

My father nodded. 'Yes.'

The man pushed his broad-brimmed cowboy hat back on his head, revealing the crow-black hair. 'I hear tell you might be looking for a hand.'

The man's smile remained expressionless. He glanced slowly across the front of the house and out on the desert. He looked back at my father. 'I could ride herd but you ain't got no cattle. I can mend fence, but you ain't got none of them, either.'

My father was silent for a moment. 'You any good with that?'

For the first time, I noticed the gun on the man's thigh. He wore it real low and tied down. The handle was black and worn and the hammer and metal shone dully with oil.

(Harold Robbins, *The Carpetbaggers*, ch. 1)

It is no coincidence that in the story the character Nevada Smith is also known as Max Sand, Robbins punning on the actual western novelist Max Brand (Frederick Schiller Faust, d. 1944) whose books began appearing in the pulp magazines of the 1920s and were being reprinted in the 1940s. In the figure of Rina, Robbins returns to the language of 1940s crime fiction – woman as erotic object of desire:

But Rina was a girl. You couldn't miss that. Especially in a bathing suit, the way she was the first time I saw her. She was slim, all right, and her shoulders were broad, maybe too broad for a woman. But her breasts were strong and full, jutting rocks against the silk-jersey suit that gave the lie to the fashion. You could not look at them without tasting the milk and honey of their sweetness in your mouth. They rested easy on a high rib cage that melted down into a narrow waist that in turn flared out into slim but rounded hips and buttocks.

(Harold Robbins, *The Carpetbaggers*, ch. 5)

By linking what were essentially numerous short stories, by mixing in glamour, power and eroticism and by constantly changing scenarios in an action-based plot, Robbins fulfilled many of the basic tenets of pulp writing. Such stories appealed to a generation of women readers (although written from a male perspective) who were more adventurous in lifestyle and opinion, likely to be able to enjoy a holiday where escapism and glamour would add interest around the hotel pool. Despite *A Stone for Danny Fisher* being first published in the UK in 1955 (by Robert Hale) and *The Carpetbaggers* in 1963 (by Anthony Blond), Robbins's success was due to the vast sales possible from paperback publication: *A Stone for Danny Fisher* was first produced in paperback in 1967 and thence continuously re-issued until 1975; *The Carpetbaggers* enjoyed paperback sales from 1964 to 1975, going on to be the biggest paperback title of all and making Robbins the most purchased American author of all time (before Stephen King).* Robbins successfully converted pulp fiction into a legitimate romance genre.

The British pulp 'mushroom' publishers of the late 1940s and early 1950s were often provincial printers with an eye to a quick profit. They were rarely legitimate in their means or methods. Using numerous pseudonyms, authors who could write quickly and to a word length and format would churn out 'novels' to order, exploiting as much of the erotic, violent and fantastic as they could get away with. 'Authors' such as 'Ben Sarto', 'Al Bocca', 'Darcy Glinto', 'John E. Muller' and many others became paperback bestsellers – one writer often behind many names, or writing different genres under a variety of names, or a 'team' of writers masquerading behind a single name. Books such as *Road Floozy*, *Crazy to Kill* or *Blonde Dynamite* were sold on their 'erotic' cover art and suggestive 'blurbs' at every railway station newsstand, every corner newsagent, every back-street 'bookseller' and every market book barrow, only to quickly and quietly disintegrate as they were passed from reader to reader in offices, army barracks (especially among those doing National Service) and mechanics' shops across Britain in the bleak post-war years. Most famous of all of these writers was 'Hank Janson', who had sold 5 million books by 1954 and inspired a new song, 'The Hank Janson Blues', which was played on the BBC.

The mushroom publishers, often family firms producing other printed ephemera, soon found themselves under pressure from police prosecutions, rising costs, and mainstream competition. Their legacy, however, continued into the 1970s. They were especially influential in promoting science fiction and fantasy for instance, often competing with American paperback imports and American science-fiction magazines produced under licence in the UK. Badger Books produced a steady supply of supernatural and science-fiction thrillers into the late 1950s, launching the career of cult authors such as Lionel Fanthorpe who, writing under numerous names including his own, was always under the pressure of time, work length and perceived market fads. Books were rarely properly copy-edited, often poorly printed and occasionally abruptly finished when binding demands overrode narrative needs. Science fiction flourished in such publications and if Nal Rafcam, author of *The Troglodytes* (published by Digit), was instantly forgettable the name and stories of Isaac Asimov were not (*I Robot* was available in Signet between 1956 and 1964).

---

* Robbins's novels were all re-issued in the 1990s.

Sensation and sexuality also continued to prosper. Reprinted nineteenth-century pornography continued to have a ready market into the 1970s and many paperbacks cashed in on sleazy titles such as *Target for Their Dark Desire* (a Carter Brown Mystery, 1966), *Shanty Town Tease* (Florence Stonebraker), *Kitten with a Whip* (Wade Miller, 1960) and *Pampered Passion* (Paul Renin). By the late 1970s, New English Library had the monopoly of more sensational titles, reprinting works such as Daniel P. Mannix's *The Hell-Fire Club* (1970) and new titles by best-selling English authors such as Richard Allen, whose *Skinhead* (1969) was the first in a highly successful series of 'bovver boot' adventures.

The line between pulp, commercial entertainment and avant-garde literature soon became blurred. Pulp publishers realised that packaging was all, and that many avant-garde writers were, in their terms, sensational and pornographic. By the mid-1960s, mainstream paperback reprints were looking towards these writers to 'spice up' their lists. The hype around Penguin's production in paperback of D. H. Lawrence's *Lady Chatterley's Lover* (1928) is well known. What is less well know is its relatively quiet life in hardback; paperbacks, because cheap, were morally dangerous. Penguin was soon publishing William Burroughs's *Junky* (1977), though it had been around over twenty years, in what they announced as 'the first and unexpurgated edition', whilst Burroughs's *Dead Fingers Talk*, which had originally been published by avant-garde entrepreneur John Calder in 1963, was revived in a Star paperback edition in 1977 with a sensational pulp cover sporting a bloody hand and heroin syringe – eagerly quoting the *Guardian*'s comment that the book was a 'build-it-yourself obscenity kit'.

By the late 1980s controversial books which may once have only found a pulp publisher were produced by mainstream publishers, erotic and pornographic work was freely available in high street bookshops under Black Lace and other imprints, and sleazy teen exploitation was being re-issued as 'cult fiction'. By a twist of fate, Richard Allen's cult pulp 'skinhead' and 'suedehead' books were being re-issued during the 1990s precisely because avant-garde writers like Stewart Home recognised their *subversive* qualities.

The ascendancy of paperbacks* was nowhere more assured than in the world of women's romance. By the 1970s the books of Sidney Sheldon, Jackie Collins, Jacqueline Susann and Harold Robbins could

---

* The Beatles even wrote a song about the phenomenon. *Paperback Writer* was released on 30 May 1966 in the United States and 10 June 1966 in the United Kingdom.

be read at leisure on holidays in Spain and Greece or while waiting for delayed flights to Benidorm or Corfu. On 17 July 1976 the *Bookseller* was able to announce an agreement between Mills and Boon and Chaucer Press (made in April of that year) for one and a half million paperbacks per month on a three-year agreement.

Censorship

Public reading habits have always been monitored by censorious moralists, librarians, magistrates and policemen. Such surveillance and censorship can kill books or make their authors a fortune. The difference is clear when we compare prosecutions from the 1950s to those of the 1960s. Concern regarding the subversive nature of reading was a reasonably subdued theme before the Second World War, but the appearance of cheap paper-bound fiction and its full impact during the 1960s led to a continuous debate regarding liberalisation. The debate focused upon a number of seizures of titles, interdictions placed upon certain titles, and an increasing trickle of publishers and booksellers being prosecuted for indecency and immorality. Calls during the 1950s to strengthen the law on obscenity, with its rather ambiguous phrasing, had led to the successful prosecution of the 'mushroom' industry and writers such as Stephen Francis (aka 'Hank Janson'). During 1951 there were nineteen successful prosecutions of publishers and booksellers, and watchdog groups such as the Catholic Association kept a keen eye for violators. Suggestions were even put forward to create a Home Office list of banned books, to be enforced by undercover policemen.

Action had also been taken against American-style children's comics which were said to be full of depraved (usually horror) material. In a bizarre alliance the morality of rather puritanical parent–teacher associations joined forces with the Communist Party of Great Britain (with its dislike of the United States) to call for reform of the law following the example of Canada and France. Debates through 1952 resulted in the Children's and Young Person's (Harmful Publications) Bill of 1955. 'Indecent literature' was now anything moral watchdogs deemed it to be – the reading habits of the British entered the Cold War. 'Depravity' might mean erotic content, gothic horror storylines or the advocacy of a counter-cultural lifestyle with drugs, according to whether one was at one magistrate's court or another, in London or the provinces.

In mid-May 1954 French pornographic books were seized at a Soho bookshop and raids were stepped up around Soho, Charing Cross, Tottenham Court Road and Farringdon, centres of the 'seamier' side of bookselling.* By mid-June six more trials actually caused *The Times* to run an article on banning certain books. At the same time two more publishers and a printer found themselves behind bars. In August 1954 Lord Russell's forthcoming history of Second World War atrocities, *The Scourge of the Swastika*, was the centre of a furious row, with calls to have it destroyed, much of the hysteria being aroused by local library committees. When Boccaccio's *Decameron* was also destroyed by order of the public magistrates, the *Evening Standard* was prompted to comment that such actions made 'England the laughing stock of civilised nations'.

On March 29th [1957] the revised and simplified Obscene Publications Bill prepared by the Herbert Committee, under the sponsorship of the Society of Authors, passed its second reading unopposed in the House of Commons, and was sent to a select committee. The Bill was introduced by Viscount Lambton (Conservative), and support was forthcoming from both sides of the House. The proposed measure removed the common law misdemeanour of obscene libel, replacing it by a new statutory offence, that of *wilfully and knowingly producing or distributing any matter which was to the knowledge* of the producer or distributor obscene within the meaning of the Act. An all-important change in the Hicklin test is included, making the test of the *dominant effect* of the publication on those among whom it was *intended* to circulate.[51]

The final reform of the obscenity laws in 1959, far from saving them, simply brought them into greater disrepute.

The challenge that Penguin Books offered to the laws on obscenity during the notorious and much written about trial of D. H. Lawrence's book *Lady Chatterley's Lover* (first published in 1928) was the result therefore of much public debate, often of an hysterical nature on both sides. Heinemann had already gone through a trial when it finally printed the book in 1956 and this had led to Pyramid Books publishing *The Complete and Unexpurgated Edition* of *Lady Chatterley's Lover* in the USA three years later. A censored paperback already existed in Britain published by Ace. The hardback had been around in the United States since 1932.

The book was, therefore, available in certain British bookshops before

---

* The prosecution of the unexpurgated *Fanny Hill* (John Cleland, 1749), released in paperback by Mayflower in 1963, began at a magic shop in Tottenham Court Road when bookstock was seized.

the Penguin trial of 1960. Penguin's motives were as much commercial as moral when they decided to publish. The real fear of the prosecution and those it represented was not Lawrence's language but the publisher's format. For the first time the work would be cheaply available in paperback and therefore easily purchased by the young and the working class, who could read it in privacy. The ability of librarians to restrict its borrowing would also, therefore, be bypassed. (Much was made of the corruptive influence of such books on working-class readers and thus much snobbery was revealed.) It sold two million copies and went on to sell many millions more for Penguin.

More than one critic (including F. R. Leavis) smelled something fishy in the self-righteousness of its defence and the commercial potential of a 'pornographic' and scandalous book. The trial and its outcome created the atmosphere for further debate, but this time debate centred around liberalisation or outright repeal of the laws on obscenity. Capitalising on the new atmosphere, Mercury Books published a paperback series for liberal-minded readers. By 1969 books by writers such as Henry Miller could be marketed as 'unexpurgated', challenging a set of laws that were now apparently meaningless. The Arts Council sponsored conferences during 1969 with representatives of the Publishers and Booksellers Associations, the Library Association, the National Book League, the Society of Authors and the Society of Young Publishers, whilst the Society of Young Publishers held its own forum with guest speakers Robert Maxwell and Sir Basil Blackwell defending the conservative position.[52]

Reaction was mounting. Three Labour MPs called for the banning of Harold Robbins's *The Carpetbaggers* on nothing more than the meagre grounds that it was literary rubbish.[53] At other times censorship was morally and commercially much more serious. Thus W. H. Smith had decided not to display 40 to 50 titles for 'reasons of taste', blacklisting Alan Burn's book *Babel* even though it had received an Arts Council grant. By October 1969 it was being reported that even the Russian writer Kutznetsov was complaining that British censorship was as bad as in the Soviet Union. Despite the belief that any move towards liberalisation of the obscenity law would be a 'pornographer's charter' the Arts Council continued throughout the summer of 1969 to call for its complete repeal, whilst publishers like John Calder and Marion Boyars consistently challenged the limits of free speech by publishing titles that immediately offered themselves for prosecution.

By 1969 the appearance of 'sensational' titles amongst the lists of mainstream publishers (especially paperback and magazine publishers) had re-opened debates about the moral responsibility of publishers and the centrality of books to culture. The debate reached Parliament, with lobbying on both sides for either stiffening or liberalising the Obscene Publications Act. During July the Arts Council of Great Britain had called for a repeal of the Act but this had been fiercely opposed.

> The dilemma facing Parliament and, of course the police, was the definition of obscenity and corruption. The 1964 Act followed a Select Committee report on the working of the 1959 Acts; the problem of definition was as apparent then as it was [during 1969], and the Select Committee considered it carefully. The committee's recommendations had been embodied in the 1964 legislation.
>
> Unless they could decide at what stage an article not merely shocked or disgusted, but had a tendency to corrupt or deprave, other measures dependent on definition became useless. Mr Bishop went on to quote the Children and Young Persons (Harmful Publications) Act 1955 [many will remember this as the 'Horror Comics' Act]. He had been told, in answer to a question which he had asked in the House, that no cases had been brought under this Act for five years; he understood that in fact no prosecutions had been taken under this Act since it became law in 1955. He would like to think that this implied that the measure had not been operated because no publications considered likely to corrupt children and young persons had fallen into their hands. 'What a blissful situation, suggesting that children read only Mr Plod the Policeman.'[54]

The then Home Secretary, Jim Callaghan, made it clear that the problem of the law's enforcement was the rapidly shifting boundaries of public taste and decency.

Despite all such pressures the power of the conservative lobby remained strong. Growing liberalisation in reading habits could still fall foul of private or criminal prosecutions. By the late 1960s many of the liberalisers and democratic reformers who had helped create an atmosphere for a more liberal censorship had begun to repent their 'naivety' and the slackening of the law that they had helped reframe in 1959. Revenge for lost ground led to the successful prosecution of *OZ* magazine in 1971, an obscenity trial that was not only the longest in British history but which saw prison sentences for the editors being prosecuted.

Private prosecutions continued during the 1970s, vociferously led by the redoubtable Mary Whitehouse (after whom a pornographic magazine was named). Further actions in the 1980s led to the seizure of drug-related titles that had been on shelves in libraries and bookshops for years and were just then appearing on university syllabi. During 1989 there were calls for *American Psycho* by Bret Easton Ellis to be banned and for paperback copies to be seized and destroyed.

Contemporary Publishing

The steady recovery of the book trade after World War Two was virtually complete by 1955 (even if less fiction was published in that year than in 1937). It continued to increase throughout the 1960s with books being marketed through book clubs, in serialisations, and in condensed form as well as hardback and paperback. When recession came it was not until the mid-1970s. With the general economic downturn came cutbacks in public-sector publishing. The old commercial libraries had long ceased to trade: W. H. Smith ended their library lending in 1961, Boots in 1966. The 1964 Libraries and Museums Act reaffirmed the place of public libraries in the cultural transmission of the country and gave them greater respectability. With the demise of the commercial libraries, public libraries took over sole responsibility for lending out fiction. The public-library system became an essential guardian of the novel and any recession was bound therefore to impinge upon the purchase of new fiction. With libraries accounting for 20 per cent of all book sales, a change in their book purchasing policies was bound to have immediate repercussions.

> Libraries account for about 20 per cent of the total British sale of books. They're important sales because they free publishers from the fickle taste of the public and sheer commercialism of trade. They have meant that creative, experimental, academic, worthy, even dull books can be published. Peter Owen summed up many publishers' view of the situation as disastrous. 'We cannot now publish fiction unless it's by a well-known writer. An average first novel will be lucky now to sell 200 copies. And yet you can't print much fewer than 2,000. We've an author who used to sell in the thousands; now he's selling 500 or 600. We may have to drop him . . .' A publisher used to be able to reckon that a 2,000 print order on a little-known novel, or non-fiction book, would sell at a price so that 1,500 was his break even point. He would be able to expect 1,200 library sales and so had only to get 300 bookshop sales to cover his costs. An acceptable situation. Now though, with libraries buying perhaps only 50 copies of that same book, the publisher is in trouble.[55]

Forced to make financial cutbacks and faced with a mountain of dubious new fiction, librarians went for conservative and well-tried authors. Financial conservatism therefore actually militated against conservative good taste when a librarian had to decide which authors would provide most borrowings: established bestseller authors were a certainty in an uncertain world.

As the century progressed, the search for the bestseller became relentless, more so in periods of recession when publishers and booksellers were looking for larger profits from a shorter list of products. In 1976 for instance, bestsellers were seen as a way of avoiding redundancies! Although the fall and rise of production remained fixed to economic decline and advance, the search for the bestseller increased during the recession of the mid- to late 1970s but continued thereafter at the same level. It remains unexplained why bestsellers become so, their appearance being serendipitous rather than predictable, a result of 'nous' rather than market production. A bestseller, once identified, could however be boosted by tie-ins with television and film or with branded products and could be packaged for book clubs, a condensed novel, serial rights and a paperback version. Authors identified as best-selling could now earn very large incomes. In 1978, Futura published Colleen McCullough's *The Thorn Birds*, paying £160,000 for the rights and using a £60,000 promotional budget. Two million copies were sold in less than two years, ensuring a guaranteed advance for the author's next book and an almost guaranteed next bestseller for the company. Authors became brands and some became celebrities.

In the 1950s, Ian Fleming was already 'sold' as a brand name; this was unusual at the time, but by the 1990s, Stephen King, John Grisham or Catherine Cookson had become brands in themselves. As such, it is no surprise that by the 1990s bestsellers were sold as any other products in supermarkets, where female purchasers spent 80 per cent of their book purchasing on impulse buying of a famous named 'author' brand.[56] The bestseller on supermarket shelves ceased to be a piece of literature sold in a specialist shop (i.e. a bookshop) and instead became a product like any other. Thus, a spokesman for Tesco could point out that 'every product has to fight for its space against very competitive items, especially food'.[57] Supermarket sales are equally affected by marketing, so displays, good covers and clear 'blurb' (user instructions!) help, but the effect must be immediate because:

> Booksellers fail to realize how few people buy books, adding that the books bought as groceries [sic] are impulse buys – books do not go on a shopping list with baked beans, butter and bread.[58]

Throughout the mid-1990s, much emphasis was placed, therefore, on good jacket designs which could be clearly displayed on shelves, tables and in store windows.

> Ten years ago, publicizing books never went beyond puffery: you phoned up a literary editor and told him or her how super a writer was, how wonderful, how innovative. Today you send a T-shirt, issue invitations to a launch party in beautiful country houses, put your author in a bed, and produce glossy, pouting pictures of the writer.[59]

It had taken ninety years to get to this stage, ninety years of periodic calls to modernise an industry whose healthy profits were based on a shrewd mixture of pragmatism and gentlemanly clubbishness (virtuousness carefully maintained). As late as 1965, critics of the trade were attacking its 'abysmal ignorance' of marketing and branding, a cry which resulted in a lack-lustre attempt by some publishers to find specialist niches rather than mass readership. From 1965 onwards W. H. Smith and the Booksellers' Association carried out periodic market research but even in 1992 the *Guardian* could still talk of a 'gentleman's business' (even though 70 per cent of employees were female!). Greater sophistication in understanding the market would often only lead to cheap stunts such as publisher Michael Joseph using Desert Orchid the racehorse to publicise Richard Burridge's novel *The Grey Horse* when the book went on sale in Harrods.

The often heard accusation of cultural critics (especially in the 1930s) that publishing was like any industrial, mass-consumer process was only to come close to reality as late as the 1980s. The fact was that publishers and booksellers used tradition and instinct, used almost no marketing, had no clear statistics, failed to correctly report sales and kept poor records of both numbers sold and money made in a variety of book categories. The complexity of calculating the volume of the British book trade is amply demonstrated by the following paragraph: taken from the *Bookseller*, February 1969.

> (ii) *Volume*:   No official figures are produced of numbers of copies of books printed, but some estimates have been made. For 1950 Marjorie Deane calculated average printing runs per book at 5,000, which would give a total figure of 85 million copies for the 17,000 books published that year. Since then the paperback has meant greatly increased production runs. Richard Findlater suggested in 1965 that book output had reached 300 million volumes. In 1952

R. E. Barker calculated average UK book production at a total of 286 million copies. An indirect calculation can be made using recent Unesco figures.

The *Statistical Yearbook* gives figures of titles and copies produced in 1965. This was for twenty-four countries under a recently agreed convention for standardised information on publishing, which this country is apparently unable to fulfil. These reveal that the average run per title is about twelve thousand. Some of the nations recorded are developing countries, but Russia had an average of only seventeen thousand and other European countries ten thousand. If we apply the figure of 12,000 to Britain, our output would have been 316 million copies in 1965. For comparison, sales in the United States may have been about 1,226 million in 1963. Divided by titles published, this would suggest runs of 47,000 copies each.

Estimates of British paperback production do appear from time to time. For sales, 100–110 million copies was the figure given in 1967 by Hans Schmoller. Hardcover output was estimated for 1964, on trade information, to be 130 million copies and is calculated at 150 million for 1958. Putting these two together suggests UK output may have been about 250 million books in 1967, of which a substantial proportion were probably children's books. Any figure much in excess would suggest large numbers of unsold copies. Schmoller calculated home paperback sales to be 50 to 60 millions, i.e. about 60 per cent of production. If the same ratio applied to hardcovers, we would have a total of say, 150 million copies plus say, in proportion, 30 million imports, 180 million altogether.

The author blamed the complexity on secrecy, ineptitude, ignorance and miscalculated figures!

Whilst the *New York Times* bestseller lists were composed 'with a certain puritan scrupulousness, by an independent polling organization', the British lists were produced 'on a whim by a panel of bibulous *bookmen*' using booksellers whose 'cynical' replies were sometimes merely an attempt to sell slow movers 'cluttering the bookseller's shelves'. In short, 'the lists were corrupt' with many fewer hardbacks selling than declared. The British lists were only regularised in the late 1970s. There are also no *cumulative* bestseller lists. Thus, for instance, the 1995 bestseller list did not include Peter Hoeg's *Miss Smilla's Feeling for Snow*, which sold 400,000 over a two-year period. There were also hidden bestsellers such as Annette Heidcamp, whose *Hummingbird in My House* sells almost 30,000 copies per year. The trade was and remained confused by its own unclear findings, which offered nothing to explain the various movements of a market that was relatively stable, conservative, and steadily enlarging. Seasonal panics were offset by seasonal windfalls and happy forgetfulness.

By the end of the century on-line sales via the Internet had also become a challenge to traditional bookshops (and indeed were promoted by them eventually). Amazon was soon joined by Waterstone's and Barnes and Noble. During 1999 one on-line business, Bol.com, gave away 20,000 books at a cost of £100,000. In return, 40,000 'customers' registered their e-mail addresses – it was a 'cheap deal' as the *Bookseller* fearfully noted. In 1998, the Internet market for books was worth £30 million, yet with a proposed growth of 15 to 20 per cent the predictions were for a book market worth £600 million by 2003. Yet cause for alarm may have been overstated:

> Although the demise of the book at the hands of new media has been predicted for many years, most commentators agree that, while electronic media are well suited to – and are being increasingly used for – reference materials, there is a long way to go before consumer books – particularly novels – are replaced. . . . It is thought that 'real' books will survive because of their flexibility, and the emotional attachments consumers have to reading.[60]

The main potential threat was not against the bookseller but against the rights of authors in the electronic age.

> For publishers, the problem is one of protecting their territorial copyright; they stand to lose out when overseas – principally US – editions of books to which UK publishers have rights are sold over the Internet to UK customers. Protecting these rights in a global market is becoming increasingly difficult, and some commentators feel that the territorial boundaries may eventually disappear . . . the implications of the potential 'opening out' of the market . . . [including] negative effects for authors, whose royalties currently tend to be negotiated by their agents individually for each territory, and vary according to local demand; the erosion of territorial rights would no doubt mean that royalties would revert to the lowest level . . . the owner of [one] specialist bookshop . . . asserted that the opposite was the case, in that authors received 'home royalties' from books imported through US wholesalers, rather than the lower export royalties.[61]

Although accounting for only 0.008 per cent of all books published, the bestseller could guarantee huge profits and act as an insurance policy against failure elsewhere. A tiny number of authors each selling a great many books can subsidise a very large number of poorer selling titles. By the late 1970s and throughout the late 1980s and early 1990s a few select authors such as Dick Francis, Stephen King, Catherine Cookson, Michael Crichton, Tom Clancy, John Grisham, Jeffrey Archer and Jilly Cooper were guaranteed huge advances and vast sales. Fifty elite authors controversially dominated the bestseller lists at the beginning of the 1990s, approximately one-third of whom were women. As early as 1976 research had shown that between 20 and 60 per cent of all books were bought by women, with fiction almost exclusively bought by women readers. Of the top ten books in 1991, eight were by women – the top two being by one author – Thomas Harris. Women purchasers dominated the reading public too, accounting for the £320 million book gift market for instance. Such a market seemed to suggest infinite possibilities for sales, with best-selling author's names becoming business properties. Top authors became investments, but not merely investments of a gilt-edged variety, rather stocks and shares to gamble with: commodities in a financial market. In October 1994, Nicholas Evans accepted a record advance for rights to his new novel *The Horse Whisperer* (published 1995). Robert Redford was soon jockeying to make the film of the book as a vehicle for himself, and all rights, including translation into seventeen languages, was said to total $8 million.

Yet such huge exchanges of money and such considerable gambles could cause serious problems. This was particularly true in the celebrated case of [Joan] *Collins vs. Random House,* that began one freezing day in New York City in Supreme Court 60. The case (which opened in October 1994) centred on *Dynasty* star Joan Collins.

Collins had had a long and varied career since starting as a Rank starlet in the 1950s. Following a lull in her film career, the leading role in *Dynasty* made her an international star and this had allowed her to branch out into popular fiction. Her sister, Jackie Collins, had been a consistently popular writer since the 1960s and Joan and her publishers had soon realised her own potential. Her publications, though not as successful as her sister's, had, nevertheless, already sold 50,000 copies in Britain and America, but with 'Joan Collins fever sweeping the UK' (as one publisher put it at the trial), any new work was set to be the biggest blockbuster *of all time*, surpassing even Jackie's extraordinary sales. A two-book deal with Random House having been brokered,

Collins was the recipient of advances worth $4 million, to be paid in stages as manuscripts arrived.

The case revolved around one of the manuscripts, *The Ruling Passion*, that Random House asserted had been delivered 'unfinished' (i.e. not a complete manuscript) and which Collins and her attorneys argued had been delivered finished and complete as required under contract. Random House, eager to recover half a million dollars paid out on a worthless collection of disconnected pages, sued for breach of contract at the Supreme Court in New York. What the argument was about was clear: When is a manuscript 'complete'?

The question in law was one of the contractual obligation, but it could not be resolved 'in law' without a lengthy courtroom debate determined by questions of narrative, style, and literary 'quality'. Indeed, the legal niceties of the case turned precisely on the relationship between business and aesthetics – the entrepreneurial authoress versus the corporate giant, the qualitative value of a narrative and its quantitative presence (as a delivered manuscript). Just what, in anybody's opinion, constituted a properly delivered novel? Was it the author's opinion or the publisher's? Was a *finished* manuscript an object or an aesthetic judgement, or both? Here, the judgement of law met the judgement of literary criticism (itself doubling as good *business* acumen).

It is true that there might have been little to debate if Joan Collins's agent had not, with uncanny prescience (of both aesthetic judgement and business sense), renegotiated contractual obligations so that the US contract required only that the manuscript of *The Ruling Passion* be delivered *on time* and regardless of quality! If Collins met those requirements Random House would have no right to withhold payment of advances even if they thought the manuscript was 'rubbish'! Random House's interpretation of this clause was that a *complete* manuscript was one ready for editing and then publication: a complete narrative without narrative gaps or gaffes, produced to the author's 'best efforts' and agreed by all parties as ready for a public readership. Thus, Collins's attorneys, led by Ken Burrows, argued that *full* was a quantitative term referring to a delivered object whilst Random House's attorneys, led by Robert Callagy, argued that full meant *complete* qualitatively (i.e. publishable). When is a novel a novel and when does it become a blockbuster? The next days would decide.

The trial witnesses, almost all of whom were Random House employees, were all quizzed on the 'state' of the delivered work. What, in their opinions, was the status of the delivered manuscript? How, in short, could one separate a qualitative and aesthetic judgement about fiction from a legal and contractual question determined by money? For Random House and its editors, the answer lay in the aesthetic values and technical skill displayed in the writing – the definition of popular fiction itself. Joannie Evans felt the work 'over-the-top, dated, melodramatic [and] not credible', the writing 'jumbled and disjointed', and of Collins's previous manuscript of *Hell Hath No Fury*, that it was 'alarming, frankly'. Leah Boyce could see nothing but 'tangles' that were 'far from resolved', a story without coherence and reliant on a mess of 'genres'. Rosemary Cheetham, Random House's British representative, found merely 'disjointed scenes', adding that Collins had chosen subject matter she knew nothing of: 'magazines [and] the New York business world!' Moreover, Collins's setting was also problematic as 'none of [them] knew anything about Monaco' (a comment which drew laughter).

With the appearance of Lucianne Goldberg, Collins's agent, questions of literary value turned rapidly to farce. Asked about narrative inconsistencies, which she could not answer, Goldberg parried with wit. Of one character's drug habit, which was suddenly dropped in the narrative, she replied 'It's a miracle!' When the same character (Desirée) contracts cancer but is later suddenly cured, Goldberg was asked, almost facetiously, by Random House's attorney Robert Callagy, when chemotherapy had occurred. Her reply that 'she (Desirée) must have been very sick. She didn't tell anybody!' brought further humour to proceedings, as did her ironic insistence that all inconsistencies be put down to divine providence – yet 'another miracle!'

Defending Collins's integrity as an author, her attorneys were happy to concede that she was 'not James Joyce or Proust' and that her intention was to write 'commercial fiction . . . like . . . Jackie Collins', intended to have 'fancy and fantastical plots', and be obsessively concerned with 'money, sex, power and sex, and intrigue and sex'. Indeed, when Collins herself took the stand, indignant, hurt and self-consciously 'English', she freely admitted her work was 'over the top', 'melodramatic' and 'more colourful'.

When is a novel a novel? When is a manuscript complete? Summing up, Judge Ira Gammerman found no grounds to suggest that Joan Collins had welched on her contract even if it needed 'editors', 'book doctors' or 'ghost writers'. A novel is a novel when it is delivered on time, when complete means a coherent (or semi-coherent) narrative, and when 125,000 words is not mere gibberish. Random House was ordered to pay Collins one million dollars, and Dutton published her ninth book, *Infamous*, during March 1996. The multi-million-dollar advance blockbuster had (temporarily) ceased to exit, but Joan Collins hadn't. Her personal triumph was also something more. Acquitted by a female literate jury it was also the vindication of popular fiction.

The closing years of the twentieth century also saw the emergence of 'serious' literature as best-selling fiction. Nowhere was this more so than through the growing media interest in, and market importance of the literary prize to, serious fiction sales to the general public. The major literary award became a sub-species of marketing technique, ensuring that there would be, for a short time at least, definite focus on a small group of 'literary' works that otherwise, despite merit, might have been overlooked by purchasers. Prizes such as Booker (established 1968), Whitbread (1985) and Orange (1996), as well as a host of lesser awards ensured literary values and large sales, effectively protecting the serious novel and guaranteeing its popularity (especially in hardback).

Concentration had also come to the booksellers, competition having greatly increased with the discounting that followed the collapse of the Net Book Agreement.[62] By the 1980s the domination of W. H. Smith was challenged by rising competitors in an evolving market in which,

> There were several significant acquisitions, led by the demerger of Waterstone's from W. H. Smith. . . . For WHS the move was designed to make it a mid-market 'popular specialist retailer.' WHS strength-ened its hand in this market by buying the 232-branch John Menzies chain for £68m, bringing the total number of WHS outlets to 741 . . . . The demerger of Waterstone's resulted in the formation of the HMV Media Group, which combined the retail operations of HMV, Waterstone's and Dillons. . . . Immediately the rebranding of 44 Dillons branches as Waterstone's was announced. But Waterstone's and Dillons were not the only ones under new ownership this year. Hammicks was bought by South African conglomerate Mega in July [1998]. Backed by its new owner, the 28-shop bookseller announced an ambitions scheme to treble in size to 75 outlets.[63]

Between 1994 and 1998 book-selling advertising rose by 71 per cent with retail giants closely packed in city centres vigorously competing for customers.

> US giant Borders embarked on a rapid roll-out with its first store openings in London, Glasgow and Brighton. . . . Not to be out-done, sister company Books Etc. opened four new shops in 1998.

Waterstone's and Dillons fought back with an extra 70,000 sq ft and revealed plans for more superstores, including 40,000 sq ft close to Oxford Circus and 54,000 sq ft in the Simpsons building, Piccadilly. . . . W. H. Smith increased its high street presence by 58,500 sq ft. Ottakars also grew its retailing space by 70,000 sq ft.[64]

Bookselling superstores offered books as 'lifestyle' and sold music, magazines and coffee. Waterstone's at Gower Street claimed two million 'visitors' per year buying books, drinking coffee and using eight Internet terminals. Such 'visitors' might be attracted as much by events, signings and concerts as by book discounts. By the end of the twentieth century it had become impossible to disentangle the elements of retail bookselling and the publishing industry.

It was during the 1980s that most of the old publishing houses either amalgamated or were taken over and absorbed within larger international media empires. Such mergers and takeovers left old imprints in place but radically altered the boundaries (and therefore the opportunities) of publishing houses in the United Kingdom. Pyramidal-shaped companies were the result of 'verticalization' from the 1980s to the late 1990s. Macmillan/Pan, HarperCollins/Fontana, Bantam/Transworld, Hodder/Coronet and Vintage/Penguin control all the processes of publishing from hardback to paperback. By 1994 News Corps had purchased Collins and HarperCollins, and as the decade progressed Pearson had taken over Penguin, Michael Joseph and Simon & Schuster. Macmillan was bought by the German media group Holzbrinck, whilst the other German media giant, Bertelsman, bought Jonathan Cape, Secker & Warburg, and Chatto & Windus. Time Warner and Hodder Headline owned most of the rest.

By the early nineties cut-price competition amongst hardbacks produced a depressed paperback market. To avoid losing both markets six publishers, under the leadership of W. H. Smith, created paperback 'originals', titles no longer tied to hardback publishing. This led to a decrease in hardback production costs and a shortening of recovery time for outlays.

The age of the mass multi-media publisher had arrived, with best-selling authors changing hands as if they were sports celebrities.

The high profiles given to a small number of best-selling writers have led to their commanding a high degree of public loyalty – and even higher advances and 'transfer fees' from publishers. High-profile deals during 1998 included Nick Hornby's move from Gollancz to

Penguin in a £2m two-book deal, and the £1m paid to Martin Amis when he moved from HarperCollins to Random House.[65]

At the turn of the new century, the children's author J. K. Rowling had established herself as Britain's top author with her tales of Harry Potter, a character whose appeal crossed the boundaries of age and class. Rowling's talents were a gift to publishers and merchandisers alike.

3
Genre: History and Form

When I first came across *Captain Corelli's Mandolin*, I was walking down the Uxbridge Road in tears. As soon as I'd finished, I realised I had just read B-movie twaddle. Louis de Bernières [the author] managed to punch every button. It was let's have nice Mediterranean peasants, nasty Nazis, positive gay characters and two people who aren't allowed to shag for 500 pages. It's Barbara Cartland and I bought it. You want to throw it across the room with a smile of admiration on your face.

(James Hawes [author of *White Merc with Fins*], in *Metro*,
10 January 2000)

The most popular genres at the end of the twentieth century were virtually the same as at its beginning – an overwhelming percentage of fiction concentrated either on crime detection and mystery or on women's romance. Such fiction accounted for at least 50 per cent of all genre purchases, whilst 'general' fiction and other series accounted for the rest.

Such divisions hide more than they reveal. Books could be endlessly subdivided according to subject matter or style, yet display other characteristics which united them according to theme or moral outlook. Genre categorisation slides uneasily between the vaguenesses of aggregation and dispersal, a game of percentages as well as stylistic or thematic nuances. Thus in 1956 readers could find romances and historical novels, 'exotic' novels, sea stories and naval adventures, tales of childhood and growing up, country novels and novels about women, adventure stories and science-fiction romps, novels of religion and novels of business, novels of modern stress and novels about 'relationships'. To these were added true crime, school novels, radio and television adaptations and a subgenre that year – novels about Australia. In 1965, by way of contrast, the romance, historical thriller and war novel had to make way for 'race' novels, psychological dramas, 'man-in-crisis' novels, tales of homosexuality, tales of the media and of the macabre, whilst medical sagas jostled with tales of the business world, working-class social realism and tales of action. Endless subdivisions and variations, however, left general genre divisions much as in 1956 or, for that matter, 1906 or 1996.

Genre stability demonstrates the innate *conservatism* of writing in two ways. First, publishers like books that fit shelves, that need little explanation and that are easy to categorise. This leads them to stick to winning formulae. Secondly, authors work in traditions and often attempt to 'compete' with past authorial influences. Thus Frederick Forsyth, the author of *The Day of the Jackal* (1971) and *The Odessa File* (1972), felt an affinity with past writers such as John Buchan, Jeffrey Farnol and G. W. Henty, whilst Barbara Cartland remembered her childhood devotion to Berta Ruck, E. M. Hull and Ethel M. Dell. Moreover, best-selling authors tend to be aged between their late thirties or (more likely) mid-forties and mid-sixties, revisiting and revising much that came from their own childhood and teen years earlier in the century.

The contemporary division of popular fiction into a variety of 'genres' according to style, theme or content was unknown to Victorian and Edwardian readers and publishers. For them, if they considered the problem at all, it would have been the classical definition of genres, inherited from Greek and Latin writers, that they would have understood. The current version of genre as a means of categorising fictional formulae gained its modern usage quite late in the last century, by which time it had replaced other meanings of the word. Before the First World War there was simply too little popular fiction to need categorising, almost all popular writing being designated with the vague title of 'romance', which had not itself become a term used exclusively for women's fiction. By the 1920s, the new deluge of popular publishing made it obvious that a bewildering variety of themes had begun to emerge. Most, if not all these themes had their origin before or during the war but now the sheer volume of titles made division inevitable.

The division of popular fiction into 'genres' may have been an accomplished fact by the mid-1920s but it did not exercise readers or publishers except in a pragmatic way. It interested critics not at all. Nevertheless, by the 1930s the now familiar categories of popular fiction had emerged (except science fiction, 'fantasy' and women's romance) sufficiently to have a sense of origins and tradition. Readers, of course, had long been used to going to the local bookshop or tuppenny library and asking for a good whodunit or the latest 'weepy'.

Researchers during the late 1930s began to use the now-familiar genre categories when library users were interviewed or followed, but the fully fledged re-categorisation of popular writing by commercial publishers, booksellers and critics only really emerges in the 1960s when certain categories, such as women's romance and science fiction, become more prevalent and when paperbacks begin to take up most of the book-shelves in shops. Genre categorisation was convenient for booksellers selling a product rather than an author (facilitated by paperback demand), for publishers looking for a niche market to dominate, and for critics keen on categorising popular (or mass) consumption.

During the 1980s, the genre categories that are now most familiar became the most popular form in which to list writers and their work in bookshops and in academic papers. Indeed the serious study of popular fiction despite its tentative beginnings in the 1970s became a small academic industry by the mid- to late 1980s. It is no coincidence that shops began re-labelling popular fiction (paperback) shelves to conform to this pattern at the same time. Academics and booksellers alike talked of crime thrillers and detective fiction, women's romance and the historical novel, science fiction and fantasy, horror and west-erns; moreover new sub-categories then began to emerge during the 1980s: 'Aga' sagas; erotica; gay fiction; 'cult' fiction; graphic novels.

Such categorisation organised and directed customers and focused academic minds. Yet this still left a vast residue of what became known as 'modern' fiction as well as forcing some writers into categories they thought diminished and pigeonholed them. Most notable amongst such writers was Catherine Cookson, who insisted she was a historical novelist (i.e. serious), not a women's romance writer (i.e. frivolous), although in most bookshops her work was shelved under 'romance'.

To categorise books into popular genres before the 1920s is in some way a false labelling, unrecognisable to the readers of that age; never-theless, it is clear that certain stories were likely to prove most popular. These included detective fiction, romance, adventures of the empire and 'family' sagas. Above all, however, were Christian and temperance morality tales, whose messages infused everything, producing some of the era's most popular writers: Hall Caine, Ouida, Marie Corelli and Mrs Henry Wood. With the more liberal climate of the 1920s (heralded by writers like H. G. Wells and Elinor Glyn), these highly successful moralists were almost entirely forgotten by a newer generation of younger readers who had grown up during the war. Some Christian moralists did, however, survive. Lew Wallace's *Ben Hur: A Tale of the Christ*, although published in 1880, was not only performed on stage but also catered to the epic pretensions of an emerging Hollywood, which made a hugely popular silent version and an equally popular full-colour talking version. Lloyd Douglas could still exploit the potential of the genre with books like *The Robe*, published as late as 1942. A small sub-genre of highly successful 'Christian meets lions in Coliseum' films continued to attract cinema audiences throughout the period from the 1920s to 1960s when the genre petered out, to be revived briefly (if in pagan disguise) by Ridley Scott in *Gladiator* (2000).

The modern 'Christianised' morality tale (albeit bereft of an overtly religious message) was exemplified in the work of Florence L. Barclay, one of Britain's most successful writers. In her work, religion is replaced by religiosity. Author of *The Rosary* (1909), Barclay wrote books that were both contemporary in theme (in attitude) and *consolatory* in times of confusion or trouble. *The Rosary* is typical in this regard. Published simultaneously in Britain and America in 1909, it immediately sold 150,000 copies, which by 1924 had risen to a million with numerous translations. *The Times* called it a book 'which should attract lovers of wholesome fiction' and the *Sphere* suggested all Barclay's books were 'inspired by true religious feeling'. The book ends on consolation, repose, acceptance and the transcendence of wedded bliss infused with an aura of religiosity ('allusion to religion [but] . . . never dragged in').

'Hush, sweetest wife,' he said. 'Neither light nor darkness can sepa-rate between you and me. This quiet moonlight cannot take you from me; but in the still, sweet darkness you will feel more com-pletely my own, because it will hold nothing we cannot share. Come with me to the library, and we will send away the lamps, and close the curtains; and you shall sit on the couch near the piano, where you sat, on that wonderful evening when I found you, and when I almost frightened my brave Jane. But she will not be frightened now, because she is so my own; and I may say what I like; and do what I will; and she must not threaten me with Nurse Rosemary; because it is Jane I want – Jane, Jane; just *only* Jane! Come in, belovéd; and I, who see as clearly in the dark as in the light, will sit and play *The Rosary* for you; and then *Veni, Creator Spiritus*; and I will sing you the verse which has been the secret source of peace, and the sustaining power of my whole inner life, through the long, hard years, apart.'

'Now,' whispered Jane. 'Now, as we go.'

So Garth drew her hand through his arm; and, as they walked, sang softly:

> 'Enable with perpetual light,
> The dullness of our blinded sight;
> Anoint and cheer our soiléd face.
>
> Keep far our foes; give peace at home;
> Where Thou art guide, no ill can come.'

Thus leaning on her husband; yet guiding him, as she leaned; Jane passed to the perfect happiness of her wedded home.

(Florence L. Barclay, *The Rosary*, ch. 4)

The maudlin sentiment and message of spiritual consolation found continuous appeal for forty years: years of civil unrest and uncertainty, changing morals and values and two world wars. It took the Cold War to finally kill *The Rosary*! Barclay's books were, however, harbingers of the new fiction, not only because we see in *The Rosary* a thousand Mills and Boon romances (Barclay overwhelmingly appealed to women) but because her work was inherently modern in its approach to writing fiction (and especially women's domestic fiction):

My aim is: Never to write a line which could introduce the taint of sin, or the shadow of shame, into any home. Never to draw a character which should tend to lower the ideals of those who, by means of my pen, make intimate acquaintance with a man or a woman of my own creating. There is enough sin in the world without an author's powers of imagination being used in order to add even fictitious sin to the amount. Too many bad, mean, morbid characters already, alas! walk this earth. Why should writers add to their number, and risk introducing them into beautiful homes where such people in actual life would never, for one moment, be tolerated?

... [I]n according so generous a reception to *The Rosary*, and to other books of the same tone and calibre, the public has frankly given its assent to this divine precept, and this verdict in favour of writers who are humbly, yet earnestly, endeavouring to make it their rule and guide, and who may, therefore, with glad assurance take courage and go forward.[1]

Her biographer and daughter concluded:

> But I believe the reason why people *bought* the books in so unusual
> a way was just because . . . the books so exactly fulfilled the require-
> ments of a novel, that people were ready to buy them and take them
> home to read again when they wanted to be refreshed after the dust
> and heat and weariness of the day. A problem novel may be inter-
> esting; a novel with a teaching purpose may be a necessary form of
> education; a book that is a piece of remorseless realism may be stimu-
> lating; but people do not want to *possess* books of that sort; they
> feel a little doubtful about lending them to their friends; they do not
> feel drawn towards reading them a second time, or dipping into them
> when the world's sunshine is, for awhile, absent; in short, they do
> not care to have them as part of the permanent furniture of their
> homes. I think it was this meeting of a public need that gave the
> books their big sales; and I emphasise the point because it was a quite
> conscious aim of my mother's. She loved to think that she was bright-
> ening the lives of millions of unknown people, resting the minds of
> the world's workers. It was for them she wrote – not for the critics.[2]

Yet there was something else that attracted readers: *The Rosary* was set
in a world essentially *mundane*, a prosaic paradise in which ordinary
women recognised their own circumstances idealised.

> She was out to supply her fellow men with joy, refreshment, inspi-
> ration. She was not out to make art for art's sake, or to perform a lit-
> erary *tour de force*, or to rival the makers of fiction of the past. By
> eschewing tragedy, by forgoing the depiction of the more violent
> human emotions, by substituting a delicate fancy for a burning
> realism, she sacrificed the dramatic opportunities her vivid imagina-
> tion could easily have supplied.[3]

This was a legacy that would soon be developed by writers such as
Ethel M. Dell and Barbara Cartland. *The Times* suggested on her death,
that,

> A writer who appealed to and won the affection of so many of her
> fellow countrymen and women is no negligible quantity. Indeed
> there is reason to think that Mrs Barclay understood the tendency of
> her age better than many contemporary novelists whose technical
> skill exceed hers.[4]

Although consolatory and spiritualist books did particularly well in the early 1920s, the First World War released other more violent and exciting passions. It is in this period that the thriller, and the spy thriller in particular, take on a modern form; that modern, empire-threatening villains make their appearance; that technology becomes a contemporary theme and western heroes ride over the horizon. It is noteworthy that Sax Rohmer's Dr Fu Manchu made his first appearance in a novel in 1913, Edgar Rice Burroughs published his first Tarzan tale in 1914, John Buchan (in imitation of American 'dime' novels and British 'shockers') created the character of Richard Hannay (and thereby the modern spy novel) in 1915, and that Herman Cyril McNeile ('Sapper') created Bulldog Drummond and Agatha Christie created Hercule Poirot both in 1920. Whereas before the war Elinor Glyn's *Three Weeks* had caused a scandal, by 1925 Anita Loos's *Gentlemen Prefer Blondes*, 'the illuminating Diary of a Professional Lady' (as it proclaimed on the British edition with the innuendo attached), had become 'probably the funniest book that [had] appeared in England or America' (Rose Macaulay). As the cover 'blurb' pointed out, 'You may blush as you laugh at it, but you cannot help laughing.'

Technology, adventure, mystery and a tinge of the erotic became the staple of thrillers, westerns, crime novels and tales of the supernatural, creating a huge market for writers such as Sidney Horler, William Le Queux, Dornford Yates, Leslie Charteris and Edgar Wallace. Between 1913 and the mid-1930s such writers rose to pre-eminent positions, the crime thriller/adventure thriller coming to dominate the market.

Tales of airmen and airships abounded as did stories of 'death rays' wielded by inscrutable (German or French) enemies, becoming part of a subgenre of thriller writing which continued into the 1930s and beyond, into tales of Cold War super-weapons. William Le Queux was an early proponent of such tales, which followed in the tradition of Jules Verne and H. G. Wells from the previous century. Le Queux's *Terror of the Air*, produced just after the First World War, suggested the sensational possibilities of the new air warfare brought about by a reinvigorated and militant Germany.

> A few short years ago such a story as *The Terror of the Air* would have been characterised as wildly improbable if not absolutely impossible. But to-day we are well into the Aerial Age. Such a great pirate aircraft as Mr Le Queux imagines is by no means beyond the realms of possibility, and a story such as he tells must cause thoughtful people to realise very forcibly the immense power which command

of the air gives. The author describes vividly how the great pirate aeroplane terrorised the world, destroying aircraft and shipping, bombing London, New York and Paris, and spreading poison gas, disease germs and other horrors over its helpless victims. The account of the long war between the forces of order and the raider is full of breath-taking incidents, culminating in the thrilling and graphic description of the pirate craft's ultimate destruction. At this time, when aviation is making such vast strides daily, this story is of immense interest. . . .

To make my story clear, and to give an adequate idea of the paralysing effect of the appearances of the *Terror of the Air* on the mind of the public all over the world, I must, much as I detest ancient history, go back a few years. The great world war into which the nation were flung in August, 1914, by the unbridled rapacity of Germany, and the unbounded megalomania of her half-crazed ruler, came to an end in November, 1918. Germany – utterly crushed in the field, slowly starving to death, a prey to famine and Bolshevism – appeared before the Council of the Allies, an unblushing mendicant, begging relief from the very peoples whom for years she had outraged and robbed without mercy. The world has seldom beheld a more nauseating spectacle. It was, and is, unpleasant to contemplate, and I mention it only to make my story clear. The bully of Europe fawned and cringed when thrashed in the manner of bullies of all ages. Of course, it is only fair to say that the German people as a whole knew nothing of what was being prepared; the secret could not have been kept had it been otherwise. None the less, as was fully established later, it was German cunning, German hatred, and German money which sent the *Terror of the Air* upon his fell mission. And behind him were the very men who planned and prepared the world war – the uncivilised and uncivilisable Junkers of Prussia.

(William Le Queux, The Terror of the Air, ch. 1)

The cover of the shilling edition shows a girl flyer and her hero boyfriend standing, clench fisted, as a huge multi-engined red bomber flies overhead and crowds of fear-driven people flee from the wreckage of another bombed-out city. The megalomaniac villain (with a Jewish name and abetted by the German government) finally commits suicide to avoid arrest.

Late twentieth-century writers have continued this early technological thriller tradition, most notably Michael Crichton, Tom Clancy and Ian Fleming, whose work is directly indebted to it. Le Queux's contemporary Edgar Wallace and his influence on film history also cannot be ignored (he created 'King Kong'). The contemporary Hollywood block-busters of the 1990s and twenty-first century are direct descendants of such writers and their (usually) long-forgotten books. During the 1950s and early 1960s television would rediscover many of these stories and use them as short dramas or series. The last of the buccaneering heroes of the 1920s, Leslie Charteris's hero Simon Templar ('The Saint') created in 1927, remained a firm favourite of television audiences from the 1950s to the 1970s.

Popular writers of the 1920s, especially those writing thrillers, continued to find popularity right through until the end of the Second World War but as might be expected the tensions of the late 1920s and throughout the 1930s produced both an edgier literature devoted to social commentary and a more escapist literature determined by nostalgia for historical romance. History books and technical or scientific books also became extremely popular.

> While fiction was thus becoming more factual, factual books were being written in a fictional style. Lytton Strachey's *Queen Victoria*, which started the fashion, had been 'as good as a novel', and Philip Guedalla's coruscating biographies were 'as good as a modern novel'. In 1930, several publishers brought out series of short, lively critical biographies of famous men and women, commissioned from noted authors. At least two hundred such appeared, and sold very well. Their subjects ranged from Lord Byron to the Indian Emperor Akbar, and from Saint Paul to Mozart. This desire for readily assimilable factual truth was met in the department of science by simply written, rather sentimental books by Professors Jeans and Eddington on physics and astronomy, and by such encyclopedia compilations as *The Outline of Science* by H. G. Wells, and his biologist son, and Professor Julian Huxley the zoologist. There was still a great demand for scientific vistas of the future, especially the 'To-day and To-morrow' series of essays; and Aldous Huxley's *Brave New World* and H. G. Wells's *The Shape of Things to Come* were their fictional counterpart.[5]

Novels dealing with the nature of Britain's future, whether science fiction or social prediction, coincided with books more evidently concerned with Britain's failed sense of community. A. J. Cronin's *The Citadel* (1937) chronicled the failure of medical provision in a Welsh community before the coming of the Welfare State. Its tone is one of outrage at cynicism and complacency.

'Science apart, doctor, you might satisfy my curiosity. Why have you come here?'

By this time Andrew's temper was rising rapidly. He answered grimly.

'My idea was to turn Drineffy into a health resort – a sort of spa, you know.'

Again Denny laughed. His laugh was an insult, which made Andrew long to hit him. 'Witty, witty, my dear doctor. The true Scots steamroller humour. Unfortunately I can't recommend the water here as being ideally suited for a spa. As to the medical gentlemen – my dear doctor, in this valley they're the rag-tag and bobtail of a glorious, a truly noble profession.'

'Including yourself?'

'Precisely!' Denny nodded. He was silent a moment, contemplating Andrew from beneath his sandy eyebrows. Then he dropped his mocking irony, his ugly features turned morose again. His tone, though bitter, was serious. 'Look here, Manson! I realise you're just passing through on your way to Harley Street, but in the meantime there are one or two things about this place you ought to know. You won't find it conform to the best traditions of romantic practice. There's no hospital, no ambulance, no X-rays, no anything. If you want to operate you use the kitchen table. You wash up afterwards at the scullery bosh. The sanitation won't bear looking at. In a dry summer the kids die like flies with infantile cholera. Page, your boss, was a damn good old doctor, but he's finished now, finished by overwork, and'll never do a hand's turn again. Nicholls, my owner, is a tight little money-chasing midwife. Bramwell, the Lung Buster, knows nothing but a few sentimental recitations and the Songs of Solomon. As for myself, I better anticipate the gay tidings – I drink like a fish. Oh! and Jenkins, your tame druggist, does a thriving trade, on the side, in little lead pills for female ills. I think that's about all.

(A. J. Cronin, *The Citadel*, ch. 2)

For all its romanticism and mystery, Daphne du Maurier's *Rebecca* (1938) reflects a tone of emptiness, loss and pointlessness punctuated by death, madness and arson. It ends in barren and lonely continental wandering. The tone is consistent with the age. Best-selling authors in 1937 called on Britons to 'reclaim their roots' and to remember that people came before machines, to be in touch with nature. J. B. Priestley reminded his readers:

We cannot seek grace through gadgets. We can be just as unhappy in spun-glass trousers as we were in worsted ones. In a bakelite house the dishes may not break, but the heart can. Even a man with ten shower-baths can still find life stale, flat and unprofitable.

(*Midnight on the Desert*, 1937)

Stanley Baldwin even established himself in the public eye as 'Farmer Stan'. In 1935 he coined his most frequently quoted statement, 'England is the country and the country is England.' His main message was one of values and traditions which marked a certain 'Englishness', which he wished to recapture. Baldwin had a particular liking for Winifred Holtby's 1936 book *South Riding*. The story followed a country squire who defeats a plan for a housing estate that was to be built by cheating others out of their money. Baldwin saw work as, and considered himself as, 'standing up for the values of an older England against the inroads of inhumane and mechanistic commercialism', which was grounded in what he saw as 'the greatest peril of our age, the peril of materialism'.

Most famous of all 'the state of the nation' books during the 1930s was H. V. Morton's *In Search of England*, originally published in 1927 but running through twenty-five editions by 1938. So popular was this book that almost every secondhand book dealer in Britain has numerous copies even now.

A writer on England to-day addresses himself to a wider and a more intelligent public than ever before, and the reason is, I think, that never before have so many people been searching for England. The remarkable system of motor-coach services which now penetrates every part of the country has thrown open to ordinary people regions which even after the coming of the railway were remote and inaccessible. The popularity of the cheap motor-car is also greatly responsible for this long-overdue interest in English history, antiquities, and topography. More people than in any previous generation are seeing the real country for the first time. Many hundreds of such explorers return home with a new enthusiasm.

The roads of England, eclipsed for a century by the railway, have come to life again.

Since James Watt invented a new world on Glasgow Green, the town and the country have grown apart. They do not understand one other. Since the so-called Industrial 'Revolution' – evolution is surely a better word – English country life has declined, agriculture has fallen on bad times, and the village has been drained to a great extent of its social vitality. . . .

It is difficult at first for the unaccustomed eyes of the townsman to understand that behind the beauty of the English country is an economic and a social cancer. An old order is being taxed out of existence; 'our greatest industry' – as the experts call it – employs fewer men than those on the dole, and, struggling along, is facing insuperable difficulties with a blundering but historic stolidity. While our cornland is going back to grass year after year, our annual bill to the foreigner for imported foodstuffs is four hundred million pounds. Everywhere is the same story: mortgages on farms; no fluid capital; the breaking up of famous estates when owners die; the impossibility of growing corn because of the expense of labour and the danger of foreign competition; the folly of keeping cattle when the Roast Beef of Old England comes so cheaply from the Argentine.

(pp. vii, ix)

The narrative of 'a motor-car journey round England' (p. vii) was an attempt to harness new technology ('the cheap motor-car') in order to find an older, more permanent and better England. The theme re-emerged during World War Two and then later formed the basis for Kazuo Ishiguro's hugely successful book *The Remains of the Day* (1989), itself a commentary on the previous 'yuppy' decade of Thatcherism (see especially the section 'Day One – Evening: Salisbury').

'Unbearable pessimism' does not sell books, as the *Bookseller* noted in November 1957 of that particular year's crop, so it is not surprising to find that readers looked for escapist and uplifting reading, something they found in J. B. Priestley's *The Good Companions* (1929) and in the genre of historical romance provided in aces by Margaret Mitchell's *Gone with the Wind* (1936), a book whose phenomenal success became legendary. It was followed by an even more famous film, which gave the book a status that sharply elevated it above all the other bestsellers of the period.

One area of innovation is worth noting. The steady rise in the popularity of the thriller had paralleled the slow decline of ghost and horror tales during the late 1920s. Ghost and horror tales had remained popular since the Victorian age but, on the whole, this was confined to short stories or collections of short stories. When Hollywood utilised the genre for its classic versions of *Frankenstein* and *Dracula* it had to look for substantial tales from the nineteenth century. Dennis Wheatley's *The Devil Rides Out* (1934) was something new – a supernatural thriller combining black magic (information supplied by Aleister Crowley), car chases and a mysterious villain, Mr Mocata (based upon Aleister Crowley himself). Mocata and his servant are direct descendants of the imperial villains of Conan Doyle and Sax Rohmer.

> 'Have you ever seen this bird – Mocata I mean?'
>
> 'Yes, I called one evening about six weeks ago. Simon was out so Mocata received me.'
>
> 'And what did you make of him?'
>
> 'I disliked him intensely. He's a pot-bellied, bald-headed person of about sixty, with large, protuberant, fishy eyes, limp hands, and a most unattractive lisp. He reminded me of a large white slug.'
>
> 'What about this servant that you mention?'
>
> 'I only saw him for a moment when he crossed the hall, but he reminded me in a most unpleasant way of the Bogey Man with whom I used to be threatened in my infancy.'
>
> 'Why, is he a black?'
>
> 'Yes. A Malagasy I should think.'
>
> Rex frowned. 'Now what in heck is that?'
>
> 'A native of Madagascar. They are curious people, half-Negro and half-Polynesian. This great brute stands about six foot eight, and the one glimpse I had of his eyes made me want to shoot him on sight. He's a "bad black" if ever I saw one, and I've travelled, as you know, in my time.'
>
> (Dennis Wheatley, *The Devil Rides Out*, ch. 1)

The nature of Mocata's villainy nevertheless is not attached to imperial defence but to current political change in Europe – a situation that in the novel produces certain esoteric commentaries, of which this is the most bizarre (and perverse) example.

> De Richleau extended the thing he had taken from the drawer. It was a small golden swastika set with precious stones and threaded on a silken ribbon.
>
> 'Simon Aron,' the Duke spoke again. 'With this symbol I am about to place you under the protection of the power of Light. No being or force of Earth, or Air, of Fire, or Water can harm you while you wear it.' With quick fingers he knotted the talisman round Simon's neck. . . . Fancy hanging a Nazi swastika round the neck of a professing Jew.

'My dear Rex! Do please try and broaden your outlook a little. The swastika is the oldest symbol of wisdom and right thinking in the world. It has been used by every race and in every country at some time or other. You might just as well regard the Cross as purely Christian, when we all know it was venerated in early Egypt, thousands of years before the birth of Christ. The Nazis have only adopted the swastika because it is supposed to be of Aryan origin and part of their programme aims at welding together a large section of the Aryan race.

(ch. 3)[6]

The Second World War delayed further changes or innovations (people went to older familiar books) but once it had finished and publishing had again settled down, changes did occur. Of most obvious interest were the momentous events of the war itself, creating an insatiable taste for fiction and non-fiction dealing with the conflict. Christopher London's *Ice Cold in Alex* was published in 1957 as was Alistair MacLean's *The Guns of Navarone*, but these were both upstaged by the success of books like Paul Brickell's *The Dambusters* (1965) and Nicholas Monsarrat's *The Cruel Sea* (1951), which became the first two books officially to reach one million paperback sales in Britain, *The Dambusters* selling a quarter of a million copies after the release of the film. Tales of the war remained popular throughout the late 1950s to mid-1970s; MacLean's *The Guns of Navarone* (1957) and *Where Eagles Dare* (1967) also became hugely successful films whilst *Ice Cold in Alex* (film: 1958) became one of the great classics of British cinematography. It is noteworthy that C. S. Forester's *The African Queen* (1935), a tale of the First World War, was brought out in a Penguin edition in 1956. Slowly diminishing in importance through the 1970s, the war story was still capable of producing bestsellers, as Jack Higgins proved in *The Eagle Has Landed* (1975), a tale about a plot to kidnap Winston Churchill. Sven Hassel's *Wheels of Terror*, which first appeared in 1959, told the story of a vicious SS Penal Regiment on the Russian front. It created a minor *œuvre* that had a huge male readership by the 1970s, when it went through numerous editions. Sam Peckinpah's film *Cross of Iron* (1977) was not only based upon the work of Willi Heinrich (*Das Geduldige Fleisch*) but was directly indebted to Hassel and his followers, such as Leo Kessler.

If the war story provided excitement, adventure and sometimes heroics during the Cold War then the spy story provided contemporary commentary. Robert Harling's *The Enormous Shadow* (1955) provided a story of sordid detections and misguided traitors. Its style is intentionally downbeat and anti-heroic as this exchange suggests.

> 'I always imagine these M.I.5 characters skipping round the world in false beards, burnous and sandals. Perhaps I'm wrong.'
> 'You're as wrong as you know you are,' I said. 'A desk, dockets, stacks of card indexes, a brief-case and a job as dreary as a pay clerk's in the army.'
>
> (ch. 1)

And the reason for this pessimistic downgrading of the language of thrillers was clearly a new demand for a realism which could compete with daily news.

> Devotees of escapist literature are in danger of losing one of their mainstays – the psychological thriller. Gone, as if it had never existed, is the Dornford Yates world of Rolls-Royce chivalry. Mr Usborne's clubland heroes have had it. Even the Saint or Mickey Spillane's American toughs now only raise a mild smile and a knowing reference to Freud. And why? Real life has caught up with them. Burgess and Maclean, Pontecorvo, Nunn May – grim and all too genuine figures of our time, they bang their way on to the stage.
>
> (Peter Green, *The Broadsheet*, 'blurb' on the cover of
> *The Enormous Shadow*)

Such 'new realism' in popular thrillers also owed a considerable debt to the political fables of George Orwell whose *Animal Farm* (1945) and *1984* (1949) proved enormously influential throughout the 1950s and 1960s. John le Carré's *The Spy who Came in from the Cold* (1963) follows this 1950s tradition of realism in Berlin's 'half-world of ruin' (ch. 1), in which 'our methods . . . and those of the opposition – have become much the same' (ch. 1) and in which spies are a 'squalid procession of vain fools, traitors . . . pansies, sadists and drunkards' working to protect 'the great moronic mass' (ch. 25). It remained for Ian Fleming to pull together the thread of imperial adventure, the craving for luxury and travel and the harsh realities of East/West antagonism. Fleming's James Bond had, by the 1970s, become the most significant creation in modern English literature, yet early on he too had succumbed to the new realism. In *From Russia with Love* (1957) Bond meets his nemesis on a mission to 'pimp for England' (ch. 12).

If some genres were doing well then others were in terminal decline.

John Creasey, on the results of a straw poll of publishers, found that the 'western' novel seemed to be read by an almost negligible market segment. Most publishers sold less than 3,000 copies per title and the most famous authors contented themselves with top sales of 6,000 copies. British readers who remained loyal to westerns preferred 'bang bang yarns' as Creasey put it, to the frontier tales preferred in the United States. The popularity of the film and television version of 'cowboys and Indians' which saturated much viewing in the 1950s may have contributed to the feeling that it was no longer necessary to read what could be seen in Technicolor (at least on the big screen). Nevertheless, westerns remained a coterie interest into the twenty-first century.[7]

One genre that found its first large popular readership in Britain was science fiction. The genre had, of course, existed since the late nineteenth century but 'romances of the future' had remained the property of writers like H. G. Wells, who had moved on to sociological novels, or were 'sports' like Huxley's *Brave New World* (1932). The age of space exploration began to change this as popular fiction explored the possibilities of technological progress and space travel and looked at the darker possibilities of atomic and radiation meltdown. Technological change was the overwhelming interest of writers like Arthur C. Clarke, in books like *Childhood's End* (1954). Clarke found lasting fame, however, with the novelisation of his screenplay for Stanley Kubrick's *2001* (1968), which mixed technological evolution with psychedelic personal evolution. It was John Wyndham, however, who came to epitomise 1950s British science fiction with his doom-laden tales *Day of the Triffids* (1951), *The Kraken Wakes* (1953) and *The Chrysalids* (1955). Wyndham's *œuvre* provided the basis for numerous film and television adaptations.

The 1960s confirmed rather than changed the genres that had existed before. The paperback revolution meant authors on the bestseller list could reach unprecedented numbers of readers. Film and television adaptation were often central to a writer's longevity, nowhere more so than in the literary careers of Ian Fleming and Agatha Christie (and, coincidentally, D. H. Lawrence). J. R. R. Tolkien also found a ready audience and with the rediscovery of R. E. Howard (d. 1936), H. P. Lovecraft (d. 1937) and Lord Dunsany (d. 1957) a whole 'sword and sorcery' subgenre came into being.

The 1970s saw the dominance of two genres: women's romance, and crime and detective fiction, but these two had largely dominated the market before. What changed was the number of disposable paperbacks, which created a publishing industry for Mills and Boon. The 1970s health boom also created a greatly enlarged readership for Barbara

Cartland and 'Miss Read', whose wholesome historical dramas attracted women to whom liberal values did not appeal. Crime fiction became more diverse but essentially remained divided between classical puzzle stories and gangster violence. Police procedurals and forensic detectives remoulded the genre for a readership keen on greater 'realism'. Elsewhere the sea adventures of C. S. Forester were attracting writers like Alexander Kent (Douglas Reeman) and Patrick O'Brian (d. 2000), and the war novel was a palpable influence on writers such as Richard Adams, whose *Watership Down* (1972) used his own experiences of the horrors of war (the strangulation of Bigwig in the wire snare). Even imperial adventure was revived with Wilbur Smith's *Shout at the Devil* (1968).

By the 1960s genre divisions, however vaguely defined, had been determined by over sixty years of publishing. The romances, historical novels, thrillers, crime and detective tales, horror and fantasy genres which ended the century all had origins before or during the First World War. If the erotic novella, in the 1990s (both heterosexual and gay), usurped space given over to romance it did not replace the more conservative and moral 'Aga sagas' and historical romances of writers like Catherine Cookson. New writers exploited rather than invented new ways of thinking about genre. The most successful of all such writers was Thomas Harris.

For all its pseudo-realism, *Silence of the Lambs* (1988) combined police procedural and forensic detection, gothic horrors and a memorable villain, Hannibal Lecter.

> Behavioural science, the FBI section that deals with serial murder, is on the bottom floor of the Academy building at Quantico, half-buried in the earth. Clarice Starling reached it flushed after a fast walk from Hogan's Alley on the firing range. She had grass in her hair and grass stains on her FBI Academy windbreaker from diving to the ground under fire in an arrest problem on the range. . . .
>
> The fire lights glowed red in the Insect Zoo, reflected in ten thousand active eyes of the older phylum. The humidifier hummed and hissed. Beneath the cover, in the black cage, the Death's-head moth climbed down the nightshade. She moved across the floor, her wings trailing like a cape, and found the bit of honeycomb in her dish. Grasping the honeycomb in her powerful front legs, she uncoiled her sharp proboscis and plunged it through the wax cap of a honey cell. Now she sat sucking quietly while all around her in the dark the chirps and whirs resumed, and with them the tiny tillings and killings.
>
> (ch. 40)

> Dr Hannibal Lecter himself reclined on his bunk, perusing the
> Italian edition of *Vogue*. He held the loose pages in his right hand
> and put them beside him one by one with his left. Dr Lecter has six
> fingers on his left hand. . . .
> His cultured voice has a slight metallic rasp beneath it, possibly
> from disuse.
> Dr Lecter's eyes are maroon and they reflect the light of pinpoints
> of red.   (ch. 22)

Lecter is a villain born of Dr Fu Manchu and Dr No; a monster straight
from the glorious days of imperial adventure.

The foremost name in genre publishing remains the company of Mills
and Boon who by the 1930s had realised the value of packaging and
target marketing.

> Before 1950 and the advent of the mass-market paperback, Mills
> and Boon was not the largest publishing house in Britain, nor was
> it the most successful (as it is today). But the firm exemplifies the
> major structural changes in the publishing industry in Britain at
> this time and in this respect is of importance to the historian. First
> and foremost a commercial enterprise, Mills and Boon was the
> pioneer in the promotion of books as commodities and the rational-
> ization of established publishing houses into library suppliers in the
> 1930s.[8]

The company had been founded in 1908 by Gerald Mills and Charles
Boon, both of whom had previously worked for Methuen. Although for
many years a general publisher with interests not only in fiction but in
educational and scientific work, the company also

> specialized in its most successful type of novel, the romance.
> Romantic novels had already been a strong feature of its lists
> throughout the 1920s, with Sophie Cole, Joan Sutherland, Louise
> Gerard, and Dolf Wyllarde big sellers. In 1923 Mills and Boon pub-
> lished Georgette Heyer's first novel, under the pen-name Stella
> Martin.[9]

Although not yet producing paperbacks, by the 1930s the company had
a strong library readership, including readers at Boots and the vast tuppenny library network.

The firm became a master of the 'personal touch', a device which promoted sales by encouraging close contact with the readership. By the early 1930s, for example, the endpages of each Mills and Boon romantic novel, which usually featured the current publication list, opened with a full-page notice headed 'To the reader: Why you should choose a Mills & Boon novel':

The Fiction Market is overburdened with new novels, and the ordinary reader finds it most difficult to choose the right type of story either to buy or to borrow. . . . Really the only way to choose is to limit your reading to those publishers whose lists are carefully selected, and whose fiction imprint is a sure guarantee of good reading. . . . Mills and Boon issue a strictly limited Fiction List and the novels they publish all possess real story-telling qualities of an enduring nature.[10]

The company also encouraged readers to send in manuscripts (a feature of its promotions today), a shrewd move which produced new best-selling authors such as Sara Seale, Mary Burchell and Jean S. Macleod. By the 1940s, with a flourishing mail-order business and a loyal female readership, the company was not just a publisher but a household *brand*.

Mills and Boon's prominence in the tuppenny libraries is demonstrated in two surveys. In 1935 *The Bookseller* analysed the stocks of 'one of the largest and newest' of the commercial libraries. Among the Mills and Boon authors listed in the 'best-seller' class were Denise Robins (thirty-six titles), Joan Sutherland and Sophie Cole (twenty-six to thirty titles each), Louise Gerard (twenty-one to twenty-five), Elizabeth Carfrae (sixteen to twenty), Deirdre O'Brien and Marjorie M. Price (ten to fifteen each). A comparison of these figures with those in stock in Mudie's Library in 1935 reveals equal, if not higher numbers; Sophie Cole, for instance, had thirty-eight titles in Mudie's. In another survey, in 1950, Mills and Boon, in association with W. H. Smith, approached library owners across Britain in an attempt to determine the frequency of borrowing of Mills and Boon titles, calculated by the total number of date stamps inside a given volume. On average, a Mills and Boon novel was issued 165 times: the highest borrowing figures were recorded in Scotland, in coastal towns in England, and in the West Country. Seaside places such as Portsmouth had particularly high lending frequencies; Mills and Boon attributed this to the lonely sailors' wives 'left behind' who took up reading, and the influx of holiday-makers during the summer months. Town libraries in Taunton reported the highest number of issues of any Mills and Boon novel (740) for a 1935 novel, *Anchor at Hazard* by Ray Dorien. Originally priced at 2s.6d., over fifteen years this title had generated nine pounds in profits.[11]

By the 1980s the world publishing market was dominated by English-language books, and of the paperback share of this domination, Mills and Boon commanded a ninth of all new titles, its command of the romantic fiction market challenged not by rival publishers but by the success of the authors Barbara Cartland and Catherine Cookson.

This dominant position had been guaranteed by the merger with the Canadian firm Harlequin, a small paperback publishing house that had started up in 1949 and approached Mills and Boon for North American rights to their Doctor/Nurse series. In the early 1970s the two companies merged, thus opening the North American market,

> which in 1977 consumed 100 million Harlequins, 10 per cent of the total mass paperback sales. The books were translated into as many as 23 languages, which, with English-language export editions and foreign licensee deals soon brought the total number of markets to almost 100 and sales rose from 3 m in 1970 to world-wide total sales of over 200 million in 1984. This enormous expansion was made possible by a comparable increase in editorial output that rose from 8 titles per month in 1970 to 60 titles a month organised under 14 stories, representing an 80 per cent share of the market.[12]

In 1981, Harlequin Mills and Boon was purchased by Torstar, a Canadian media giant.

By the mid-1980s Mills and Boon had a number of paperback collections from which readers could choose. These ranged from 'contemporary romances', with 'modern international settings' and 'happy endings' to 'temptation romances' where heroines encounter the 'dilemmas of modern-day life'. Other series included reprints of old favourites, back-to-back romances, tales of love in 'busy hospitals' and historical romance 'from Saxon times to the turn of the [twentieth] century' (quoted from Mills and Boon publicity). The *Temptation* series was a 'line of sensually charged romantic fantasies' concentrated on the theme of female 'destiny', American in viewpoint, containing a 'high level of sexual tension' and written from the heroine's point of view.

Although continuously updated with regard to plot, setting and gender relations, all the Mills and Boon range endorsed a conservative, if more liberated, traditionalism. The books remain relaxing melodramas of personal destiny in which a heroine overcomes obstacles of esteem, social position and income to get her man. Upholding middle-class values of hard work, decency and family where virtue is rewarded, the romance focuses upon 'events . . . affecting the sentiments'.[13] The moment of the 'kiss' is not only erotically charged, it is also a moment of transformation and the exchange of power, confirming in its sensuality the inherent worth of femininity.

> The significance of romantic fiction, as a cultural phenomenon, cannot be exaggerated. The market leader, Harlequin Enterprises Ltd sells 200 million books per year, the company's international readership numbers about 50 million women and their books display a remarkable facility to cross cultural boundaries. Written overwhelmingly by Anglo-Saxon authors, the books are translated into 26 different languages and sold in 100 different countries. Initially ignored or summarily dismissed by academics, from the 1980s onward the genre became the focus of a considerable body of academic criticism and analysis, especially from feminists because of its implications concerning the relationship of women and culture.[14]

The very end of the 1990s gave rise to two 'decadent' or corrupt genres. The first, 'cult' fiction, was generated by the emergence of nostalgia for the rebelliousness of the late 1950s and 1960s and included books as diverse as those by Jack Kerouac (d. 1969), Joseph Heller (d. 2000), and Ken Kesey (d. 2001), Anthony Burgess (d. 1993) and Charles Bukowski. Cult fiction was no real genre but a bookshop ploy to increase sales of back-listed, but famously 'radical' titles from forty years previously. As cult fiction included many 'classic' books it was an excellent way of reintroducing important or forgotten titles.

The other genre was pornography dressed as women's *erotica*. This was created as the extreme edge of romance, as an answer to women's fantasies. Virgin's *Black Lace* imprint was first on the market, shelved as 'respectable' fantasy reading for women, yet Virgin's marketing unanimously reported that over 90 per cent were sold to men! At least one Black Lace author pointed out that 'erotica [was] a middle class validation of pornography'. Put off by 'problematic' covers and unwilling to purchase such books from open shelves (if at all), women's response rapidly declined, whilst gay erotic remained a male preserve. It remained entirely true, however, that an erotica paperback title could (in the early years, at least) pull together a readership of almost half a million. Such numbers suggest a lucrative, if diminishing market share.

If the 1960s tended to produce diversity rather than innovation, then by the late 1990s, the nascent diversity of the 1960s suggested to some critics that the age of genre was over, reduced to a mass of competing subgenres and specialist areas, including such divisions as cyberpunk, post-modern historical sagas, metaphysical crime, serial-killer who-dunits and vampire lesbianism.

The phenomenal success of J. K. Rowling's tales of Harry Potter (*Harry Potter and the Philosopher's Stone*, 1997, onwards) marks a certain change in reading patterns. Although written for children aged between nine and eleven the tales of Harry and his magical life at Hogwart's Academy were soon being read by adults and marketed as 'novels'. An adult edition of the stories (same text, more adult covers) was directed at older readers, whilst children could enjoy the original tales, games and merchandise. Rowling was able to fill a gap left by the death of Roald Dahl, producing stories whose gothic suburbanism was grafted onto the very traditional public school children's adventure (with clear echoes of Angela Brazil and Enid Blyton). The fantasy elements of the tales owe much to Tolkien's 'Gandalfian' sensibility. Rowling's work is a clear example of the retention and reiteration of traditional themes and the conservatism of all popular fiction and at the same time an illustration of the idea of literature as lifestyle (through the creation of a parallel 'world' which can be 'lived' by a group of readers).

With the ethnographic changes in the population which came from mass immigration between the late 1940s and the 1970s also came the possibility of the appearance of differently inflected literary voices. Such voices had, to a large extent, to wait for the writing of second- and third-generation authors whose first language is English but whose perceptions are determined by newer cross-cultural possibilities. Of these writers Salman Rushdie emerged as the most significant and most controversial. Rushdie was lionised in the West but vilified elsewhere for *The Satanic Verses* (see author entry).

On the whole, however, other writers whose immediate family origins may be Asian or Caribbean have concentrated on metropolitan landscapes and especially the muti-cultural neighbourhoods of London. Such writers include Hanif Kureishi, Meera Syal and Zadie Smith and their work makes clear the shift of focus of regional authors (especially those in Scotland) towards the landscape of the city. These voices represent possibilities for bestsellers of the future.

4
Best-selling Authors Since 1900

There were two types of best-selling authors in Britain during the twentieth century. There were those like Margaret Mitchell or Grace Metalious who gained bestseller status through a single work, and there were others like Ian Fleming or Agatha Christie who consistently sold very large numbers of copies. Some best-selling authors never seemed to feature in the historical records. Writers such as Edgar Wallace and Edgar Rice Burroughs had no obvious best-selling titles, yet were clearly very important in terms of their *overall* sales. Others, such as Stephen Francis (Hank Janson), succeeded in the pulp market where few, if any, records were kept or have been preserved; still others wrote virtually anonymously for romance publishers and the records for their sales are still kept relatively secret. Other writers have had sales assured through their adoption by teachers and academics; such is the case with Virginia Woolf and Aldous Huxley.

In the following section I have included writers whose bestseller status was assured through purchasers' choice rather than any other criterion and so those writers who have sold very large quantities of books to schools and universities have been excluded, as have writers who died before the twentieth century but who still enjoyed excellent sales.

Figures relating to book sales must, of course, always be approached with considerable caution, if only because they usually cannot be reliably checked and rest upon approximations suggested by orders from booksellers. In the early years of the twentieth century book 'booming' meant the unscrupulous promotion of works that might be selling poorly, whilst the constant issue of new editions might disguise sales of fewer than two hundred copies an edition. However, publishers have their own views on what constitutes a bestseller or best-selling line. Publisher Michael Joseph suggested in 1957 that a base limit of 50,000 sales for a hardback original edition would produce a bona fide best-seller, although 'Miss Read' never sold more than 20,000 copies in hardback for each new title whilst, nevertheless, enjoying huge success in paperback.

Finally, it should not be forgotten that records of accurate sales figures from publishers and bookstores are notoriously contradictory and incomplete when not actually lost or falsified for 'industry' consumption. Caution is essential where booksellers were known for 'puffing' slow sellers and publishers were declaring double entries and weren't showing returns. Moreover, public records of any sort really only came into existence in the late 1970s and remained problematic until the 1990s. Even then, publishers like Mills and Boon are not included. Best-selling authors are therefore not always obvious and their sales not always commensurate with their influence. Discrimination between dubious claims (especially from 1900 to 1919) means that no clear picture is likely to emerge although we can make some assured assumptions. These assumptions are based on gross sales of first editions, reprints, cheap editions and paperbacks seen as a totality and such sales are almost impossible to calculate accurately. Last, but not least, of course, although all of these authors are bestsellers, the difference in sales figures between the highest and the lowest may amount to millions of copies and so the range of best-selling writers itself becomes a calculus of popular taste and specialist interest.

The following selection of best-selling authors has been divided into the historical periods in which they enjoyed their greatest fame. Some, like Edgar Wallace, Ian Fleming or Agatha Christie, cross eras but these have been situated in the period of their greatest success. Thus D. H. Lawrence, who died in 1930, became a bestseller in Great Britain only posthumously from the 1960s onwards. In some cases authors fit easily into a period (for instance Grace Metalious or Catherine Cookson) but where they do not and sales indicate longevity a note has been attached to the relevant period.

Some readers may be concerned that favourite authors have been omitted who, they believe, have a legitimate place, and that some choices seem eccentric in their inclusion. I probably stand guilty of omission and eccentricity. I have, for instance, included Irvine Welsh, whose novel *Trainspotting* (1993) is, in reality, a series of strung-together short stories (and whose later work has met with less success), but, in a different vein, I have not included Angela Carter (d. 1992), who despite much applause for her magic realism and feminist stance remains popular because of the needs of the academic syllabus rather than through popular mandate. The same is the case with Virginia Woolf and James Joyce. (This does not impugn the quality of these writers' works.) Equally, I have not attempted to be encyclopaedic in my approach to entries. These sometimes offer factual information and at other times combine this with consideration of the author's contribution to a genre. The list is only intended as a quick pen-portrait reference to the last hundred years of best-selling fiction, nothing more. Thus, some writers such as Sheila Holland (Charlotte Lamb) are included as much in their own right as examples of the success of a genre exemplified by a different author or group. Simple cumulative sales have been used as only one criterion amongst others to determine an entry. I have gone for typicality where possible and used my selection as an illustration rather than the sort of comprehensive guide that is available elsewhere. Where an author produced a very large number of titles but no one title is of great significance, I have either noted their output or simply mentioned an indicative title or two, usually omitting comprehensive lists easily located in other publications dedicated to one specific area of genre fiction.

Roald Dahl (but not J. K. Rowling) has been left out because his original (if far from total) appeal has been to the children's market, whilst John Wyndham and Ethel M. Dell have been included because, although their work was devoured by adolescents, they considered themselves as authors writing for adults. Equally, it should be noted that where an author (however good) sells his or her books because of celebrity status gained elsewhere (primarily through television) then, they too have been omitted from the selection. Thus Ben Elton, Stephen Fry and Alan Titchmarsh do not appear. This is also the case with authors from the beginning of the century whose status as bestsellers seems hardly in question. Bram Stoker died in 1912, his most famous book, *Dracula*, had appeared long ago in 1897 and despite its extraordinary success Stoker remained a late Victorian who published nothing of significance in the twentieth century. H. G. Wells was, alongside Arthur Conan Doyle, Britain's most famous novelist during the first forty years of the century but his great novels were all written in the previous century, his fame resting on a back catalogue and on his major works of non-fiction and social commentary.

An Age Passes, an Age Begins: 1900 to 1918

The sixpennies in paper covers probably represent what is most widely read. Here [Charles] Garvice, who had six titles to his name in 1908, now has 53, Effie Rowland [*sic*], unrepresented ... in 1909, has 30; but all living writers are headed by the sporting novelist, Mr Nat Gould with 60. . . .

(*The Athenaeum*, 10 June 1911)

Florence L(ouisa) Barclay

b. 1862   d. 1921

PSEUDONYM: Brandon Roy

Guy Mervyn (1891)
The Rosary (1909)

Barclay was a writer of romance stories, and much of her work is concerned with semi-religious issues. On their honeymoon in the Holy Land she and her husband, the Reverend Charles W. Barclay, discovered the mouth of Jacob's Well, on which Christ is believed to have rested, and which was covered by the ruins of a fourth-century church.

Her first novel, *Guy Mervyn*, was published under her pseudonym in 1891, and Barclay began writing *The Rosary*, her best-selling novel, in 1905 while recovering from a serious illness. Barclay sent a copy to her sister in America and when it was published in New York the book sold 150,000 hardback copies in the first nine months after publication. It was translated into eight languages, and sold over a million copies by 1921, continuing to appear on the bestseller lists for twenty years.

Barclay believed that writing should have a positive effect, and wrote that

There is enough sin in the world without an author's powers of imagination being used in order to add even fictitious sin to the amount. Too many bad, mean, morbid characters already, alas! walk this earth. Why should writers add to their number and risk introducing them into beautiful homes where such people in actual life would never, for one moment, be tolerated?[1]

(Enoch) Arnold Bennett

b. 1867   d. 1931

Anna of the Five Towns (1902)
The Grand Babylonian Hotel (1902)
The Old Wives' Tale (1908)
Clayhanger (1910)
The Card (1911)
Riceyman Steps (1923)

Arnold Bennett was a novelist, short-story writer, journalist, and critic. He was born in Hanley, Staffordshire, in 1867 and grew up in the earthenware-producing community of towns dubbed the 'Potteries', a setting which appears in his novels and short stories as the fictitious 'Five Towns'. He was educated at Burslem Endowed School and the Middle School in Newcastle-under-Lyme before graduating from London University. After training as a solicitor's clerk in London, he became assistant editor of the journal *Woman* in 1893 and editor in 1896. His first novel, *A Man from the North* (1898), drew on his own experiences in the Potteries, and was followed in 1900 by his resignation from *Woman* in order to pursue writing novels and articles professionally, although as a journalist he remained the most influential critic of his generation.

Bennett admired realistic authors such as Flaubert, Maupassant, Zola, and Balzac, and his own realistic style emerged in his novels of the 'Five Towns' such as *The Old Wives' Tale* (1908) and the Clayhanger series: *Clayhanger* (1910), *Hilda Lessways* (1911), and *These Twain* (1915). During World War One he wrote propaganda literature for the Ministry of Information, which possibly inspired his political novel *Lord Raingo* (1926). Bennett also wrote humorous novels about wealth and luxury, such as *The Grand Babylonian Hotel* (1902). Bennett received the James Tait Black Memorial Award for *Riceyman Steps* (1923) in 1924.

John Buchan

b. 1875   d. 1940

Prester John (1910)
The Thirty-Nine Steps (1915)
The Power-House (1916)
Greenmantle (1916)
Mr Standfast (1919)
Huntingtower (1922)
The Three Hostages (1924)
John Macnab (1925)
The Dancing Floor (1926)
The Courts of the Morning (1929)
Castle Gay (1929)
The Island of Sheep (1936)
Sick Heart River (1941)

> ... I have long cherished an affection for that elementary type of tale which Americans call the 'dime novel,' and which we know as the 'shocker' – the romance where the incidents defy the probabilities, and march just inside the borders of the possible.

Thus Buchan dedicated *The Thirty-Nine Steps* (1915) and in so doing created the modern spy thriller and its first great hero Richard Hannay.

Buchan was born in Perth in Scotland in 1875, the son of a minister of the free church. Schooled in Fife and Glasgow, he went to university in Glasgow and Oxford where he won several awards including the Newdigate Prize for Poetry, published in the avant-garde magazine the *Yellow Book*, wrote books and gained a First. A barrister and Member of Parliament, he was also a soldier and publisher. Created Baron Tweedsmuir of Elsfield in 1935, he was Governor General of Canada until his death in 1940.

Although Buchan's first success was with *Prester John* (1910), it is with his spy thriller-adventures that he will be remembered, most especially for the creation of his hero Richard Hannay.

Richard Hannay is the adventure-seeking hero of John Buchan's novel *The Thirty-Nine Steps* (1915) and its sequels. A stalwart upholder of the British Empire, Hannay has made his fortune in South Africa. At one point he expresses the opinion: 'perhaps the Scots are better than the English, but we're all a thousand percent better than anybody else'. He feels a continuing need to test his own courage, and the Great War gives him plenty of opportunities. In the affair of the '39 steps' he becomes embroiled with a spy ring and is pursued across the hills of Scotland. His further adventures are recounted by Buchan in *Greenmantle* (1916), *Mr Standfast* (1919), *The Three Hostages* (1924), *The Runagates Club* (1928; short stories, not all of which feature Hannay) and *The Island of Sheep* (1936). By the time of this last novel he had become Sir Richard Hannay.[2]

Buchan's work must also be seen in the context of the thriller genre; for instance, 'Sapper' (see entry), Dornford Yates (Cecil William Mercer, b. 1885, d. 1960), William Le Queux (see entry), Edgar Wallace (see entry), and Sidney Horler (see entry) were all,

> Essentially romantic (in the widest sense of the word) thriller writers [and] dominated the British literary scene during the inter-war years . . . all held vaguely similar views on the role of their mother-country in the greater scheme of things, all were highly proficient at spinning the kind of yarns (what Buchan himself, in a faintly embarrassed throwaway, used to refer to as 'shockers') that sold in their tens of thousands on first publication, their hundreds of thousands in reprint.[3]

All of these writers owe a debt nevertheless to Anthony Hope (Sir Anthony Hope Hopkins, d. 1933), whose most famous romance thrillers (set in mittel-European Ruritania), *The Prisoner of Zenda* (1894) and *Rupert of Hentzau* (1898), belong to the nineteenth century and create the style for the escapist adventure set within an international political crisis.

Edgar Rice Burroughs

b. 1875   d. 1950

Tarzan of the Apes (1914)
The Return of Tarzan (1915)
A Princess of Mars (1917)
The Gods of Mars (1918)
The Warlord of Mars (1919)
Thuvia, Maid of Mars (1920)

Tarzan the Terrible (1921)
The Chessmen of Mars (1922)
At the Earth's Core (1922)
Pellucidar (1923)
Tarzan and the Ant Men (1924)
The Land that Time Forgot (1924)
The Moon Maid (1926)

Burroughs was born on 1 September 1875 (the same year as Rafael Sabatini [see entry]), the son of a distilling entrepreneur who later manufactured electric batteries. Although expected to join the army, Burroughs was expelled from one academy and failed when at West Point, ending his 'career' as a cavalryman in Arizona. After numerous (and pointless) jobs Burroughs began to write for the early pulp magazines, his second short story, 'Tarzan of the Apes' (1912), made him instantly famous and turned him into a professional author.

Burroughs's creation of Tarzan in a tale for *All-Story* magazine in 1912, and in twenty-four subsequent books, beginning with *Tarzan of the Apes* (1914), has been an extraordinary influence on film, television, comic books, and popular culture in general. Tarzan films were produced throughout the twentieth century, with a musical cartoon Disney version (1999). The character of Tarzan can be seen as a major influence on 'superhero' figures, especially Conan the Barbarian and Batman, as well as in the continuing 'lost world' tradition of Sir Arthur Conan Doyle and Michael Crichton. The concept of alien 'green men' may well originate with *A Princess of Mars* (1917).

(Sir Thomas Henry) Hall Caine

b. 1853   d. 1931

The Shadow of a Crime (1885)
The Deemster (1887)
The Bondman (1890)
The Scapegoat (1891)
The Manxman (1894)
The Christian (1897)
The Eternal City (1901)
The Prodigal Son (1904)
The White Prophet (1909)
The Woman Thou Gavest Me (1913)

Hall Caine was born in Runcorn, Cheshire, in 1853. He attended primary school in Liverpool and on the Isle of Man before becoming an architect's clerk in Liverpool at the age of fourteen, already exhibiting interest in reading and spending much of his spare time in the local library. He became a teaching assistant and then a teacher at his uncle's school on the Isle of Man for about a year before returning to Liverpool to his job as a clerk. He soon became consumed with writing, principally articles in journals like *The Builder*, along with lecturing and organising literary societies. At the age of twenty-five, he met and became friends with the poet D. G. Rossetti, who was a major influence on Caine and his writing career. Caine worked as Rossetti's secretarial assistant until the poet's death in 1882. He wrote a remembrance of their relationship in the same year, titled *Recollections*. Hall Caine continued writing, gaining steady employment with the *Liverpool Mercury*, writing articles for newspapers and journals, and editing the anthology *Sonnets of Three Centuries* (1882) until his first novel *The Shadow of a Crime* was published in 1885. Many of Caine's novels are set on the Isle of Man, such as *The Deemster* (1887), the first of some of his most popular works. Hall Caine also wrote propaganda literature pertaining to the Russo-Polish persecutions of the Jews from 1892 to 1893 and he edited *King Albert's Book* during the War of 1914–18. He died in 1931.

By 1904 Hall Caine was so famous that *Punch* suggested he might be a new literary disease!

HALL CAINE [*sic*], There seems to be no escape. I go to a bookshop and the shopman insinuates a volume into my hand, *Cobwebs of Criticism* by HALL CAINE. It is a shrill plea for the sanity of the mob and I do not want it. I am taken to the theatre, and the play is *The Christian* by HALL CAINE. I open *The Chronicle* and find an article by Mr Begbie daring to question if Mr HALL CAINE's chromolithographic view of Christianity is a true one and asking if there is not a finer ideal than he puts before the playgoers. I shudder to think of the morrow.[4]

Marie Corelli (Mary Mackay)

b. 1855   d. 1924

A Romance of Two Worlds (1886)
The Sorrows of Satan (1895)
The Secret Power (1921)

Born in London on 1 May 1855, Corelli was educated privately and showed a considerable ability in music, debuting in 1884. Nevertheless, in 1885 she became a full-time writer and later settled in Stratford-upon-Avon.

Corelli's work is now forgotten, but she was easily the best-selling woman writer of the early twentieth century, churning out books that mixed pious sentiment with sensation, theosophy and comments on marital relations. She was especially good at writing for a readership that wanted consolation, hope, and thrills, mostly a female readership but from all classes. The extraordinary success of her work suggests the need felt at the time for a literature of assurance in an age of rapid change, especially for women. In 1909, Corelli could still command the vast sum of £9,500 in advances.

How did she do it? It is not easy to answer that question. Perhaps the nearest we can come to it is by noting the fact that her stories all have an element of sensationalism in them, plus a dose of vague, mystical, other-or-ideal worldly religion; and that this was almost bound to go down well in an age which had not lost its religious impulse, even though the discoveries and arguments of Darwin and his followers had denied that impulse orthodox expression. Queen Victoria herself praised the *Sorrows of Satan*, and Amy Cruse, in *After the Victorians*, points out how often it was used as a text by fashionable preachers of the day. A Father Ignatius praised the novel to a packed congregation at the Portman Rooms, Baker Street, and wrote to Marie Corelli, calling her 'a prophet of good things to come in this filthy and materialistic generation.' She had thrillingly portrayed, he told her, 'the utter misery of being without Christ in life and death, the daring blasphemies of popular poets and other writers, and the consequences in the lives of their readers.'[5]

(Sir) Arthur Conan Doyle

b. 1859   d. 1930

'Sherlock Holmes' series:
6 novels (from 1888 to 1914) including:
  The Hound of the Baskervilles (1902)
21 volumes of short stories (1889–1927; 5 published posthumously, 1959–81)

Other novels:
  Micah Clarke (1890)
  The White Company (1891)
  The Parasite (1895)
  Sir Nigel (1906)
  The Lost World (1912)

Arthur Conan Doyle was the son of Charles and Mary Doyle and was born in Edinburgh on 22 May 1859. His grandfather was the highly talented artist HB, whose political lampoons graced the Regency, and all his uncles seemed to possess considerable artistic gifts, Richard Doyle creating Mr Punch.

The young Conan Doyle finished his schooling at a Jesuit school in Austria and then went to Edinburgh University where he graduated in 1881 and signed on as a ship's surgeon on voyages to the Arctic and Africa. On his return he practised as a doctor in Plymouth and Southsea, where the first Sherlock Holmes story was written. Success as a writer came late and Doyle left medicine in his thirties.

Doyle catered to the vast literate public of the late nineteenth and early twentieth century through inexpensive and hugely popular magazines such as the *Strand*, each issue of which contained complete short stories. From 1888 to his death in 1930 Doyle produced novels, short stories, plays, poetry, two histories, books of autobiography, and ten works on spiritualism. On top of this he wrote campaigning pamphlets, played world-class cricket and managed his various business enterprises including his spiritualist bookshop in Westminster.

Of Doyle's vast output the science fiction tales, including *The Lost World* (1912), are now seen as amusing curiosities, enjoyable in themselves (and a clear influence on writers like Michael Crichton; see entry) but perhaps lacking the darkly logical predictions of H. G. Wells. This leaves what Doyle considered his masterworks, *Micah Clarke* (1890), *The*

White Company (1891) and *Sir Nigel* (1906), which belong to a genre out-dated as serious fiction even when they were written and which can be regarded as enjoyable only in terms of the limitations they labour under as minor romances rather than the status that Doyle claimed for them as works of epic seriousness.

It is upon the much more than merely literary reputation of the sixty stories of Sherlock Holmes and Dr John H. Watson that Doyle's reputation rests. Produced between 1888 and 1927, the tales were published either as complete short stories or as two-part novels, mostly in the pages of the *Strand* in Britain and a variety of magazines in America, including *Harper's*, the *American Magazine*, *Liberty* and others. The stories were then anthologised following the usual practice of the age and can be listed alongside the four novels as: *A Study in Scarlet* (1887); *The Sign of Four* (1890); *The Adventures of Sherlock Holmes* (1892); *The Memoirs of Sherlock Holmes* (1894); *The Hound of the Baskervilles* (1902); *The Return of Sherlock Holmes* (1905); *The Valley of Fear* (1915); *His Last Bow* (1917); and *The Case-Book of Sherlock Holmes* (1927).

Numerous films have used the Holmes stories as their basis and there is a growing number of works by other writers who have borrowed characters from or enlarged upon Doyle's original conception. Enthusiasts talk of 'Sherlockiana' to describe the vast literature, both serious and ephemeral, that has come into being.

Charles Garvice

b. 1833   d. 1920

PSEUDONYMS: Charles Gibson; Caroline Hart

150 titles including:
Woman's Soul (1902)
Love's Dilemma (1902)
When Love Meets Love (1906)
The Gold in the Gutter (1907)
Story of a Passion (1908)
Dulcie (1910)
The Earl's Daughter (1910)
He Loves Me, He Loves Me Not (1911)
Nellie (1913)
The Call of the Heart (1914)

Charles Garvice rose to fame in the nineteenth century with romances and romance adventures read by both men and women. He was particularly popular in the United States, producing over 150 novels, twenty-five of which were written under the pseudonym Caroline Hart. His work, although containing the usual romance or mystery elements, was written in a naturalistic style and often displayed an acute awareness of social problems and divisions.

Elinor (Sutherland) Glyn

b. 1864   d. 1943

> *The Visits of Elizabeth* (1900)
> *Three Weeks* (1907)
> *His House* (1910)
> *The Career of Catherine Bush* (1916)

Elinor (Sutherland) Glyn was born in Jersey, the Channel Islands, on 17 October 1864 and was privately educated. She married Clayton Glyn in 1892, and they had two daughters. Elinor helped as a canteen worker and war correspondent during the First World War. She is best known for her highly romantic tales filled with luxurious settings and unlikely plots. She began writing society novels, which, at the time, were greatly admired for their content, but which now have their greatest worth in Glyn's storytelling abilities. She soon turned her attention towards passionate romance literature. In 1916, after the death of her husband, she found herself in debt and was forced to write from necessity. From this point on, her stories were simply meant to entertain audiences in Europe and America. In 1920, Glyn moved to America where she began her career in screenwriting in Hollywood. Her short story entitled 'It' was made into a film, after which 'it' became synonymous with sex appeal. Elinor Glyn returned to England in 1929 and published her autobiography, *Romantic Adventure*, in 1936. Her novel *Three Weeks* (1907) made her name as a risqué writer whose erotic suggestiveness was considered highly immoral but also highly tittilating to young female readers.

Nat(haniel) Gould

b. 1857   d. 1919

Banker and Broker (n.d.)
Racecourse and Battlefield (n.d.)
and many others

Prolific author of sporting books, editor of the short-lived *Sporting Annual* (1900) and *Nat Gould's Annual* (first published in 1903) as well as writing an autobiography, *The Magic of Sport* (1909), and numerous travel books relating to Australia and Europe. In all Gould produced 130 titles and published 126 during his lifetime.

Nat Gould was born on 21 December 1857 in Manchester, England. He first encountered the future loves of his life in school. On the way to school he rode on the box next to the omnibus driver and listened to the old man reminiscing about racing. He loved sports, captaining the school cricket club and playing football and rugby. Although Nat was only a mediocre student, a teacher who once caught him sneaking a minute to write a piece of drama told him he would 'probably write something decent'.

Early in the boy's life, his father, an enterprising tea trader and churchwarden, suddenly died. Young Gould left school and followed his father's work. He hated the drudgery of the tea trade but enjoyed the frivolities of Manchester. Later, he moved to live with his uncle in Derbyshire. He found the hearty work of farm life a welcome change, and he particularly enjoyed driving the horses to get supplies. When he was twenty his mother convinced him to try the tea trade again, so they returned to Manchester. Still disliking the tiresome job, Gould quit but then grew listless through lack of work.

At his mother's suggestion, he began reporting for a newspaper in Newark. He relished his return to the country and gained valuable experience because the small size of the publication required him to cover a variety of fields. After six years, he grew restless. His mentor and editor suggested that he try life in Australia, so Gould left for another continent in 1884. He worked for several newspapers, including the *Brisbane Telegraph* and the *Sydney Referee*. He reported largely on racing, thus continuing a passion he had pursued while in Manchester. Aware of his interest, Gould's editor at the *Referee* urged him to begin a serial about horse racing. A representative of George Routledge happened upon this serial and snapped up the rights to it. Shortly thereafter, the publisher made Gould an offer for two more books, although Gould had not yet published a novel in England.

After eleven years in Australia Gould returned to England with his wife, a woman he met during his travels. He began to publish for George Routledge, but when the publisher died, Gould signed with John Long.

In his autobiography *The Magic of Sport* (1909) Gould comments on sitting down to write his first book, which was actually the first instalment in what became a long-running serial in the *Sydney Referee*.

> When I commenced the first chapter of 'Within the Tide,' I sat down at my table without the least idea of what I was going to write about, except that it was to be a racing story. I had no plot mapped out, no lines upon which to work, no idea that a long novel was required; I merely set out to write a short story.

The comment went on to reflect on Gould's awareness of attacks on his work by literary reviewers.

> Some of my critics have said I know nothing about literature. That is quite unnecessary information, for I never pretended I did. We can't all write classics. . . .
>
> It is rather amusing to be told I have 'no pretensions to style' when I don't profess to have any. The object of writing a novel is to tell a story that will hold the reader from start to finish – a story that grips him so that he will not put the book down until he has read the last page. That is the object I have in my view when I write, and I think I may fairly claim to have succeeded, if I may judge by press and personal comment on my work.

It was Gould's love of sport, especially horse racing (see also Dick Francis), as well as his ability to offer 'masculine thrills', which made him the best-selling men's author during the First World War, indeed as one hospital librarian commented in 1916,

> We soon learnt to invest in a large number of detective books, and any amount of Nat Gould's stories. In fact, a certain type of man would read nothing except Nat Gould. However ill he was, however suffering and broken, the name of Nat Gould would always bring a smile to his face. Often and often I've heard the whispered words: 'A Nat Gould – ready for when I'm better.'

Gould died on 25 July 1919 aged 61, at New Haven, having completed 115 novels on horse racing, numerous articles and short stories. On his death, *The Nation* (9 August 1919) commented:

> In the way of sale, his wares surpassed all others. To millions they were the bread of mental life. We have heard that men at the front yearning for a 'bit of a read,' would ask for Nat Gould, and, in default of him, would go empty away to sit brooding in the monotonous dug out scornfully disdaining the allurements of Charles Garvice, Florence Barclay, or even Marie Corelli. We have heard that a newspaper purchasing the serial rights to one of his stories could promise itself an increased circulation of 10,000 a day, no matter what its politics or principles.

During his lifetime, Gould exemplified the new phenomenon of the best-selling author, as *Truth* (22 January 1913) pointed out:

> Who is the most popular of living novelists? It will astonish a great many people to learn that Mr Nat Gould, judged by the sales of his books, easily and indisputably takes first place. His stories are read with avidity by a vast public for whom the novels mostly in demand at the libraries have no attraction. It is to readers who love tales of the sporting world above all others that Mr Gould appeals, and how successfully he does so is shown by the fact that in the past eight years or so upwards of 8 million copies of his books have been sold.

Robert Hichens

b. 1864   d. 1950

The Green Carnation (1894)
The Garden of Allah (1904)

Son of a cleric, Hichens was a gifted musician but chose to travel and write, living a 'bohemian' lifestyle which took him, amongst other locations, to Egypt, which inspired his mystic tone and approach. Hichens's novel *The Garden of Allah* (1904) combined the exotic landscape of the Sahara with the enthusiasm and overheated passionate spiritualism of Marie Corelli (see entry), and in doing so created a bridge between the late nineteenth-century romance and its post-World War One incarnation in works like E. M. Hull's *The Sheik* (1919). The book was turned into a play and filmed three times.

The protagonist of *The Garden of Allah* is a young aristocratic Eng-
lishwoman, Domini Enfilden, who is travelling in North Africa. Her
journey is no mere tourist trip; from the very beginning (when we
encounter her reading Cardinal Newman's verse epic about the soul's
journey to judgement, *The Dream of Gerontius*), it is represented as
a kind of pilgrimage: a flight from the distractions of civilization
in quest of some unspecifiable spiritual truth. The Sahara Desert –
the 'garden' of the title – features throughout the book as a quasi-
supernatural landscape whose immanent godhead is more funda-
mental and less distorted than the supposedly-derivative images
reflected in the major world religions and pagan beliefs which they
replaced.

The plot of the novel initially follows a pattern which has since
been enshrined as the principal formula of mass-produced romantic
fiction. Domini meets a man named Androvsky, whose behaviour
towards her is at first offensive and disdainful. She is attracted to him
anyway, even though she glimpses in his eyes what appear to be
'unfathomable depths of misery or of wickedness.' She observes him
secretly for some days, during which she notices that he has a curious
aversion to priests and other symbols of religion.

The antagonism between Domini and Androvsky gradually
changes into a fierce erotic attraction, which is mirrored in a whole
series of atmospheric effects. Carried away by their passion, they
decide to be married, in spite of Androvsky's antipathy to all things
religious. This antipathy appears to be mutual; it is reflected not only
in the dark suspicions of the local priest but in the literally ominous
behaviour of a silver crucifix which hangs in his church.

After their marriage, Domini and her husband go on into the
deepest heart of the desert. Androvsky has in his possession a quan-
tity of a liqueur called Louarine, which is recognized by a priest they
happen across as the unique product of a particular Trappist
monastery, the secret of whose manufacture is the privilege of only
one man – a man who disappeared from the monastery in question
some time before, in stark violation of both his holy vows and his
duty to confide the formula of the liqueur to a new custodian.
Androvsky, of course, is that man.

Androvsky eventually confesses his sin to Domini, and then to the
priest who married them – and having purged himself of guilt and
achieved true repentance, he returns whence he came, feeling that
his love for Domini would be fatally diminished could he not love
honour more. Domini fully endorses this decision; although she is
left to bring up their as-yet-unborn son alone, she feels that every-

thing has now been set to rights, and that her fierce spiritual hunger has been fully and properly appeased. . . . Domini ultimately receives the same magical endowment of contentment.[6]

William (Tufnell) Le Queux

b. 1864   d. 1927

Guilty Bonds (1891)
The Temptress (1895)
Zoraida: A Romance of the Harem and the Great Sahara (1895)
Devil's Dice (1896)
The Great White Queen (1896)
The Veiled Man (1899)
The Bond of Black (1899)
Wiles of the Wicked (1899)

This British novelist, who claimed to have intimate knowledge of the secret service operations of several European nations, was one of the first contributors to the spy fiction genre. A former consul to the Republic of San Marino, he was foreign editor to the *London Globe*, and correspondent for the London *Daily Mail* during the Balkan War from 1912 to 1913. His first novel, *Guilty Bonds* (1891), a fictional account of his observations as a journalist, was banned in Tsarist Russia. He authored 150 novels about international intrigue as well as books warning of Britain's vulnerability to European invasion before World War One.

Le Queux's 'shockers' paved the way for John Buchan, Dornford Yates, 'Sapper' and Sidney Horler but they were, to a large extent, eclipsed and forgotten by the 1940s.

W(illiam) J(ohn) Locke

b. 1863   d. 1930

The Morals of Marcus Ordeyne (1905)
Beloved Vagabond (1906)

William Locke was born in Demerara, then British Guiana, the son of a Barbados banker, whose move to Trinidad meant that his son would be sent to school in Britain and not see his father for nine years. Locke did finish his schooling in Trinidad before going up to Cambridge in 1881. After graduating, Locke travelled in France before returning to teach French (a job he hated) and write novels that were not successful enough to let him escape. In 1897 he was able to leave teaching to become Secretary to the Royal Institute of Architects, a post he held for ten years. By 1907, Locke's writing career had taken off, with his ninth and tenth novels, *The Morals of Marcus Ordeyne* (1905) and *Beloved Vagabond* (1906), making him wealthy as well as famous. The books epitomise his 'gay romanticism' (summed up by the figure of the vagabond) – light-hearted, charming, witty and without purpose except to entertain.

A(lfred) E(dward) W(oodley) Mason

b. 1865   d. 1948

'Inspector Hanaud' series
  The Watchers (1899)
  The Four Feathers (1902)
  Running Water (1907)
  At the Villa Rose (Hanaud) (1913)
  The Witness for the Defence (1913)
  The House of the Arrow (Hanaud) (1924)
  No Other Tiger (1927)
  Fire over England (1936)
  Konigsmark (1938)

A. E. W. Mason was born in Camberwell in London in 1865 and educated at Dulwich College in South London between 1878 and 1884. He graduated from Trinity College, Cambridge, in 1886 with a degree in Classics and later served in the First World War with the Royal Marine Light Infantry and on secret service missions across the world, for which he was promoted to Major. Having become an actor with a touring company, Mason took up writing from 1895 and even became a Liberal MP (Coventry) during 1906 to 1910. Like Sir Arthur Conan Doyle, Mason was a fine sportsman especially in yachting and mountaineering.

Mason specialised in exciting thrillers, historical romances and detective fiction. His most famous adventure, *The Four Feathers* (1902), is a tale of imperial thrills and personal redemption during the war in the

Sudan and it has proved a popular subject both for films (1939; 1955) and spoofs: *Carry on Camel* (1967).

Mason is also the creator of Inspector Hanaud who first appeared in *At the Villa Rose* (1910). Ernest Hemingway recalled Mason's work in *The Sun Also Rises*:

> It was a little past noon and there was not much shade, but I sat against the trunk of two of the trees that grew together, and read. The book was something by A. E. W. Mason, and I was reading a wonderful story about a man who has been frozen in the Alps and then fallen into a glacier and disappeared, and his bride was going to wait twenty-four years exactly for his body to come out on the moraine, while her true love waited too.
>
> (Ernest Hemingway, *The Sun Also Rises* [UK: 1927])

E. Phillips Oppenheim

b. 1866　d. 1946

PSEUDONYM: Anthony Partridge

Over 100 novels from 1892 to 1943, including:
Expiation (1887)
Millionaire of Yesterday (1900)
The Survivor (1901)
The Great Awakening (1902)
The Double Traitor (1915)
The Great Impersonation (1920)
Jacob's Ladder (1921)
Murder at Monte Carlo (1933)
Last Train Out (1940)

Oppenheim was born in London on 22 October 1866 but educated in Leicester where his father owned a business. He served in the Ministry of Information during the First World War.

Oppenheim was one of the great writers of thriller romances and one of the most popular novelists in both Britain and America. Although his work brought him vast wealth and a Riviera lifestyle he is now almost totally forgotten and none of his vast output of novels remains in print. Known as 'the Prince of Storytellers' for his fast-paced escapist stories, Oppenheim may be considered the precursor of the glamorous international thrillers and spy adventures of a later era with his combination of descriptions of conspicuous wealth, exotic luxury, secret intrigues and plans for world domination concocted by foreign, evil-genius villains.

Baroness ('Emma' Magdalena Rosalia Maria Josefa Barbara) Orczy

b. 1865   d. 1947

> *The Emperor's Candlesticks* (1899)
> *The Scarlet Pimpernel* (1905)
> *By the Gods Beloved* (1905)
> *I Will Repay* (1906)
> *Beau Brocade* (1907)
> *The Elusive Pimpernel* (1908)
and many others

Although British, Orczy was born in Tarna-Orsi in Hungary. Educated in Brussels and Paris, Orczy studied at the West London School of Art and Heatherley School of Art. She married Montagu Barstow in 1894 and had one son.

Orczy's fame rests on the novel *The Scarlet Pimpernel* (1905) and its subsequent production in play form (1905; 1910).* The story centres on the foppish Sir Percy Blakeney whose exploits saving aristocrats from the French revolutionary guillotine form the basis for numerous short stories, novels, adaptations and television shows.

> The piece of doggerel with which Sir Percy mocks the baffled Chauvelin was once known to every schoolboy [sic] in England: 'They seek him here, they seek him there, / Those Frenchies seek him everywhere. / Is he in heaven or is he in hell, / That damned elusive Pimpernel?'[7]

Orczy was also the creator of the Old Man (Bill Owen), one of the central figures of early detective fiction.

---

* It was first produced as a play in 1903.

Sax Rohmer

b. 1883   d. 1959

PSEUDONYM: Michael Furey

'Fu Manchu' series:
About 15 novels (1913–59) including:
  The Mystery of Dr Fu Manchu (1913)
  The Yellow Claw (1915)
  Dope (1919)

Arthur Henry Sarsfield Ward was born in Birmingham in 1883. Moving first to London, where he combined journalism with a talent for writing songs and sketches for the music hall, he later moved to New York. Looking for a more exciting name than his own he chose Sax Rohmer, the name under which he wrote his Fu Manchu tales.

Rohmer created Dr Fu Manchu in the short story 'The Zayat Kiss' for *The Story-Teller* magazine in 1912, and this, combined with ten more tales, formed the first 'novel', *The Mystery of Dr Fu Manchu* (1913). In an endless war with secret agent Nayland Smith, Dr Fu Manchu (demonic mixture of German and Chinese blood) works on behalf of a secret Chinese society dedicated to the overthrow of the British Empire and the capture of India.

Although clearly a product of the Western (especially American) 'Yellow Peril' obsession – 'a brow like Shakespeare and a face like Satan, a close shaven skull, and long, magnetic eyes of the true cat-green . . . [an] awful being . . . the yellow peril incarnate' – Fu Manchu fights fascism in the 1930s and communism in the 1940s. The character has been reproduced in many guises but most notably in Ian Fleming's version as Dr No.

Effie A. Rowlands (Effie Adelaide Maria Albanesi)

b. 1859 (or 1866)   d. 1936

  Beneath a Spell (1990)
  An Unhappy Bargain (nd)
and many others

Rowlands was a prolific British romance writer, who produced over 200 novels, all variations on a true-love-with-complications theme, though none with any marked note of religious, political or moral quest. Her novels illustrate upper-class Edwardian concerns for physical comfort and material value. Many of her novels and novelettes offer early examples of paperback production aimed at a mass female market.

(Amy) Berta Ruck

b. 1878   d. 1978

His Official Fiancée (1914)
The Wooing of Rosamund Fayre (1914)
The Bridge of Kisses (1917)
The Girl who Proposed (1918)
Kneel to the Prettiest (1925)
Money for One (1928)
One of the Chorus (1929)
Half-Past Kissing Time (1936)
and many others

Ruck was born at Murree in India, the daughter of an army officer and one of eight children. When her father became chief constable of Carnarvon the family moved to Wales where Ruck went to school in Bangor. She later studied art at the Slade and then went to Paris. In 1909 she married the writer Oliver Onions, whose short stories enjoyed some success.

Abandoning illustration as a career, Ruck published her first novel, *His Official Fiancée* (1914) – a tale of love and romance originally serialised in *Home Chat*. Five further novels were produced during World War One, giving hope and enjoyment to both combatants and those left behind. In 1919, Ruck visited the United States, setting one of her books there, but equally many are set on the banks of the Thames and all have happy endings. Ruck only stopped writing at 96 after a lifetime of novels, serials, short stories and autobiographical reminiscences. She died aged 100.

(Richard Horatio) Edgar Wallace

b. 1875   d. 1932

The Four Just Men (1906)
Sanders of the River (1909)
and many others

Wallace was born in Greenwich on 1 April 1875 to extremely poor parents and forced to leave school at twelve years old to go and earn a living. He joined the army (1893 to 1896) and went to South Africa until buying a discharge. Previously he had worked in a number of menial jobs. Nevertheless, Wallace was able to secure journalistic work in South Africa for Reuters and the *Daily Mail*, which allowed him to move on and up the ladder of journalism, especially as a racing correspondent and editor. By the end of his life he had risen to become editor of the *Sunday News*, Chairman of the British Lion Film Corporation and Chairman of the Press Club. He was also Britain's most famous popular novelist of his time.

Wallace's output was enormous, and he could claim that in many ways he helped create the modern thriller, especially with the appearance of the vigilante novel *The Four Just Men* (1906). His creation of the detective 'J. G. Reeder' was a notable addition to the crime genre but '(Commissioner) Sanders' of *Sanders of the River* (1909, short stories; 1911, novel) sums up all the unpleasant racism of the imperial adventure.

> Mr Commissioner Sanders had graduated to West Central Africa by such easy stages that he did not realize when his acquaintance with the back lands began. Long before he was called upon by the British Government to keep a watchful eye upon some quarter of a million cannibal folk, who ten years before had regarded white men as we regard the unicorn; he had met the Basuto, the Zulu, the Fingo, the Pondo, Matabele, Mashona, Barotse, Hottentot, and Bechuana. Then curiosity and interest took him westward and northward, and he met the Angola folk, then northward to the Congo, westward to the Masai, and finally, by way of the Pigmy people, he came to his own land.
>
> Now, there is a subtle difference between all these races, a difference that only such men as Sanders know.
>
> It is not necessarily a variety of colour, though some are brown and

some yellow, and some – a very few – jet black. The difference is in character. By Sanders' code you trusted all natives up to the same point, as you trust children, with a few notable exceptions. The Zulu were men, the Basuto were men, yet childlike in their grave faith. The black men who wore the fez were subtle, but trustworthy; but the browny men of the Gold Coast, who talked English, wore European clothing, and called one another 'Mr', were Sanders' pet abomination.

(Sanders of the River, ch. 1)

Dolf Wyllarde (Dorothy Margarette Selby Lowndes)

b. *c.*1870   d. 1959

Tropical Tales (1909)
and many others

We know almost nothing about this popular author except that she was born in about 1870, was a university graduate, and that she lived at Old Mixon Manor near Weston-super-Mare.

Lowndes was one of a number of popular and strongly promoted authors who flourished between 1900 and the 1930s but whose background and life have faded into almost complete obscurity. She was a romance author and general-subject novelist who worked with a number of publishers, including Mills and Boon.

The Interwar Years: 1919 to the Early 1930s

> You and your Scotland Yard. If it wasn't for Edgar Wallace no one
> would ever have heard of it.
>
> (Alfred Hitchcock, *Blackmail*, 1929)

(Dame) Agatha Christie

b. 1890   d. 1976

PSEUDONYMS: Mary Westmacott; Agatha Christie Westmacott

The Mysterious Affair at Styles (1920)
The Murder of Roger Ackroyd (1926)
and 31 others featuring Hercule Poirot

Murder at the Vicarage (1930)
and 11 others featuring Miss Jane Marple

Agatha Christie wrote more than seventy detective novels, her name
becoming synonymous with the genre. She was made a Dame of the
British Empire in 1971.

In her fiction Christie created two detectives who have become central
figures within the genre: the eccentric Belgian detective Hercule Poirot
(introduced in her first novel, *The Mysterious Affair at Styles*, 1920) and
the very English elderly spinster Miss Jane Marple (first introduced in
Murder at the Vicarage, 1930). Her last novel, *Sleeping Murder*, which again
featured Miss Marple, was published in 1976.

Christie's genius was to combine the novel of manners (with a strong
hint of women's romance) with the classic 'locked room' mystery.
This was a combination successfully exploited by A. A. Milne in *The
Red House Mystery* (1920) but one which Christie made her own, not
least because of the introduction of Hercule Poirot, an egg-shaped,
effete, over fussy detective from Belgium who relies on the 'little
grey cells'. He is the opposite of Sherlock Holmes, being a creature
made for the little details of suburban crisis and middle-class mayhem,
combining a taste for domestic detail familiar to Christie's female
readership with a nose for gossip and unexpected décor or household
management. If James Bond was the greatest fictional action hero of the

twentieth century then Poirot was the greatest fictional expert on bourgeois lifestyle.

Christie's play *The Mousetrap*, first produced in 1952, set a world record for the longest continuous run at one theatre. A significant number of her novels have successfully been adapted for television and film, including *Murder on the Orient Express* (1933, book; 1974, film) and *Death on the Nile* (1937, book; 1978, film).

Agatha Christie also wrote six romantic novels under her pseudonym Mary Westmacott, and four non-fiction books including her autobiography, which appeared posthumously in 1977.

In 1926, following the death of her mother, and her husband's request for a divorce, she famously disappeared for several days. After a highly publicised search, she was finally discovered in a hotel, registered under the name of the woman her husband wished to marry. Agatha Christie remains the most famous of all the twentieth-century women detective writers, a group which includes Dorothy L. Sayers (b. 1893; d. 1957), Margery Allingham (b. 1904; d. 1966), P. D. James (see entry), Ellis Peters (Edith Mary Pargeter; [see entry]) and Ruth Rendell (see entry).

Warwick Deeping

b. 1877   d. 1950

Love among the Ruins (1904)
Sorrell and Son (1926)

Deeping studied medicine at Trinity College, Cambridge, where he also achieved a Master of Arts. He practised medicine for several years at the Middlesex Hospital in London, where he qualified as a doctor, but he subsequently left to become a full-time author. He and his wife lived in Sussex where they designed and constructed their own house and gardens.

Deeping initially wrote historical romances, a very popular genre at the end of the nineteenth century. However, his approach shifted after World War One, which he spent as a doctor in the Army Medical Corps in Belgium, Egypt, France, and at Gallipoli. He summed up his approach to writing in his entry in *Twentieth Century Authors* (1942): 'One set out to see life and its realities, its pathos and heroism, and I have managed to find it more splendid than sordid. A negative cynicism seems to me a form of cowardice.'

Ethel M. Dell

b. 1881   d. 1939

The Way of an Eagle (1912)
The Lamp in the Desert (1919)
The Black Knight (1926)
Sown among Thorns (1939)

Ethel Dell, one of the great writers of women's romance, was born in South London, into comfortable surroundings, on 2 August 1881. Dell moved to Streatham, South London, in 1890 – a genteel suburb next to Brixton where she was born. She attended Streatham College for Girls, after finishing which she moved with her family to Knockholt, Kent, her father Vincent joining the new breed of suburban and country commuters into London.

Despite publishing some early short stores, Dell's success rests with *The Way of an Eagle* (1912), which was refused by eight publishers before re-typing and final acceptance by T. Fisher Unwin. By 1915 the book accounted for half Unwin's turnover! By the end of the First World War, Dell was earning a huge income from her books – one of the weathiest authors in Britain. Her easy style and clear eroticism made her an illicit favourite with middle-class adolescents and working-class servants and gained her the title of 'the housemaid's choice' for her success in writing what Rebecca West called 'tosh'. In a memoir of her adopted aunt, Penelope Dell could point out, however, that Ethel Dell was also an early 'modern':

> [She] was a child of late Victorian England, yet her stories abound in explicit and passionate detail. In order that they should be acceptable, she made them highly moral. . . . It is titillating to be told . . . of the very things which are taboo.[8]

During the 1930s Dell was still one of the most popular women's authors to be asked for at the 'tuppenny' libraries (alongside Elinor Glyn and Marie Corelli). Although 'spiritual' and conservative, Dell's stories also contained the violent passions so enjoyed by women (especially young girls) before World War Two. Her influence on women's romance is still evident and can be seen clearly in the 'sexier' women's writers of a later age, but also in works like E. M. Hull's *The Sheik* (1919). She was also an early influence on Barbara Cartland and Catherine Cookson; she is one of the great progenitors of Mills and Boon.

Alongside Ethel Dell there were other equally successful romance authors. **Ruby M(ildred) Ayres** (b. 1883, d. 1955) was one of the most popular writers of 'good, clean love stories', popular between the two world wars, and she was still writing in 1953 (*Dark Gentleman*). Her stories were often serialised and filmed and had great appeal for school-age and adolescent girls. As with all writers of commercial fiction of her period, Ayres was prolific, producing over 150 titles.

Jeffrey Farnol

b. 1878   d. 1952

The Broad Highway (1910)
The Amateur Gentleman (1913)

Born in Warwickshire in 1878, Farnol enjoyed a private education before being apprenticed to a Birmingham brass foundry. Having studied at Westminster School of Art, he nevertheless moved to New York to become a scene painter at the Astor Theatre but returned to England in 1910.

Farnol's fame lay in his ability to produce historical romances and escapist adventures. Like W. Riley (see entry) he might combine this with a real location. *The Broad Highway* is subtitled 'A romance of Kent' where the reader is invited to 'read . . . of country things and ways and people . . . of blood . . . and love [and] when [the reader] shall have turned the last page . . . you shall do so with a sigh'.

Farnol's books combined such sentiments with a strong sense of the romance of history. The past becomes for the historical novelist a land-scape *into* which one escapes in search of adventure. Thus the past is less a lost time than a *geographical* space peopled with individuals, where lives are more exciting than our own. In this sense the past of roman-tic historical novels is both more interesting than now and much safer. Yet Farnol was only too aware of how easy it is to pastiche such writing (the writing indeed from which he earned his living).

'... trees and such like don't sound very interestin' – leastways – not in a book, for after all a tree's only a tree and an inn, an inn; no, you must tell of other things as well.'

'Yes,' said I, ... 'to be sure there is a highwayman –'

'Come, that's better!' said the Tinker encouragingly.

'Then,' I went on, ticking off each item on my fingers, come Tom Cragg, the pugilist –'

'Better and better!' nodded the Tinker.

'– a one-legged soldier of the Peninsula, an adventure at a lonely tavern, a flight through woods at midnight pursued by desperate villains, and – a most extraordinary tinker. So far so good ... and it all sounds adventurous enough.'

(*The Broad Highway*, Ante Scriptum)

Sidney Horler

b. 1888   d. 1954

PSEUDONYMS: Peter Cavendish; Martin Heritage

Series: a number, including 'Paul Vivanti' and 'Tiger Standish'
The Breed of the Beverleys (1921)
The Mystery of No. 1 (1925)
False-Face (1926)
The House of Secrets (1926)
The Secret Service Man (1929)
Tiger Standish (1932)
Tiger Standish Comes Back (1934)

Sidney Horler was born in Leytonstone, Essex (now London).* He served in the Propaganda Section of Air Intelligence during the First World War (1918) after beginning a career as a journalist, first as a reporter on the *Western Daily Press* (1905–11) then as a special writer on the *Daily Mail* and *Daily Citizen*. After the war he acted as a sub-editor for *John O'London's Weekly* (1919) before turning to novel writing.

Horler was a journalist by profession but a thriller writer by temperament. A competitor for the readers of Edgar Wallace and E. Phillips Oppenheim, his thrillers are exciting adventures in which diabolical

---

* The birthplace of Alfred Hitchcock eleven years later.

villains, often foreign or 'homosexual' (by suggestion), are defeated by manly and virtuous heroes like the Honourable Timothy Overbury 'Tiger' Standish. Despite being sold with the emblazoned motto 'Horler for excitement' his novels could not survive changes in taste nor his style make up for prejudice, his work being neither quaint, amusing, nor witty and his thrills not quite as thrilling as those of Sapper, whom he resembles in moral tone.

E. M. Hull (Edith Maude Hull)*

b. 1880   d. 1947

> *The Sheik* (1919)
> *The Shadow of the East* (1921)
> *The Desert Healer* (1923)
> *The Sons of the Sheik* (1925)
> *The Lion-Tamer* (1928)
> *The Captive of Sahara* (1931)
> *The Forest of Terrible Things* (1939)

Edith Hull was a pig farmer's wife living in Derbyshire and had never seen a desert when she wrote *The Sheik* in 1919. She was following a long line of writers who found the romance of the desert irresistible, including Robert Hichens (see entry) and Elinor Glyn (see entry).

The Sheik is a work full of violence and eroticism set in an exotic location. It is the first great erotic popular novel of the post-World War One period and its film version, with Rudolph Valentino (1921), was extraordinarily influential. Hull's tale formed a background to a fashion for 'the desert' in books like *Desert Love* (1921) by Joan Conquest and Arthur Weighall's *The Dweller in the Desert* (1920).

A(rthur) S(tuart) M(enteth) Hutchinson

b. 1879 or 1880   d. 1971

> *If Winter Comes* (1921)

A. S. M. Hutchinson was born in India before moving back to Britain.

* The details of Hull's birth and death remain matters of some debate. A reclusive personality, Hull also avoided being photographed.

If Winter Comes (1921) was his most famous work, translated into ten languages and running to forty-five editions by 1924. It told the poignant story of Mark Sabre trapped in a loveless marriage to the snobby and conventional Mabel in the little village of Penny Green, and the effect of the momentous social and personal changes that accompanied the period just before and after the First World War.

J(ohn) B(oynton) Priestley

b. 1894   d. 1984

> *The Good Companions* (1929)
> *Angel Pavement* (1930)
> *Let the People Sing* (1939)

J. B. Priestley was born in Bradford, went to a local school, fought in the First World War and later took a degree at Trinity Hall, Cambridge. He was a jounalist and critic as well as a prolific playwright. Although he began writing in 1918, his novel *The Good Companions* (1929) made his name, with its life-affirming message coming during the worst years of The Slump. His play *An Inspector Calls* (1947) was still running in the West End of London, after a successful revival, during 2001.

Priestley's moral vision was defined by the decline, both economic and social, that he saw around him. His books were intended as a social programme as much as works of fiction. In *The Good Companions*,

> a disparate group becomes unified as its members find fulfilment in a common cause. Elizabeth Trant, a wealthy spinster, befriends the hapless Dinky Doos, a group of stranded players, transforming them into the successful Good Companions. They recognize however, that their success cannot last; travelling theatre and concert groups will soon be replaced by the talking picture, but they have shared a glorious moment which has enriched their lives and made them wiser. Beneath the romantic sentiment, the Dickensian characters and setting, lies a hard core of realism, as Priestley insists that determination, hard work, and cooperation underlie happiness.

In *Angel Pavement*, which followed *The Good Companions*, Priestley first attempted a serious novel with symbolic structure and probing characterization. Whereas the Dinky Doos travelled the open road, the characters of *Angel Pavement* inhabited London's claustrophobic business world during the Great Depression, an economic nightmare-reality that Priestley would later explore in his social [documentary work].[9]

Priestley's work also exemplified his concept of 'liberal socialism', 'that a spirited nation of good, hardworking people has not fulfilled its capability to realize the ideal community of men [*sic*] working in harmony'.

W(illiam) Riley

b. 1866   d. 1961

Windyridge (1913)

Known as the 'Yorkshire Novelist', Riley found fame with his first work, *Windyridge* (1913), the novel being also the first publication of Herbert Jenkins. In the early years of the 1920s, Riley's books proved extremely popular. *Windyridge Revisited* appeared in 1928.

Windyridge is typical of the 'consolatory' romances of the early twentieth century, providing a romantic storyline in a rural retreat. The tone of the book is elegiac and wistful and the story is infused with a religiosity that centres on homely values of the type exemplified by 'Mother Hubbard', one of the characters. The romanticism of the storyline is not seriously disturbed by the realisation that the sins of the city may also exist in a rural setting, and the 'happy ending' returns the reader to a sense of peace only to be found in the countryside. Riley's evocation is both nostalgic and sentimental and falls easily into mawkishness. His heroine's meditations are those of an emancipated mature woman whose desire for a (substitute) mother, family and husband allows the author to dramatise the 'fate' of a spinster following her heart. The book combines the reality of a newly independent womanhood with a conservative desire for home and peace. Thus the reader is led to understand that one must follow one's heart and turn one's back on materialism.

The book also relied on its regional flavour to win readers. The realisation of a region (in this case, Yorkshire) is to be found in writers as diverse as Catherine Cookson (see entry), Winston Graham (see entry) or Daphne du Maurier (see entry) and it provides not only an anchored and realistic setting but also a sense of locatedness and attachment that offers the reader a *fantasy* of a real location greater than the actuality of the location itself. Such imaginative locatedness is found also in works of other regionalist novelists and it connects the reader to a sense of *national homecoming*. On her arrival, Grace Holden (the heroine of *Windyridge*) exclaims, 'surely . . . it is good to be here; this people shall be my people' (chapter 1). A sense of being lost and searching for a home (both literally and figuratively) is a component of many popular novels written before World War One.

Rafael Sabatini

b. 1875   d. 1950

40 novels including:
  The Sea Hawk (1919)
  Scaramouche: A Romance of the French Revolution (1921)
  Captain Blood, His Odyssey (1922)
  Captain Blood Returns (1931)
  The Gamester (1949)
  In the Shadow of the Guillotine (1955)

Born in Jesi, Italy, Sabatini was educated in Switzerland and Portugal. Like so many other writers he was a member of British intelligence during World War One.

Sabatini's historical romances were sagas of love and revenge, sometimes using real historical personalities and sometimes using an historical milieu for a swashbuckling adventure. The books sold in millions and the film versions became minor classics of their genre – *Captain Blood* (1935); *The Sea Hawk* (1940); *Scaramouche* (1952).

Sapper (Herman Cyril McNeile)

b. 1888   d. 1937

  Bulldog Drummond: The Adventures of a Demobilized Officer who Found Peace Dull (1920)
  The Black Gang (1922)
  The Third Round (1924)
  The Final Count (1926)
  The Female of the Species (1928)
  Temple Tower (1929)

Tiny Carteret (1930)
The Island of Terror (1931)
The Return of Bulldog Drummond (1932)
Knock-Out (1933)
Challenge (1937)

Herman McNeile was born in Bodmin in Cornwall on 28 September 1888 and was educated at Cheltenham College in Gloucestershire before going to the Royal Military Academy at Woolwich, South London. He served during the First World War, rising from a Captain to a Lieutenant-Colonel and winning the Military Cross.

As 'Sapper', McNeile created the adventure hero Bulldog Drummond, whose exploits against the diabolical Carl Peterson and other exotic villains were the most extreme expression of the 1920s adventure-thriller genre, with a high level of violence, xenophobia and sadism. Drummond is a figure characteristic of the soldier adventurer, for whom the war was an essential expression of their temperament (morally certain, masculine, anti-intellectual) and for whom peace was intolerable if it were not an extension of battle. That Drummond has a 'fascistic' personality would be an appropriate comment.

Mary Webb

b. 1881   d. 1927

Precious Bane (1924)

Webb was born in Leighton in Shropshire, the eldest child of George and Sarah Meredith who ran a boarding school. Educated at home by her father and a number of governesses, Webb found herself mistress of a household in which her mother was slowly recovering from a violent riding accident.

Although she began writing juvenilia at finishing school, Webb only began to write seriously whilst convalescing from Grave's disease, a thyroid problem from which she never fully recovered. Nine of her essays were published in 1917 as *The Spring of Joy*. Writing came to a halt for a time when her father died, and again slowed down when she married Henry Webb, a teacher, in 1912, later helping him as a market gardener. In the meantime she had taken to book reviewing, first for the *Liverpool Post* and later the *Spectator*. Five novels followed, one of which, *Precious Bane* (1924), won the Femina Vie Heureuse for 1924–5.

Webb's novels are pantheistic and retain a natural mysticism and transcendentalism that sees the landscape as a symbolic message from God. Compared to Thomas Hardy, Webb's tales of passion and love are also tales of 'overcoming' set in the landscape of an imaginary Shropshire.

P(elham) G(renville) Wodehouse

b. 1881   d. 1975

PSEUDONYMS: P. Brooke-Haven; Pelham Grenville; J. Plum; C. P. West; J. Walker Williams; Basil Windham

Psmith (1915)
Piccadilly Jim (1917)
Their Mutual Child (1919) [published in England as *The Coming of Bill* (1920)]
Leave it to Psmith (1923)
Right Ho, Jeeves (1934)
and many other short story collections

P. G. Wodehouse, novelist, short-story writer and playwright, was born in 1881 in Guildford, Surrey, and died in Southampton, New York, in 1975. He attended Dulwich College from 1894 to 1900. After working as a bank clerk in London for a few years he assisted with and then took over the writing of a column in *The Globe* from 1902 until 1909, and was a drama critic for *Vanity Fair* from 1915 until 1919. His novels and stories are noted for their wit and style, for his engaging creation of characters, and for his adept handling of language. Wodehouse's most memorable characters are the slightly inept gentleman Bertram Wilberforce Wooster (Bertie) and his efficient valet Jeeves, who is capable of solving all problems Bertie encounters. They first appeared in a short story, 'The Man with Two Left Feet', which Wodehouse wrote for the *Saturday Evening Post* in 1917. Most of the 'Wooster' stories appeared in this form first of all. Wodehouse, a prolific writer of musical comedies, called Wooster's world, 'musical comedy without music . . . ignoring real life altogether'.

Wodehouse lived in France during World War Two and broadcast for the Nazis. However, as time passed and defenders such as George Orwell attested to Wodehouse's naïve involvement in the political and social tumult around him, the public seemed to accept him, and his work continued to enjoy wide popularity. Wodehouse received an honorary doctorate from Oxford University in 1939 and was granted the title of Knight Commander of the Order of the British Empire in 1975.

P(ercival) C(hristopher) Wren

b. 1885   d. 1941

Beau Geste (1924)
Beau Sabreur (1926)
Beau Ideal (1928)

Percival Wren was born in Devon (in a house once occupied by Charles Kingsley), a direct descendant of Sir Christopher Wren. After Oxford, Wren travelled the world as everything from a hunter to a farm labourer, a navvy and a tramp. His most significant employment was in the French Foreign Legion, until finding work in the government at Bombay. During the First World War he fought with the Indian Army in East Africa until invalided out in 1917, unsuccessfully attempting to become a secret service agent in Morocco during the 1920s.

Beau Geste (1924), loosely based upon Wren's Foreign Legion experience, was a huge success, being turned into a play and a movie, which spawned copycat movies and numerous parodies. The book also became the start of a series. Although Wren wrote other novels of war and adventure, it was these romantic and exciting tales that offered just the right blend of exotic thrills and escapist adventure. These novels were the male equivalent of E. M. Hull's *The Sheik* (1919), taking their place in a tradition going back to Ouida's *Under Two Flags* (1867).

World War Two to Suez: The Late 1930s to 1956

> The most notorious and widely read best-seller of the Second World War – among the working classes – was probably *No Orchids for Miss Blandish* by James Hadley Chase. . . . Why Chase's novel was not subject to prosecution is anyone's guess.
>
> (Joseph McAleer, *Popular Reading and Publishing in Britain, 1914–1950*, p. 29)

James Hadley Chase (René Brabazon Raymond)

b. 1906   d. 1985

PSEUDONYMS: James L. Docherty; Ambrose Grant; Raymond Marshall

  No Orchids for Miss Blandish (1939)
  You're Lonely when You're Dead (1949)
  Young Girls Beware (1959)
and 37 others

Born in London on 24 December 1906, René Raymond was educated in Rochester, Reading and Hastings. He joined the RAF, became a squadron leader and editor of the *Royal Air Force Journal*, after a number of jobs as an encyclopaedia salesman and as a wholesale publisher.

Chase found fame with *No Orchids for Miss Blandish* (1939), a work which to George Orwell exemplified a new brutishness in culture. The many thrillers that followed are set in America although Chase gained his knowledge from maps, slang dictionaries, etc., and rarely visited, going only to the obvious tourist spots. Many of the paperback authors of the immediate post-World War Two period copied his style.

Peter Cheyney

b. 1896   d. 1951

PSEUDONYM: Harold Brust

Series: Lemmy Caution; Slim Callaghan including:
  This Man is Dangerous (1936)
  Poison Ivy (1937)
  Dames Don't Care (1937)

Reginald Southouse Cheyney was born in London, trained as a lawyer, but worked in numerous jobs before taking up a full-time career as a thriller author.

Cheyney was the first British imitator of the hard-boiled pulp thriller exemplified by Carroll John Daly and, more famously, by Dashiell Hammett. His Lemmy Caution books were violent and sexy and formed a bridge between the work of Sapper (Herman Cyril McNeile [see entry]) and that of James Hadley Chase (see entry). His mock 'American' slang was also popular with actual American readers.

John Creasey

b. 1908   d. 1973

PSEUDONYMS: Gordon Ashe; M. E. Cook; M. C. Cooee; Margaret Cooee; Henry St John Cooper; Norman Deane; Robert Caine Frazer; Elise Fecamps; Patrick Gill; Michael Halliday; Charles Hogarth; Brian Hope; Colin Hughes; Kyle Hunt; Abel Mann; Peter Manton; J. J. Marric; James Marsden; Richard Martin; Rodney Mattheson; Anthony Morton; Ken Ranger; William K. Reilly; Tex Riley; Jeremy York

Gideon's Day (1955)
Gideon's Week (1956)

Creasey was a prolific novelist, publishing 562 novels, most of them organised into series, each written in a distinctly different style and under a different pseudonym. The 'Gideon' series (by J. J. Marric), for example, are authentic police procedural novels; the 'Roger West' series contains detective novels based around a police superintendent; the 'Patrick Dawlish' series (by Gordon Ashe) centres on a secret service agent; the 'Superintendent Folly' series (by Jeremy York) are country-house type murder investigations; and the 'Dr Cellini' series (written by Michael Halliday) concerns the fight against evil undertaken by an elderly psychiatrist. Although he worked in a range of related genres, his themes were connected to his belief that it is mankind's destiny to work together for the common good. His novel *Gideon's Day* was made into a film in 1958, directed by John Ford and starring Jack Hawkins.

Creasey was a founder of the British Crime Writers Association in 1935. He was also an unsuccessful parliamentary candidate when he founded the All-Party Alliance in 1967, urging voters to choose the best candidate regardless of party, and urging shared political control of nations.

A(rchibald) J(oseph) Cronin

b. 1896   d. 1981

Hatter's Castle (1931)
The Stars Look Down (1935)
The Citadel (1937)
The Keys of the Kingdom (1941)

A. J. Cronin was born in Cardross, Dumbartonshire, Scotland, and studied medicine at Glasgow University. He practised medicine for many years in South Wales and London before devoting himself to writing. From 1921 to 1924 he made a special study of industrial medicine in South Wales, where he was appointed Medical Inspector of Mines. His time at the mines was later reflected in his works, such as *The Stars Look Down*, *The Green Years* (1944), and *A Pocketful of Rye* (1969). While Cronin's novels received little critical acclaim, he was widely published and read internationally. His medical stories formed the basis for the hugely successful BBC television series *Dr Finlay's Casebook* (1959–66; 1993). Cronin was awarded the American Booksellers' Prize for *The Citadel* in 1937.

Lloyd Douglas

b. 1877   d. 1951

The Robe (1942)

Douglas wrote ten novels, each of which made the bestseller lists; six were made into films, and one was the basis for a television series. His first novel, *Magnificent Obsession* (1929), led to a huge increase in the sales of Bibles in America during the 1930s, and the adaptation of his novel *The Robe* was the first film made in Cinemascope (in 1953) and won two Academy Awards.

Lloyd Douglas was born into a religious family in Indiana; he was ordained as pastor of a Lutheran Church in 1903, and went on to become director of religious work at the University of Illinois. He later joined the Congregational Church and spent many years as a pastor of churches in the United States and Canada. In 1933 he retired from the ministry and became a full-time writer, his purpose being to present a Christian thesis in the form of a novel and to include human interest in the gospel stories. The recurrent theme in his work is that of the conversion of the atheist hero to a practising Christian. 'If my novels are entertaining I am glad,' he said, 'but they are not written so much for the purpose of entertaining as for inspiration.'

Daphne du Maurier

b. 1907 d. 1989

Jamaica Inn (1936)
Rebecca (1938)
Frenchman's Creek (1942)
My Cousin Rachel (1951)

Du Maurier was the daughter of Sir Gerald du Maurier, actor-manager, and granddaughter of George du Maurier, author of *Trilby* (1894). Although she produced her first novel, *The Loving Spirit*, in 1931, it was with *Rebecca* (1938) that she became one of the most popular authors of the century. Accorded literary status as well as enjoying popularity, du Maurier was also the author of famous short stories such as 'The Birds' and 'Don't Look Now' and many of her works were filmed. *Rebecca* is probably the greatest of women's gothic romances, tales that are

a genre of particular appeal to women readers, [and] are pure escapism. . . . They are the female equivalent of the adventure stories of the Alistair MacLean type so popular with both men and women for much the same reasons.

The stories have a woman as the main character, and contain elements of adventure, mystery, love and the supernatural, often in an historical setting, and written in the first person. The heroines encounter danger and misunderstanding, and the enmity of jealous rivals, but there is invariably a happy ending. The favourite locations for this type of novel are Cornwall, the Yorkshire Moors and Scotland, or similar wild areas of the country, and often involve stately homes with mysterious owners. They are, obviously, derived from the 'gothick' novels of the nineteenth century, and particularly from the work of the Brontë sisters. . . .

The genre does overlap, to some extent, with the family story and with the historical novel, but certain authors, such as Victoria Holt and Mary Williams, while writing about family life in rural nineteenth-century England, typify the literary style and plot of this sort of novel.[10]

Rebecca's opening paragraphs are some of the most famous in twentieth-century fiction.

> Last night I dreamt I went to Manderley again. It seemed to me I stood by the iron gate leading to the drive, and for a while I could not enter, for the way was barred to me. There was a padlock and a chain upon the gate. I called in my dream to the lodge-keeper, and had no answer, and peering closer through the rusted spokes of the gate I saw that the lodge was uninhabited. . . .
> The drive was a ribbon now, a thread of its former self, with gravel surface gone, and choked with grass and moss. The trees had thrown out low branches, making an impediment to progress; the gnarled roots looked like skeleton claws.

Du Maurier's Brontë-esque introduction to her novel was itself the begetter of numerous literary look-alikes. Take, for instance, the opening paragraph of Sara Seale's *The Gentle Prisoner* (voted 'Romantic Book of the Month' in *Woman and Home* [1945] and considered by Seale's publisher Alan Boon – of Mills and Boon – 'one of the great classic books we published').

> The house, in the soft summer twilight, looked grey and forbidding. The high wall, which completely enclosed it, rose in a straggling circle from the silent moor, and only through the tall iron gates could the house itself be seen, strong and implacable with its shuttered windows blank to the enquiring eye. . . . The man, with his hand already on the chill iron scrolling, paused and shivered. He had an instinct not to enter, a faint presage of ill-luck, should he push those hostile gates ajar and slip inside. . . . Inside the gates, it was as if the barren moorland had blossomed under some magic wand, for he found himself in a rose-garden, which was as unexpected as it was beautiful. . . . He pulled at a bell at the side of the heavy front door, and to the old man who answered it, he said:
> 'Mr Penryn, please.'
> 'I'll see sir.' The door swinging open reluctantly, revealed a dark, shadowy hall which echoed to their voices.
> 'Mr Penryn is not officially in residence,' the old man said severely, as if defending the shuttered windows, 'but if you will give me your name, sir, I will enquire.'

C(ecil) S(cott) Forester

b. 1899   d. 1966

Payment Deferred (1926)
Brown on Resolution (1929)
Death to the French (1932)
The Gun (1933)
The African Queen (1935)
The General (1936)
The 'Hornblower' series including:
The Happy Return (1937)
Flying Colors (1938)
A Ship of the Line (1939)
Lord Hornblower (1946)
Mr Midshipman Hornblower (1950)

C. S. Forester, born in Cairo and educated at Dulwich College in England, was a prolific journalist and novelist of historical fiction. The settings of his early work range from World War One, as in *Payment Deferred* (1926), to the Peninsular War, as in both *Death to the French* (1932) and *The Gun* (1933). His later novels, however, are set within the naval conflict of the Napoleonic Wars, and chronicle the life of his most popular fictional character Horatio Hornblower, a British naval officer. Forester narrates Hornblower's career, from midshipman to admiral, with his succession of a dozen novels ultimately culminating in *Lord Hornblower* (1946).* This series re-articulates the typical Forester theme of personal forbearance in war.

Forester's novels of the Napoleonic War remain the male equivalent of the Regency romance aimed at women readers (see entry under Georgette Heyer). They spawned a host of imitators including Patrick O'Brian's 'Jack Aubrey' series (see entry), Douglas Reeman's 'Richard Bolitho' series (see entry) and Dudley Pope's 'Nicholas Ramage' and 'Ned Yorke' series (see entry) amongst a number of others.

---

* Confusingly, the novels were not written in the chronological order of Hornblower's life.

Stephen Francis

b. 1917   d. 1989

PSEUDONYM: Hank Janson

'Hank Janson' series: 50 books including:
  Cactus (1956)
  Framed (1956?)
  Flight from Fear (1958)

Stephen Francis was born in South London in 1917, the son of Stephen Francis and his wife May. Stephen senior was killed during World War One leaving his wife to struggle in poverty. After leaving school at fourteen, Francis became an office boy for a Fleet Street trade paper and thence drifted between jobs but not before joining the Labour Party League of Youth and the Communist Party (from which he was expelled). During World War Two he was a conscientious objector publishing a magazine called *Free Expression* from his home – an abandoned bus. In 1945 he began a small publishing business with a friend, but later went on alone, writing western novelettes and later crime stories based on Chicago reporter 'Hank Janson'. *When Dames Get Tough* (1945) was followed by *Scarred Faces* (1945). These were very short 'novels' dictated to an assistant over weekends, which capitalised on the lack of American crime magazine imports. Their length was dictated by the availability of paper during rationing. It was not until Francis began his second series that he found wider success, becoming 'South London's Best Selling Author' as one placard at Elephant and Castle announced.

Despite (or even because of) his growing popularity amongst young male readers and directly because of the lurid erotic covers employed, Francis became the focus for censorious magistrates. Charged with publishing obscene material at trials in 1953 and 1954, the publishers of the Janson books were sent to jail. Francis also stood trial but the prosecution was abandoned. With sales of approximately five million books (50 titles) between 1948 and 1954 and total sales to 1971 of twenty million, Francis nevertheless died in Spain poor and forgotten in 1989. His books retain cult status, however, amongst paperback collectors.

Francis was one of a number of British working-class writers who capitalised on American themes and who followed the lead in gangster-crime and erotic violence offered by James Hadley Chase (see entry) and Peter Cheyney (see entry).

Erle Stanley Gardner

b. 1889   d. 1970

PSEUDONYM: A. A. Fair

> *The Case of the Velvet Claws* (1933)
> *The Case of the Sulky Girl* (1934)
> *The Case of Lucky Legs* (1934)
> *The Case of the Howling Dog* (1935)
> *The Case of the Curious Bride* (1935)
> *The Clew of the Forgotten Murder* (1935)
> *This Is Murder* (1936)
> *The Case of the Counterfeit Eye* (1935)
> *The Case of the Caretaker's Cat* (1936)
and many others

Although he was admitted to the California Bar in 1911, Gardner's fame rests upon his fictional lawyer Perry Mason. The 82 'Mason' stories ran from *The Case of the Velvet Claws* (1933) to *The Case of the Postponed Thunder* (1973; posthumous) and form the basis of the much loved courtroom showdown genre recently revived by Scot Turow and John Grisham. The Perry Mason television series ran from 1957 to 1966.

Born in Malden, Massachusetts, in 1889, Gardner graduated in 1909, marrying twice and practising law in Oxnard, California, between 1911 and 1918. Between 1923 and 1932 he contributed stories to magazines, becoming a full-time author in 1933. A reporter on crime trials and founder of a production company, Gardner also helped create the Court of Last Resort (Case Review Committee). In 1952 he was presented with the Mystery Writers of America Edgar Allan Poe Award.

William Golding

b. 1911   d. 1993

> *Lord of the Flies* (1954)

William Golding was born on 19 September 1911 in St Columb Minor, Cornwall, England, to Alex A. Golding, a schoolmaster, and Mildred A. Golding. He attended Marlborough Grammar School before going to

Brasenose College at Oxford where he received his BA in education in 1935 and his MA in 1960. From 1940 to 1945 Golding served in the Royal Navy, in which he became a commander. During this time Golding found war to be evidence of man's brutality, and war became the prime source of his extreme pessimism. He began his career as a social worker and later taught English and philosophy at Bishop Wordsworth's School in Salisbury, Wiltshire, England, from 1939 to 1940 and 1945 to 1961. Golding became a visiting professor at Hollins College in 1961–2. *Lord of the Flies* (1954) was published to immediate acclaim and adapted for cinema in 1963 by Peter Brook. He received the James Tait Black Memorial Prize for *Darkness Visible* in 1980, the Booker McConnell Prize for *Rites of Passage* in 1981, the Nobel Prize for literature in 1983, and was knighted in 1988.

Georgette Heyer

b. 1902   d. 1974

PSEUDONYM: Stella Martin

> *The Black Moth: A Romance of the Eighteenth Century* (1921)
> *The Regency Buck* (1935)
> *Beau Wyndham* (1941)
> and numerous others

Heyer published her first novel when she was seventeen, having enjoyed an education at various expensive girls schools and having attended a history lecture series at Westminster College. In 1925 she married and accompanied her husband to East Africa and in 1928 moved to Yugoslavia for a year.

Heyer's work is to the popular historical romance as du Maurier's is to the popular gothic romance (see entry): a standard and a reference. Concerned with the 'romance' of historical fact and filled with an admiration for the work of Jane Austen, Heyer chose as her period 'the Regency', which was not only of historical interest but also contained a contemporaneous and modern sensibility that was both escapist and factual (that is, 'real'). The Regency provided civilised manners, picaresque detail, historically accurate backgrounds and actors and a mannered, Austenesque language (including accurate period slang). Heyer's novels contained some of the sentiments of Austen with the verve of Baroness Orczy (see entry) and paralleled C. S. Forester's own interest in the period and in the Napoleonic Wars, which became the male equivalent of the Regency woman's romance.

Heyer produced almost sixty romance and mystery novels between 1921 and her death in 1974, appealing to a very wide range of woman readers but especially adolescents and older women. Her work was always considered 'intelligent' if popular, but such appeal sometimes brought only grudging praise from reviewers. Of one novel *The Times Literary Supplement* tartly commented,

> *April Lady* is a tale of true love in the high society of Regency days, a genre in which Miss Heyer is accomplished. The story is exciting and gracefully told, with a liberal seasoning of the slang of the period. Such a careful writer should not introduce a Foreign Office clerk who expects to be sent abroad on a diplomatic mission; but in other respects the picture of the times is attractive and accurate.[11]

Heyer also wrote classic-style detective stories, including *Footsteps in the Dark* (1932) and *Death in the Stocks* (1935).

James Hilton

b. 1900   d. 1954

Lost Horizon (1933)
Goodbye Mr Chips (1934)
Random Harvest (1941)

Hilton began his writing career as an undergraduate at Cambridge during World War One, providing articles for the *Manchester Guardian*. He wrote his first novel at seventeen and published it two years later as *Catherine Herself* (1920). He was also contributing a twice-a-week column to the *Irish Independent*. Success, however, took until 1931 with *And Now Goodbye*. In 1933, Hilton was invited to contribute a short story to the non-conformist *British Weekly* – it became *Goodbye Mr Chips* (1934). In 1934 the *Atlantic Monthly* published the story in the United States to great praise. A play (1938) and film version (1939) followed. *Lost Horizon* (1933), an earlier novel, also now became a bestseller, bringing into general use the term 'Shangri-La'. *Random Harvest* followed in 1941. Hilton's work was extremely successful in his lifetime (especially in the

United States) and continued to find a popular readership into the 1960s. His work contained mass appeal but also won critical praise and awards.

(Ralph) Hammond Innes

b. 1913   d. 1998

> *The Doppleganger* (1937)
> *Air Disaster* (1937)
> *Sabotage Broadcast* (1938)
> *The Trojan Horse* (1940)
> *The Killer Mine* (1947)
> *The Lonely Skier* (1947)
> *Air Bridge* (1951)
> *Campbell's Kingdom* (1952)
> *The Mary Deare* (1956)

and many others

Born in Sussex in 1913 and educated at Cranbrook School in Kent, Innes worked at the *Financial News* from 1934 to 1940, serving in the Royal Artillery during World War Two and ending the war with the rank of Major. In 1978 he was awarded a CBE (Commander, Order of the British Empire).

Mystery, suspense and romance were central to Innes's successful exploitation of the theme of man's [*sic*] struggle with the natural elements. His most significant book is *The Mary Deare* (1956), which deals with a sea captain's fight to save his ship after it runs aground.

Innes was known for exciting and cliff-hanger thrillers written in a Buchanesque style. Alongside Alistair Maclean (see entry) he dominated the thriller market for over twenty years.

> No one since Buchan has kept the flag of romantic adventure more bravely aloft. . . . Innes . . . has preserved some of the Buchan values, a sense of knight errantry, the tug of landscape, a basic charity of outlook.[12]

W(illiam) Somerset Maugham

b. 1874   d. 1965

Liza of Lambeth (1897)
Of Human Bondage (1915)
The Moon and Sixpence (1919)
Ashenden; or, The British Agent (1928)
The Razor's Edge (1944)

Maugham was born in the British Embassy in Paris on 25 January 1874, learning to speak French before learning English, and orphaned at ten years old. His unhappy childhood spent with a dour uncle in Whitby formed the basis for the novel *Of Human Bondage* (1915). After going to Heidelberg University but failing to complete his studies, Maugham travelled before going to study medicine at St Thomas's Hospital in London where he qualified in 1898 although he did not practise. *Liza of Lambeth* (1897) documents the social deprivation surrounding his work in the hospital. After leaving medicine to become a writer, Maugham travelled the world and starved in Paris, success coming with his plays and with the novels completed during the First World War. Later in his career, his satiric and pungent attacks on the foibles of his class and the writers he mixed with led to accusations of libel with the publication of *Cakes and Ale* (1930). A curiosity remains his creation of secret agent Ashenden, which capitalised on the popularity of the thriller genre in the 1920s.

Maugham was one of only a few pre-war authors from Great Britain to become bestsellers in the United States. Maugham's *The Razor's Edge* (1944) totalled over 3 million sales. Other successful British exports included Daphne du Maurier (*Rebecca*, 1938; *My Cousin Rachel*, 1952; see entry), Agatha Christie (*The Murder of Roger Ackroyd*, 1926; *And Then There Were None*, 1940; see entry), James Hilton (*Lost Horizon*, 1935; *Random Harvest*, 1941; *So Well Remembered*, 1945; see entry), A. J. Cronin (*The Citadel*, 1941; see entry), E. Phillips Oppenheim (*The Great Impersonation*, 1920; see entry), P. G. Wodehouse (*Jeeves*, 1924; see entry), E. M. Hull (*The Sheik*, 1926; see entry), George Orwell (*1984*, 1949; see entry) and D. H. Lawrence (*Lady Chatterley's Lover*, 1932).

Margaret Mitchell

b. 1900   d. 1949

Gone with the Wind (1936)

Margaret Mitchell was born in Atlanta, Georgia, on 8 November 1900. Educated first at Washington Seminary, Atlanta, between 1914 and 1918, she graduated from Smith College, Northampton, Massachusetts, in 1919. Twice married, Mitchell nevertheless had a career as a journalist and feature writer. She received a Pulitzer Prize in 1937 and the Bohmenberger Memorial Award in 1938.

Mitchell's reputation rests on one phenomenonally successful work, the focus of which is a romantic saga set in the 'Old South' during America's Civil War. Scarlett O'Hara, Rhett Butler and Ashley Wilkes play out their complex relationships against the backdrop of the death of 'cavalier' and plantation Georgia. The book was made into one of Hollywood's most enduring films. The book and film, as well as Mitchell's life, continue to fascinate readers and critics up to the present day.

Nicholas Monsarrat (John Turney)

b. 1910   d. 1979

The Cruel Sea (1951)
The Tribe that Lost Its Head (1956)

Born in Liverpool, Monsarrat was educated at Trinity College, Cambridge, abandoning a law degree for literature. Having written before World War Two it was the war, nevertheless, that gave him the experiences that inspired *The Cruel Sea* (1951).

Monsarrat was one of the great novelists of the sea story – a genre much exploited during the century. He died before completing a three-volume saga of seafaring life beginning in the Napoleonic period.

George Orwell (Eric Arthur Blair)

b. 1903   d. 1950

Animal Farm (1945)
1984 (1949)

Eric Arthur Blair was born in India where his father was a civil servant. In 1907, on moving back to Britain, Blair was sent to Eton, later going out to join the Indian Imperial Police in Burma where he remained until 1928. Returning to England from time spent in Paris, he became a bookshop assistant and novel reviewer. In 1936 he fought in Spain for the Republicans, joined the Home Guard during World War Two, worked for the BBC Eastern Service from 1940 to 1943 and wrote for *Tribune*, the *Observer* and the *Manchester Evening News*. He died in 1950 aged 46 having suffered from tuberculosis.

Orwell (who took his pen name from a Suffolk river) began publishing in 1928 with an article for *Le Monde*, later following with a documentary social piece, *Down and Out in Paris and London* (1933). His fame rests not only with his documentary work but with his more famous fictional tales, the social allegory *Animal Farm* (1945) and the bleak political morality tale *1984* (1949). These two books, with their mixture of narrative and of social and political commentary represent probably the most famous two fictional titles produced by an English author in the twentieth century. Like Joseph Heller's, 'Catch 22', '1984' has entered the English language as shorthand for totalitarianism, as has 'Big Brother' (used in 2000 for a game show!), 'mini' and 'Newspeak'. Orwell is, without doubt, the most important British writer of the twentieth century even if there remains considerable debate over whether he was ever a true novelist, or a moralist who merely used fiction as a vehicle.

Mary Renault (Mary Challans)

b. 1905   d. 1983

Promise of Love (1939)
Return to Night (1947)
The Last of the Wine (1956)
The Bull from the Sea (1962)
The King Must Die (1958)
The Praise Singer (1978)

Mary Challans decided when she was young that she wanted to be a writer. She also believed that a good writer must participate actively in life and so she enrolled in a nursing school. Her experiences in nursing school provided her with material for her first novel, *Promise of Love* (1939), which was a resounding success. During World War Two, Renault continued her nursing career and wrote in her spare time. After the war she published *Return to Night* (1947), which won her the MGM prize and brought her name to the attention of American readers. Mary Renault travelled extensively in France, Italy, Africa, Greece, and the Aegean islands. Her experiences on these travels inspired her post-war novels, which were mainly historical. Renault was most impressed with Greece and it became the setting for *The Last of the Wine* (1956), dealing with the Theseus myth and taking place during the Peloponnesian War.

Nevil Shute (Norway)

b. 1899   d. 1960

A Town Like Alice (1950)
The Far Country (1952)
On the Beach (1957)
Trustee from the Toolroom (1960)

Shute served in both World Wars, was an engineer at an airship factory and the manager of an aeroplane factory. He emigrated to Australia in 1949.

At one time Shute's two most famous books were almost the most famous works in English but he has now faded in popularity.

Shute is best remembered for *On the Beach* (1957), a novel about nuclear holocaust. The book is set in Melbourne, Australia, in the year 1963 and tells the story of the few people in the world who survived the atomic warfare that completely wiped out the northern hemisphere. Together they must face the reality that the radiation is heading toward them and determine how they will handle their inevitable end. Critics claim that the novel was Shute's attempt 'to caution his readers against the unbridled proliferation of warfare technology.' Between the year it was published and Shute's death in 1960, *On the Beach* sold well over two million copies. The novel was released as a film in 1959.[13]

According to *The Times Literary Supplement*,

> *On the Beach* [was] intended clearly as a cautionary tale. Unfortunately, the characterization is so weak that the reader, faced with the extinction of the human race as represented by Mr Shute's characters, is left comparatively unmoved.[14]

Mickey Spillane (Frank Morrison Spillane)

b. 1918

I, the Jury (1947)
Vengeance Is Mine (1950)
My Gun Is Quick (1950)
Kiss Me, Deadly (1952)

Mickey Spillane was born Frank Morrison Spillane in Brooklyn on 9 March 1918. Having attended Kansas State University, he served in World War Two in the Air Force and was twice married.

Beginning in 1935, Spillane sold stories to comic books, later graduating to novels, of which *I, the Jury* (1947) was first intended as a comic-book story, in which Mike Hammer may have ended up as 'Mike Danger'.

> Spillane is the stylistic successor to Carroll John Daly; the most popular *Black Mask* writer. Mike Hammer is such a similar character to Daly's Race Williams that many have observed Hammer could well be William's literary son. Spillane's protagonists – Mike Hammer, Tiger Mann, The Deep, Morgan the Raider, Gill Burke – are direct pulp descendants of Daly's Williams (and Satan Hall). They are no-

nonsense characters who act first and think second, without exception modern avengers. In turn, they influenced contemporary pulp series, particularly Don Pendleton's Executioner paperback saga and Clint Eastwood's Dirty Harry films.[15]

It was Spillane's novels rather than those of Dashiell Hammett or Raymond Chandler which brought the hard-boiled American novel to Britain – the real McCoy compared with Peter Cheyney's comic hero Lemmy Caution or James Hadley Chase's imitation style (see entries).

> 'No, . . . I'm the jury now, and the judge, and I have a promise to keep. Beautiful as you are, as much as I almost loved you, I sentence you to death.'
>
> *(Her thumbs hooked in the fragile silk panties and pulled them down. She stepped out of them. . . . She was completely naked now. . . .)*
>
> The roar of the 45 shook the room. [She] staggered back a step. Her eyes were a symphony of incredulity. . . . She looked down at the ugly swelling in her naked belly where the bullet went in. A thin trickle of blood welled out. . . .
>
> 'How c-could you?' she gasped.
>
> I only had a moment before talking to a corpse, but I got it in.
>
> 'It was easy', I said.
>
> (I, the Jury, ch. 13)

J(ohn) R(onald) R(euel) Tolkien

b. 1892   d. 1973

The Hobbit, or *There and Back Again* [children's book] (1938)

Series: *The Lord of the Rings*:
   vol. 1: *The Fellowship of the Ring* (1954)
   vol. 2: *The Two Towers* (1954)
   vol. 3: *The Return of the King* (1955)

The Silmarillion (1977)

John Tolkien was born in 1892 in Bloemfontein, South Africa, the son of a bank manager and a pianist. Tolkien became an academic after graduating from Exeter College, Oxford, and military service in the Lancashire Fusiliers during the First World War. A period of work as an assistant on the *Oxford English Dictionary* (between 1918 and 1920) was followed by work at the University of Leeds, which led to a professorship (1924–5) and a move to Oxford where he became Rawlinson and Bosworth Professor of Anglo-Saxon (1925–45) and Merton Professor of English Language and Literature (1945–59). At Oxford, Tolkien met and collaborated with Charles Williams and C(live) S(taples) Lewis, forming a conservative, Catholic club called the 'Inklings'. Tolkien's temperament and religious convictions made him particularly anti-modern: nostalgic for a rural organic past and with a dislike of 'Americo-cosmopolitanism', Soviet 'new-townism' and the 'magia [*sic*]' of machinery. His preference for a lost and heroic age before the war and before electricity was shared by many contemporaries, although his support for Franco during the Spanish Civil War was not.

The *Hobbit* (1938) reflects much of this postwar temperament and nostalgia but it is in *The Lord of The Rings* (developed over a fourteen-year period) that Tolkien's moral vision becomes fully mature – a work for adults as much as for children. Tolkien's creation of 'Middle Earth' with its folktale and Anglo-Saxon sensibility nevertheless is a conservative and moral analogue of twentieth-century history. It represents a retreat and a critique when viewed from such a position and this is why, perhaps, Tolkien rejected any moral message, allegorical or hidden.

It is, however, impossible to reject the view that *The Lord of the Rings* is a sustained elegy on the very nature of 'Englishness' itself – a world of rural peace, harmony and yeomanly expression: England as a fairy-story land

As for the Hobbits of the Shire, with whom these tales are concerned, in the days of their peace and prosperity they were a merry folk. They dressed in bright colours, being notably fond of yellow and green; but they seldom wore shoes, since their feet had tough leathery soles and were clad in a thick curling hair, much like the hair of their heads, which was commonly brown. Thus, the only craft little practised among them was shoe-making; but they had long and skilful fingers and could make many other useful and comely things. Their faces were as a rule good-natured rather than beautiful, broad, bright-eyed, red-cheeked, with mouths apt to laughter, and to eating and drinking. And laugh they did, and eat, and drink, often and heartily, being fond of simple jests at all times, and of six meals a day (when they could get them). They were hospitable and delighted in parties, and in presents, which they gave away freely and eagerly accepted.

It is plain indeed that in spite of later estrangement Hobbits are relatives of ours.

(Prologue: *The Fellowship of the Ring*)

Tolkien's charming, absurd, helpless hobbits, along with Gandalf, the elves, dwarves, orcs and other creatures of his imagination, created an epic 'total' vision which has consistently appealed to adults as well as children, is consistently voted the most important fiction to come out of Britain in the twentieth century (in popular polls) and has formed the basis for a whole fictional industry of fantasy novels and mythic lost worlds. Tolkien's influence has been immense both in literature and in alternative lifestyles, a trend that seems set to continue with the release of the movie trilogy (2002 to 2005).

Dennis Wheatley

b. 1897   d. 1977

The Devil Rides Out (1934)
The Haunting of Toby Jugg (1948)
To the Devil a Daughter (1953)
The Ka of Grifford Hillary (1956)
and numerous black magic, adventure and historical romances

Brought up in London and educated at Dulwich College, Wheatley served in the artillery in the First World War and thence until 1919 when he was invalided out. Having joined his father's wine company in the same year, he became its sole proprietor in 1926. As a member of the Joint Planning Staff of the War Cabinet between 1941 and 1944 Wheatley knew Maxwell Knight of MI5 and may have had an association with Aleister Crowley.

Wheatley's reputation rests with *The Devil Rides Out* (1934),* in which he successfully combined two genres which were in decline by the early

---

* The Richleau books take the Duke from age 18 in 1894 to his death in 1960 at 85. They were purposely based on Dumas's 'Musketeers' cycle with the exiled monarchist (and his fondness for Hoyo de Monterrey cigars) in the role of Athos, the conservative Richard Eaton as d'Artagnan, Simon Aron (the Liberal Jew) as Aramis, and the democratic American, Rex Van Ryn, as Porthos.[16]

1930s: the 'shocker' of the First World War and the supernatural tale of the 1920s. By amalgamating these two, using knowledge of black magic rituals learned from acquaintance with Aleister Crowley, by cashing in on Nazi symbolism (Hitler had just come to power) and by appending an 'infamous' author's note about the dangers of dabbling in the supernatural, Wheatley created a uniquely exciting supernatural thriller. Although unable to compete with the more violent and erotic thrillers which became fashionable after World War Two, Wheatley's books found new readers with the mass consumption of paperbacks during the 1960s and early 1970s. In 1968 *The Devil Rides Out* was filmed (Seven Arts/Hammer Films joint production), starring Christopher Lee and Charles Gray, but Wheatley was disappointed with the result. More catastrophically, the reinvention of the supernatural horror thriller by Peter Blatty (*The Exorcist*, 1971), Stephen King (*Carrie*, 1974) and James Herbert (*The Rats*, 1974) and the subsequent films of both Blatty's and King's work relegated Wheatley's thrillers to a world that appeared nostalgic and quaint. Despite this, Wheatley's 50 books sold over 40 million copies in Britain.

By contrast, in recent years, Wheatley's relationships with Aleister Crowley, Maxwell Knight (of MI5) and counter-espionage operations have provided the biographical thrills that the fiction alone can no longer support.

The Paperback Years: 1957 to 1974

And I want to be a paperback writer.

(The Beatles, *Paperback Writer*)

H(erbert) E(rnest) Bates

b. 1905   d. 1974

PSEUDONYM: Flying Officer X

Fair Stood the Wind for France (1944)
Love for Lydia (1952)
The Darling Buds of May (1958)

Bates's early writing in the 1920s utilised his knowledge of rural English life, gained as a provincial journalist. However, it was during the 1930s that he became known as a writer about the countryside, especially for his novels *The Poacher* (1935) and *My Uncle Silas* (1940).

In 1941 he was commissioned as a short-story writer by the British government, to write about the Royal Air Force, and published several books (such as *The Greatest People in the World* and *How Sleep the Brave*) as 'Flying Officer X'. The three novels he published under his own name at the end of the war further increased his reputation as a powerful novelist (*Fair Stood the Wind for France*, and two set in Burma during the Japanese invasion, *The Purple Plain* and *The Jacaranda Tree*).

It has been suggested, however, that it was in his post-war novels that Bates more effectively demonstrated his power as a novelist, especially when he revisited the pastoral subject matter of his earlier writing, notably with *The Darling Buds of May* (1958), for which he is now probably best known, following the very successful ITV adaptation.

Sheila Burnford

b. 1918   d. 1984

The Incredible Journey (1961)

Born in Scotland, Burnford made her home in Ontario and was known primarily as the author of *The Incredible Journey*, for which she won a number of literary awards. The novel is the story of two dogs and a cat that trek through the wilds of Canada back to their home. The book was extremely popular with children and adults, one of a number of novels written in the twentieth century and centred on animals. These include *Tarka the Otter* (1927) by Henry Williamson, *Ring of Bright Water* (1961) by Gavin Maxwell, *Watership Down* (1972) by Richard Adams (see entry) and the non-fictional books by Joy Adamson.

Burnford also wrote *Mr Noah and the Second Flood* (1973), an ecological parable, and *Bel Ria: Dog of War* (1977).

(Sir) Arthur C(harles) Clarke

b. 1917

> *Prelude to Space* (1951)
> *Childhood's End* (1953)
> *The City and the Stars* (1956)
> *Master of Space* (1961)
> *The Space Dreamers* (1969)
> *Rendezvous with Rama* (1973)
> *The Fountains of Paradise* (1979)
> *2001: A Space Odyssey* (1968)
> *2010: Odyssey Two* (1982)
> *2061: Odyssey Three* (1988)

Arthur Clarke, born in Somerset, England, is Britain's most famous writer of science fiction. His style is typified by a fidelity and precision regarding the various scientific topics with which his stories deal. Clarke's first significant work was a non-fiction article entitled 'Extra-Terrestrial Relays', submitted to *Wireless World*. The article is considered to have predicted satellite communications. Drawing upon the wealth of his non-fiction publications, such as *Interplanetary Flight* (1950), *The Challenge of the Sea* (1960), and *Profiles of the Future* (1962), Clarke's fiction uniquely investigates futuristic notions of time and space travel and other themes of exploration. His work, notably with a screenplay for the movie *2001: A Space Odyssey* (1968), directed by Stanley Kubrick, found cult status. Clarke's essentially hopeful, progressive vision should be contrasted with the darker post-modern concerns of writers like William Gibson.

James (du Maresq) Clavell

b. 1924   d. 1994

> *King Rat* (1962)
> *Tai-Pan* (1966)
> *Shogun* (1975)
> *Noble House* (1980)

Clavell was born in Australia, brought up in England and became a US citizen in 1963. During World War Two he joined the Royal Artillery and in 1942 was captured by the Japanese in Java. He subsequently spent three and a half years in Changi prison camp and was one of only 10,000 out of 150,000 inmates to survive. He later used his experiences in prison as a basis for his first novel, *King Rat*. This was the first of several novels set in the Far East which concern themselves with the tensions between East and West and the struggle for wealth and power. His long and richly detailed novels are recognisable for their exotic settings and strong plotlines.

Clavell's early interests were primarily with film, and he worked in television production in New York and as a screenwriter in Hollywood. His first screenplay was *The Fly* (1958), and he later collaborated on the screenplay for *The Great Escape* (1963). He also wrote *633 Squadron* (1964), and wrote, produced and directed *Five Gates to Hell* (1959), *Walk Like a Dragon* (1960), *To Sir with Love* (1966) and *The Last Valley* (1969). He began writing novels during the 1960 screenwriters' strike.

Jackie Collins

b. 1941 (or late 1930s)

> *The World is Full of Married Men* (1968)
> *The Stud* (1969)
> *The Bitch* (1979)
> *Hollywood Husbands* (1986)
> *American Star* (1998)
> *Lucky* (1998)
and many others

Jackie Collins is an English writer living in London and Los Angeles but she is closely associated with Hollywood, which is the setting for many of her 'romances'. Her themes are sex, power, money and love, and the novels are believed to reflect her own inside knowledge of the film industry and the celebrities with whom she associates. She created a strong and beautiful heroine, Lucky Santangelo, for the novel *Chances* (1981), who has subsequently featured in many books. Collins reflects (or caricatures) the lifestyles of the rich and famous, and the accuracy of her writing in this respect has led some readers to claim that they have identified her characters as well-known real-life individuals. The novels themselves are long, racy and glossily packaged and became the prototype of the 'sex and shopping' genre of the 1970s and 1980s.

Several of Jackie Collins's novels have been successfully adapted for television and for film, notably *The Stud*, which was filmed in 1978, and starred her sister, Joan Collins, as did its sequel, *The Bitch* (1979).

Len (Leonard Cyril) Deighton

b. 1929

> *The Ipcress File* (1962)
> *Funeral in Berlin* (1964)
> *Billion-Dollar Brain* (1966)
> *SS-GB* (1978)
and many others

Deighton was born in Marylebone in London. During his National Service he worked as a photographic technician in the Royal Air Force Special Investigation Branch. Later he attended St Martin's College of Art and the Royal College of Art. Before becoming a writer Deighton had a variety of jobs including time as a waiter which gave him an interest in cooking, later put to good use when he became an illustrator for the *Observer* for which he provided an illustrated cooking guide.

The Ipcress File (1962) was to be the first of many works of espionage set in the Cold War, the Second World War or in the aftermath of the destruction of the Berlin Wall. The use of realistic detail and anti-heroic characters with burnt-out personalities is in contrast to the heroics of Ian Fleming's James Bond (see entry). In this respect, Deighton's style owes something to the fiction of the social and psychological realists of the 1950s.

Dorothy (Enid) Eden

b. 1912　d. 1982

PSEUDONYM: Mary Paradise

The Vines of Yarrabee (1962)

One of the best known gothic novelists and historical romancers, Eden was born in New Zealand but settled in Great Britain. Her most famous book was *Never Call it Loving: A Biographical Novel of Katherine O'Shea and Charles Stewart Parnell* (1966), a fictional account of two famous figures from Irish history. As Mary Paradise, she also wrote gothic romance tales. Story settings range from Edwardian London (*Speak to Me of Love*, 1972) to the Australian Outback (*The Vines of Yarrabee*, 1962).

J(ohn) T(homas) Edson

b. 1928

PSEUDONYMS: Rod Denver; Chuch Nolan

The Ysable Kid (1962)
'Floating Outfit' series (37 novels, 1961–87)
'Waco' series (7 novels, 1962–81)
'Civil War' series (14 novels, 1963–88)
'Calamity Jane' series (9 novels, 1965–79)
'Rockabye County' series (10 novels, 1968–82)
'Old Devin Hardin' series (6 novels, 1975–82)
'Cap Fog' series (6 novels, 1977–87)
'Bunduki' series (4 novels, 1975–8)
and many others (20 novels, 1965–96)

John Edson was born on 17 February 1928 in Worksop, England. An uneventful career following army service abroad included owning a fish-and-chip shop and being a postman, but his western yarns led to a free-lance writing career after 1968 (although he had written for children's comics such as *Rover*, *Hotspur*, and *Victor* previously).

　　Like Penny Jordan (see entry), Edson could write a 'novel' in four to six weeks, and like James Hadley Chase (see entry) he never needed to visit America to create one of his stories. His output of over 100 novels remains popular, and being published in paperback first ('where the money is' as Edson put it) they continue a pulp tradition in British publishing aimed at an adolescent and older working-class male readership.

Edson's western heroes were the movie versions of the real thing: John Wayne and Audie Murphy. His attitude towards the genre was essentially conservative and his influences those of the pulp authors Nelson G. Wright and Robert Cade, who were writing in the mid-1930s. Alongside Edgar Rice Burroughs (see entry) and Edgar Wallace (see entry), these authors influenced Edson's work for the comic *Victor* in the 1960s and his later novels.

Ian Fleming

b. 1908   d. 1964

Casino Royale (1954)
Moonraker (1955)
Diamonds are Forever (1956)
From Russia, With Love (1957)
Dr No (1958)
Goldfinger (1959)
Thunderball (1961)
The Spy who Loved Me (1962)
On Her Majesty's Secret Service (1963)
You Only Live Twice (1964)
The Man with the Golden Gun (1965)

The son of Major Valentine Fleming, Conservative Member of Parliament for South Oxfordshire (killed in action 1917), and Evelyn Beatrice (née St Croix Rose), Fleming went to Eton and then Sandhurst Military Training College. After a period in Austria he failed the Foreign Office exam and became a journalist with Reuters before the outbreak of war, when he joined the Royal Naval Volunteer Reserve, becoming personal foreign manager of Kemsley Newspapers and remaining there until 1957. Fleming's first novel to feature James Bond was *Casino Royale* (1953), written partly whilst at his Jamaica retreat Goldeneye. By his death in 1964 Fleming had sold over forty million books.

Fleming's reputation rests squarely with the creation of James Bond (Secret Agent 007), himself an amalgamation of the Buchanesque imperial hero and the cynical killer of a Mickey Spillane thriller. With the filming of the books from *Dr No* (1962) onwards, Bond has become the most famous fictional character of the twentieth century and this, not least because of the memorable array of villains set against him (Dr No and Blofeld amongst many others), the organisations they represent (SMERSH; SPECTRE) and the women he seduces (Pussy Galore; Rider Honeychile).

Kingsley Amis and later John Gardner continued to write 'Bond' novels after Fleming's death and Bond movies are still being made in the twenty-first century.

Frederick Forsyth

b. 1938

The Day of the Jackal (1971)
The Odessa File (1972)
The Dogs of War (1974)
The Fourth Protocol (1984)

Forsyth started writing as a reporter. He worked for Reuters and the BBC. Between 1956 and 1958 he served in the RAF as a pilot. At the time, he was the youngest pilot ever to have earned his wings (he was only nineteen years old).

The author's first bestseller, *The Day of the Jackal*, published in 1971, was based on Forsyth's own coverage of a plot to assassinate Charles de Gaulle. For the novel, he created a professional killer, 'The Jackal'. Forsyth established his writing style as journalistic, a style which carried into his second and third bestsellers, *The Odessa File* (1972) and *The Dogs of War* (1974). *The Dogs of War* drew upon Forsyth's experience as a correspondent in West Africa, where he covered the situation in Biafra. His novel deals with a military coup in the same region. Forsyth says of his novels, 'my books are 80% plot and structure. The remaining 20% is for characters and description.'

Winston (Mawdsley) Graham

b. 1909 or 1910

> *Ross Poldark: A Novel of Cornwall, 1783–1787* (1945)
> *No Exit: An Adventure* (1949)
> *Demelza: A Novel of Cornwall, 1788–1790* (1946)
> *Marnie* (1960)

Graham's style of suspense and crime attracted director Alfred Hitchcock, who filmed *Marnie* in 1961. In addition to crime fiction, Graham has also written a series of historical novels set in eighteenth-century Cornwall. A firm believer in stories with strong narratives and plenty of suspense and local atmosphere, especially in his historical romances, Graham is concerned with the interplay of the mundane and the criminal in any period or place. The atmospheric tales of Cornwall were adapted for a highly successful television series.

Arthur Hailey

b. 1920

> *Hotel* (1965)
> *Airport* (1968)
> *Wheels* (1971)

Arthur Hailey was born and brought up in Luton, Bedfordshire, attending elementary school but unable to win a scholarship to the local grammar school and thus pursue a career in journalism. After work as a junior in an estate agent's, Hailey joined the RAF during World War Two but afterwards, with little success in 'civvy' street, he emigrated to Canada in 1947.

Hailey finally found work as a real-estate agent and then as an assistant editor on the trade journal *Bus and Truck Transport*, and later as a promotion manager for *Trailmobile*. Success finally came with a play and a novel. *The Final Diagnosis* (1959) was chosen for a *Reader's Digest* Condensed Book Choice and by the Literary Guild of America. *Hotel* (1965), *Airport* (1968) and *Wheels* (1971) were each a huge success and made into successful films, confirming Hailey as the master of the corporate saga. Hailey's ten major novels account for 160 million sales.

Joseph Heller

b. 1925   d. 2000

Catch-22 (1961)
Something Happened (1974)

Joseph Heller was born in Brooklyn, New York, in 1925 and served in the US Air Force during World War Two before acquiring a degree from New York University and a Master's from Columbia, after which he spent two years studying at Oxford University as a Fulbright Scholar between 1949 and 1950. Heller taught English at Pennsylvania State University for two years, later worked in New York for *Time* (1952–6), *Look* (1956–8) and *McCall's* (1958–61) magazines before becoming a full-time writer.

Heller's first novel, *Catch-22*, was published in 1961 and is a satire on the US Air Force as a bureaucracy gone beyond its rightful limits; this novel proved to be Heller's most successful. Heller also participated in the writing of screenplays, namely, *Sex and the Single Girl* (1964), *Casino Royale* (1967), and *Dirty Dingus Magee* (1970). 'Catch 22' entered the language as shorthand for a double bind.

Victoria Holt (Eleanor Burford Hibbert)

b. 1906   d. 1993

PSEUDONYMS: Philippa Carr; Elbur Ford; Katherine Kellow; Jean Plaidy; Ellalice Tate

Together They Ride (1943)
Mistress of Mellyn (1960)
The Royal Road to Fotheringay (1955)

Eleanor Burford Hibbert was one of Britain's most popular novelists during the twentieth century, writing in a number of romance sub-genres under a collection of pseudonyms, the most famous of which were Jean Plaidy and Victoria Holt. Her writing included historical novels (as Plaidy), gothic romance (as Holt) and family sagas with historical backgrounds (as Philippa Carr). As Jean Plaidy, Hibbert took actual royal and dynastic history and retold the events through the eyes of the women involved, whether Queen Victoria, Katherine of Aragon,

Mary, Queen of Scots or Caroline of Ansbach (George II's wife) etc. When Hibbert began writing as Victoria Holt similarities between her work and that of Daphne du Maurier (see entry) suggested that Holt was actually a pseudonym for the latter author! As Victoria Holt, Eleanor Hibbert continued a gothic tradition straight from Ann Radcliffe (1764–1823) and the Brontës, and as Jean Plaidy she continued a tradition with its origins in W. Harrison Ainsworth (1805–82).

Susan Howatch

b. 1940

Penmarric (1971)
Cashelmara (1974)
The Rich are Different (1977)
Sins of the Fathers (1980)

Now resident in the United States, Susan Howatch was born in Leatherhead, Surrey, in 1940, took a degree at King's College, London, in 1961 and became a law clerk before emigrating in 1964.

A writer of 'gothic' tales and generational sagas, Howatch became a bestseller with *Penmarric* (1971). Despite its wild setting in North Cornwall, Penmarric is pointedly unlike Daphne du Maurier's *Rebecca* (see entry), the story resembling rather the Forsyte series of novels by John Galsworthy (d. 1933), the house itself being a building of 'pseudo-Gothic clumsiness'. Like *Cashelmara* (1974), the tale concerns a dynastic family struggle (over 55 years). Such fiction looks back to the nineteenth-century domestic novel and forward to the 'Aga saga' and contemporary romance.

Ken Kesey

b. 1935   d. 2001

One Flew Over the Cuckoo's Nest (1962)

Ken Kesey was born in Colorado, and studied both at the University of Oregon and Stanford University. His work as an attendant in a mental hospital served as a backdrop to his most famous novel, *One Flew Over the Cuckoo's Nest* (1962), which was subsequently made into a popular film. His vibrant characterisation of the various patients and employees of a mental ward in the 1960s adopts a dysfunctional hero as the central symbolic figure of modern American culture. He further drew on personal experience for his later novels, setting *Sometimes a Great Notion* (1964) in a small town in Oregon, whilst addressing his eclectic lifestyle with the band of so-called 'Merry Pranksters' in various works such as the loosely autobiographical *Kesey's Garage Sale* (1973) and *The Further Inquiry* (1990).

Louis L'Amour

b. 1908   d. 1988

PSEUDONYMS: Tex Burns; Jim Mayo [Under Tex Burns, L'Amour continued the Hopalong Cassidy stories of Clarence E. Mulford (d. 1956).]

Hondo (1953; UK, 1954)
and many others

Born Louis Dearborn La Moore in North Dakota in 1908, he served in the United States Army during World War Two before marrying Katherine Adams in 1956. A tough man, he worked in physically tough jobs including prize fighting and as a longshoreman, tug-boat deckhand, miner, and elephant handler. His writing made him the most distinguished western novelist since Zane Grey (d. 1939) and he was the recipient of a number of awards including the Congressional Gold Medal in 1983.

L'Amour's work is an essentially epic and traditional view of the West despite the numerous 'updating' attempts of others in both prose and on film. He produced 108 books, including 87 novels, and sold upward of a quarter of a billion copies of his work, sometimes at the rate of 15,000 to 20,000 per day!

D(avid) H(erbert) Lawrence

b. 1885   d. 1930

White Peacock (1911)
Sons and Lovers (1913)
The Rainbow (1915)
Women in Love (1921)

Aaron's Rod (1922)
Kangaroo (1923)
The Plumed Serpent (1926)
Lady Chatterley's Lover (1928)
The Virgin and the Gypsy (1930)

D. H. Lawrence was born in Nottinghamshire in 1885, the fourth child of a miner and a schoolteacher. Having attended Nottingham High School and Nottingham University College he became a schoolteacher and began writing. His first novel, *The White Peacock* (1911), coincided with the death of his mother. Suffering from tuberculosis and having formed a scandalous relationship with Frieda Weekley (née Richtofen), Lawrence could not earn a living from his novel writing even though he produced *The Rainbow* (1915) and *Women in Love* (completed 1916). Travel across Europe, Asia and America did not save Lawrence from scandal and difficulties. He died aged 44 in Vence.

Lawrence is the only really great novelist (barring Orwell) to become truly popular as well. Critical recognition failed to save his career during his lifetime but the (sometimes prurient) excitement surrounding the paperback publication of *Lady Chatterley's Lover* (1928) in 1960 by Penguin and the subsequent trial to defend liberal and artistic values made his work a *cause célèbre* for the 'Sixties generation'. Many of his books have been filmed and his reputation sets him among the most significant British novelists of the twentieth century.

Norah Lofts

b. 1904   d. 1983

PSEUDONYMS: Juliet Astley; Peter Curtis

Jassy (1945)
The Concubine (1963)
The King's Pleasure (1969)
Also the following series: Gad's Hall; Sir Godfrey Tallboys; Suffolk House Trilogy

Norah Robinson was born in Norfolk on 27 August 1904. Educated at Norwich Teaching College, she took up teaching between 1925 and 1936. In 1933 she married Geoffrey Lofts. Her reputation as a historical novelist gained her the Georgette Heyer Prize in 1978 and, like Heyer (see entry), she has an ability to create historically interesting and accurate worlds that are nevertheless also a convenient background for dramatic and romantic tensions. The tradition of the historical romance has a pedigree that takes it back to Sir Walter Scott but which in the twentieth century has largely been confined to the vague category of women's romance. For a further consideration of this phenomenon see under Georgette Heyer.

Alistair MacLean

b. 1922   d. 1987

H.M.S. Ulysses (1955)
The Guns of Navarone (1957)
South by Java Head (1958)
Fear is the Key (1961)
The Golden Rendezvous (1962)
Ice Station Zebra (1963)
When Eight Bells Toll (1966)
Where Eagles Dare (1967)
Force 10 from Navarone (1968)
Puppet on a Chain (1969)
Caravan to Vaccares (1970)
Breakheart Pass (1974)

MacLean, the son of a Scots minister, spent his childhood in the Scottish Highlands, and was educated at Inverness and at Glasgow University before joining the Royal Navy during World War Two, after which he became a school teacher. *H.M.S. Ulysses* (1955) was written at the suggestion of a publisher after MacLean won a short-story competition.

MacLean's novels are traditional adventure-thrillers often set in wartime situations. Many of his books have been made into successful films, especially *The Guns of Navarone* (in 1961), *When Eight Bells Toll* (in 1971) and *Where Eagles Dare* (in 1968). His work remains the epitome of the adventure story.

Ed McBain (Evan Hunter)

b. 1926

PSEUDONYMS: Curt Cannon, Hunt Collins, Ezra Hannon, Richard Marsten

Series: '87th Precinct'
Cop Hater (1956; UK, 1958)
The Mugger (1956; UK, 1958)

And numerous other 'Precinct' tales as well as 9 titles by Evan Hunter including:
The Blackboard Jungle (1954; UK, 1955)

Evan Hunter (born Salvatore A. Lombino) was brought up in New York, attending school and college there until entering the Navy during World War Two and thereafter teaching in high school and working for a literary agent.

The 87th Precinct novels form the longest 'police procedural' series in the world and although the tales are fictional and the city anonymous, it is clear they are set in New York, just as Dashiell Hammett (b. 1894, d. 1961) set his in San Francisco, Raymond Chandler (b. 1888, d. 1954) in Los Angeles and 'Bay City', and Elmore Leonard (b. 1925) in Florida. American crime fiction has strong attachments to location.

McBain's city has both a physical geography and a municipal organisation. Characters such as Steve Carella, Bert Kling and Mayor Meyer 'work' the city within stories that follow the bureaucracy as well as the detective ability of a team of police. McBain's stories have not only won a number of prestigious crime fiction awards, but they have also proved to be extremely popular, putting the author among the top twenty novelists writing in English in the twentieth century.

Grace Metalious

b. 1924   d. 1964

Peyton Place (US 1956; UK 1957)
Return to Peyton Place (US 1959; UK 1960)
The Tight White Collar (1960)
No Adam in Eden (US 1963; UK 1964)

Metalious was known for one book, *Peyton Place* (1956), which chronicled a small town's infidelities and secret vices. Adapted for television and for film it proved the model for the hundreds of soap operas that followed its example. *The Times* recorded of Metalious's world that it was little more than a record of characters stuck in 'sex-ridden adolescence' – a formula that has never failed to please ever since!

James (Albert) Michener

b. 1907   d. 1997

Tales of the South Pacific (1947; UK, 1951) short stories
The Bridges of Toko-Ri (1953)
Hawaii (1959; UK, 1960)
Centennial (1974)
Chesapeake (1978)
Texas (1985)

Educated in Pennsylvania and at the University of Northern Colorado and at St Andrews, Scotland, Michener went on to become a Professor before joining the United States Navy during World War Two where he rose to become a Lieutenant-Commander. In 1949 he became a freelance writer but continued to be involved with education and local and government organisations. In 1948 he was awarded the Pulitzer Prize, one of many awards and honours. *Tales of the South Pacific* (1947), a set of short stories, formed the basis for the highly successful musical *South Pacific* (1949).

Michener placed the reason for his popularity in the widened horizons offered to people because of World War Two. His work also coincided with the rise of television viewing – his books, he claimed, acting as an antidote for such undemanding entertainment. Michener, in that sense, attempted to create absorbing sagas set on a broad historical and geographic stage, which offered entertainment and education but, in their breadth and length, were Tolstoyan in sensibility. It might be argued that only in an age dominated by television and the insatiable desire for information could his books have succeeded. Michener's success may perhaps be considered the product of the very technologies he found suspect.

Michael (John) Moorcock

b. 1939

Breakfast in the Ruins (1962) and 33 others (many with alternative titles)

Numerous series including: Colonel Pyat; Corum; Jerry Cornelius Chronicles; Dancers at the End of Time; Chronicles of Count Brass; Elric; Michael Kane; Von Bek Family and others.

The only major author in Britain also to have been a successful rock musician, Moorcock was instrumental in continuing the fantasy genre after J. R. R. Tolkien (see entry). His utilisation of pulp influences, especially from the 'sword and sorcery' world of Robert E. Howard (d. 1936) creator of Conan the Barbarian, helped open up a market for writers of other-world adventures and for comic fantasists such as Terry Pratchett (see entry). Moorcock has proved a prolific author with numerous fantasy and adventure series. Currently he is also involved with the creation of virtual worlds and the interactive opportunities of web cyberspace, an area that has come to be more and more significant for a growing number of post-modern and fantasy writers.

Andrea Newman

b. 1938

A Bouquet of Barbed Wire (1969)
Another Bouquet (1978)
A Sense of Guilt (1988)

Andrea Newman was brought up in Dover, Kent, and later in Shropshire and Cheshire. She graduated from London University in 1960 to take up work as a civil servant and later as a teacher. She is best remembered for *A Bouquet of Barbed Wire* (1960) and the subsequent erotic television series that created the sort of scandal once enjoyed by Elinor Glyn. Much of Newman's work has been televised, and she continues to write television drama.

Harold Robbins (Francis Rane)

b. 1916   d. 1997

Never Love a Stranger (1948)
The Dream Merchants (1949)
A Stone for Danny Fisher (1952)
79, Park Avenue (1955)
The Carpetbaggers (1961)
The Pirate (1961)

Harold Robbins (Francis Rane) was born on 21 May 1916 in New York. He became a millionaire in his twenties and rose meteorically from being a stock clerk at Universal Pictures to being their executive director of planning and budgeting.

Robbins used male pulp genres and turned them into women's romance. He was the first of the so-called 'blockbuster' novelists and his books, when published in paperback, were eagerly bought by a generation of women who could afford holidays in Spain and Greece and who would purchase holiday thrills at airport lounge bookshops. His novels are long, complicated and filled with the sex and violence that seem to accompany his powerful, rich jet-setters. Critically derided, the novels still sold in their millions with *The Carpetbaggers* (1961) considered the fourth most read book! According to one's predilection either he or Stephen King is the biggest selling American author of all time. Jackie Collins commented, on his death,

> He was certainly my big inspiration. Really successful writers give their readers a world they know intimately, and Harold certainly knows his world. From his luxurious yachts in the south of France to his lavish jet-set parties, Harold was king. He was larger than life and a real charmer. I will miss him and his ferocious talent. But his books will go on entertaining forever.[17]

Bernice Rubens

b. 1928

Madame Sousatzka (1962)

Bernice Rubens was born on 26 July 1928 into a Welsh Jewish family living in Cardiff. After completing her education at Cardiff High School for Girls and the University College of South Wales and Monmouth, she taught at a boys' school in Birmingham (1948 to 1949), later learning to become a documentary film-maker with the United Nations. In 1968 she received the American Blue Ribbon for film-making and in 1970 the Booker Prize (for *The Elected Member*).

Using a 'plain' style and utilising numerous genres, Rubens' territory is the sometimes tragic struggle of individuals for self-realisation, suffering setbacks as often as triumphs.

> Lonely, guilty, incompetent to communicate their longing to give and to receive love, conscious of the dimensions of their failure,

[Rubens'] characters experience life as pain. The pessimism of her vision is ameliorated by two factors, however, one being the grimly farcical nature of the comic episodes which rescue her novels from sentimentality, and the other, the occasional evidence that redemption is a possibility, at any rate for some individuals. . . . Those with the strength to confront the dark forces may survive and grow, but, for the majority of Rubens' characters, the best that can be achieved is avoidance of pain through a retreat into the self.[18]

Wilbur Smith

b. 1933

When the Lion Feeds (1964)
The Dark of the Sun (1965)
The Sound of Thunder (1966)
Shout at the Devil (1968)
Goldmine (1970)
Diamond Hunters (1971)
Golden Fox (1990)
Elephant Song (1991)
River God (1993)
Seventh Scroll (1995)
Birds of Prey (1997)
Monsoon (1999)

Wilbur Smith was born on 9 January 1933 in Northern Rhodesia (now Zimbabwe) and was educated at Rhodes University before moving to live in South Africa. Authentic in their African settings, Smith's stories are adventures in an imperial mode, selling extremely well in Britain and Europe where nostalgia for African adventures, hunts, safaris and exploration is still a field to exploit. At the beginning of the 1990s Smith had sold in excess of 55 million copies translated into fourteen languages.

Scribbling school essays in Nothern Rhodesia, the young Wilbur Smith never held back on the blood and guts. 'Smith,' said his English master, reeling from pages of ritual slaying and horrible accidents, 'you're a bloodthirsty young savage. Tone it down, can't you?'

Smith never did tone it down. Over the past four decades he has published some 30 bestselling thrillers set on the African continent. ... Yet for Wilbur Smith, the gold standard of adventure fiction remains H. Rider Haggard's Victorian classic, *King Solomon's Mines*. Haggard's blockbuster was published in 1885 and advertised, without undue modesty, as 'the most amazing story ever written'. 'I'd go along with that,' says Smith. 'I was 13 when I picked up *King Solomon's Mines* and I was absolutely enchanted by it. It had everything a boy wanted to know about – hidden treasure, maps written in blood, warfare and witchcraft and mysticism. Rider Haggard was able to weave the magic carpet and I was swept along by it, and inspired by it too. It made me realise what an enormous treasure chest of stories Africa was and it has stayed with me over the years of my own writing. In fact there are echoes of *King Solomon's Mines* in a lot of my own books. . . . Still, [with a bit of sex thrown in,] Rider Haggard's basic formula has stood me in good stead for 40 years. And for that, I am profoundly grateful.'

(From *The Times*, 17 March 2001)

Jacqueline Susann

b. 1926   d. 1974

Valley of the Dolls (hardback in UK, 1966; paperback in UK, 1968)
Once is Not Enough (UK, 1973)

Born in Philadelphia the daughter of Robert Susann, a society portrait painter, and his schoolteacher wife, Jacqueline moved to New York to take up stage acting and then television acting and compering. She died of cancer in September 1974.

Susann's first book, *Valley of the Dolls* (1966), was an immediate hit (with sales of 5 million copies), taking its influence from Harold Robbins (see entry) and Grace Metalious (see entry) and influencing writers like Jackie Collins (see entry). It portrays the glamorous worlds of Broadway and Hollywood and the entrapments of sex and drugs amongst the super-successful. Its heroines, Anne Wells, Nelly O'Hara and Jennifer North, are drawn through their beauty or ability into 'the secret, drug-filled, love-starved, sex-satiated, nightmare world of show business'!

Morris (Langlo) West

b. 1916   d. 1919

PSEUDONYMS: Michael East; Julian Morrin

> *Gallows on the Sand* (1955)
> *Kundu* (1956)
> *The Devil's Advocate* (1959)
> *The Naked Country* (1960)
> *The Shoes of the Fisherman* (1963)
> *The Ambassador* (1965)
> *The Tower of Babel* (1968)
> *Vanishing Point* (1996)

West is an Australian novelist and playwright born in Victoria, who trained for the priesthood but left it before taking vows. After war service his first novel, *Moon in My Pocket* (1945), dealt with the conflicts facing a Catholic novitiate. In 1955 he left Australia for Italy, where his fourth novel, *Children of the Sun* (1957), a tale of Neopolitan slum urchins, attracted attention along with *The Salamander* (1973). However, West is best known for *The Devil's Advocate* (1959; filmed 1973), an international bestseller. His novels, some of which he dramatised, deal with significant religious and political issues in an essentially humanist context.

Joseph (Aloysius, Jr) Wambaugh

b. 1937

> *The New Centurions* (1971)
> *The Blue Knight* (1972)
> *The Onion Field* (1973) [non fiction]
> *The Choirboys* (1975)
> *The Black Marble* (1978)
> *The Glitter Dome* (1981)

Wambaugh was born in East Pittsburgh, the son of a police officer, graduated from college with a BA in 1960 and an MA in 1968, worked in the Los Angeles Police Department (between 1960 and 1974) and rose to become a detective sergeant. His first book, *The New Centurions* (1971), gave a vivid, 'objective' account of police routine and mundane work in which violence was put in an appropriate and realistic context. Special attention was paid to the lives of ordinary 'beat' cops: the men amongst whom Wambaugh served as a police officer. *The Onion Field* (1973) was a documentary true-crime narrative similar to Truman Capote's *In Cold Blood* (1963), interested in the psychology of the killers and in narrating a lost world of marginalised proletarian Americans.

Herman Wouk

b. 1915

> *The Caine Mutiny* (1951)
> *Youngblood Hawke* (1962)
> *The Winds of War* (1971)
> *War and Remembrance* (1978)

Born in New York and educated at Columbia, Wouk served in the United States Naval Reserve between 1942 and 1946. A radio writer and scriptwriter before the war, Wouk became a full-time novelist in 1946, won a Pulitzer Prize for *The Caine Mutiny* (1951) and became Visiting Professor of English at Yeshiva College (1952–8) before enjoying further academic and artistic positions and awards. His monumental novels *The Winds of War* (1971) and *War and Remembrance* (1978) are essentially family sagas set in epic mode – his sentiments conservative and traditional.

John Wyndham (John Harris)

b. 1903   d. 1969

PSEUDONYMS: John Benyon; Johnson Harris; Lucas Parkes

> *The Day of the Triffids* (1951)
> *The Kraken Wakes* (1953)
> *The Midwich Cuckoos* (1955)
> *The Trouble with Lichen* (1960)

The greatest twentieth-century British science fiction author before Arthur C. Clarke (see entry), Wyndham worked in farming, commercial art and law whilst selling stories to magazines. During the 1930s he used a variety of pseudonyms to get published in America, before joining the Civil Service and the army during the Second World War. After the war, again with an eye to American markets, he tried a new genre – science fiction, a term he disliked and a genre he tried to modify. His novels are some of the greatest works in the genre, including *The Day of the Triffids* (1951), *The Midwich Cuckoos* (1955) and *The Trouble with Lichen* (1960).

His tales are pessimistic, Cold War catastrophe epics, which include natural disasters brought about by alien forces that cannot be controlled, but which create circumstances that purge British sensibilities and leave a chastened remnant of survivors.

> 'There were only five million or so of us in the first Elizabeth's time – but we counted,' she said. . . . 'I was just thinking . . . nothing is really new, is it . . . ? . . . I think we have been here before, . . . and we got through last time. . . .'
>
> (*The Kraken Wakes*, Phrase Three)

The Last Decades: 1975 to 1999

> When did I first begin to read and write? I can't recall the
> time when I could not read. There was *Chatterbox Annual*, then
> *Rainbow Comic* every week and *Tiger Tim's Weekly*. The first book
> I owned was *Grimm's Fairy Tales*. I must have been about eight at
> the time. But at what age did I advance to Charles Garvice, Ethel
> M. Dell, and Ruby M. Ayres? Odd. But I did not read Elinor Glyn
> at this period . . . her *The Career of Catherine Bush* led me to . . .
> real reading.
>
> (Catherine Cookson, *Catherine Cookson Country:*
> *Her Pictorial Memoir*, p. 11)

Douglas Adams

b. 1952   d. 2001

> *The Hitch Hiker's Guide to the Galaxy* (1978)
> *The Restaurant at the End of the Universe* (1980)
> *Life, the Universe and Everything* (1982)
> *So Long, and Thanks for All the Fish* (1983)

Adams began his career as a producer and script editor with the BBC,
working on radio programmes and on television serials such as *Dr Who*.
His witty and whimsical science fiction fantasy spoofs became extremely
popular and found a ready audience when broadcast on radio.

Richard (George) Adams

b. 1920

> *Watership Down* (1972)
> *Shardik* (1974)
> *The Plague Dogs* (1977)
> *Girl in a Swing* (1980)
> *Maia* (1984)
> *Traveller* (1988)

Richard Adams was born in Newbury, Berkshire, England, in 1920. He
served in the British Army in the Second World War, before finishing

his education at Worcester College, Oxford, in 1948. Adams then served as a civil servant in the Department of the Environment until becoming a full-time writer in 1974. His first novel, *Watership Down* (1972), is a story of a displaced community of rabbits and their contact with the human world. It was for *Watership Down*, which has appealed to both children and adults, that Adams was presented with the *Guardian* Award for children's literature and the Carnegie Medal in 1973. His next novel, *Shardik* (1974), was a 'lost world' adventure in the style of Henry Rider Haggard and John Buchan (see entry). It is set in the 'Beklan Empire' and is the story of a sacred bear god and the characters its influence affects. While Richard Adams continued to write children's literature and use animals as main characters in his novels, he tended more towards adult readers in later years with such works as *Girl in a Swing* (1980) and *Maia* (1984). *The Plague Dogs* (1977) exposed issues of animal experimentation.

Adams served as writer-in-residence at the University of Florida in 1975 and at Hollins College in 1976. He is a member of the Royal Society of Literature and Royal Society of Arts, and was the President of The Royal Society for the Prevention of Cruelty to Animals between 1980 and 1982.

Ted Allbeury

b. 1917

PSEUDONYMS: Richard Butler; Patrick Kelly

Omega Minus (1975)
The Alpha List (1979) and many others

Allbeury was born in Stockport, Lancashire, and educated in Kent. A professional soldier, his biographers claim that Allbeury was already a Lieutenant Colonel in British Intelligence by the age of twenty!* What is certain is that he later became an advertising executive and owned shares in one of Britain's first pirate radio stations. The disappearance of his four-year-old daughter in 1970 led, ironically, to a career in crime

---

* Only a T. E. leB. Allbeury is recorded as an officer during the period 1937 to 1947, commissioned as a second lieutenant in 1942 and part of the Regular Army Intelligence Corps under 'Emergency Commissions' in 1946.

and thriller writing. Allbeury's tales are traditional spy stories often centred on Berlin.

Virginia Andrews

b. 1923   d. 1986

Flowers in the Attic (1979)
My Sweet Audrina (1982)
The Seeds of Yesterday (1984)

Andrews was an American novelist and artist born in Portsmouth, Virginia. A writer of gothic horror and melodrama, she was a great believer in ESP and reincarnation, and believed that, while writing a novel, she experienced whatever her characters experienced. Andrews' commercial success was the result of a trilogy of novels, beginning with *Flowers in the Attic* (1979) and ending with *Seeds of Yesterday* (1984), which also produced a huge and devoted following of fans.

After her death her family agreed that another writer could continue to write 'in the style of Virginia Andrews' and approximately twenty novels have been published by her original publisher, Pocket Books, in this same or similar style. The novels are credited to 'the *new* Virginia Andrews', and include the 'Cutler Family' series, the 'Landry' series and the 'Casteel' saga. It is believed all these new titles are the work of Andrew Neiderman.

Jeffrey Archer

b. 1940

Not a Penny More, Not a Penny Less (1975)
Kane and Abel (1980)
First Among Equals (1984)

As well as being a very successful author of thrillers, Archer is well known as a politician and an art collector, and he has also represented Great Britain internationally as a sprinter. In 1969 he became the youngest member of the House of Commons, as MP for Louth, but resigned in 1974 as a bankrupt, at which point he began writing. Some time later Archer suggested that this was done solely in order to make money to clear his debts. His first novel, *Not a Penny More, Not a Penny Less*, was published in 1975, after which he continued to produce a succession of best-selling novels and to be active in politics (including as deputy chairman of the Conservative Party, 1985–6); he was made a life peer in 1992 (Lord Archer of Weston-super-Mare). The revelation of an earlier scandal led to his withdrawal from the London mayoral elections in 2000 and his expulsion from the Conservative Party for five years. His prosecution for perjury in 2001 (following an earlier libel case) ended with his imprisonment and the loss of his knighthood. He nevertheless continues to write and remains Britain's most successful contemporary male author.

Jean M. Auel

b. 1936

The Clan of the Cave Bear (1980)
The Valley of Horses (1982)
The Mammoth Hunters (1985)

Auel is an American writer of what have been described as 'prehistoric romances'. Her 'Earth's Children' series of five novels, beginning with *The Clan of the Cave Bear* (1980), are sagas about prehistoric Europe and describe early tribes; they are the result of 'meticulous' research. Auel uses the 'Stone Age' setting to explore issues such as gender roles and social structures. She has received a number of awards, including the Scandinavian Kaleidoscope of Art and Life Award (1982) and the American Academy of Achievement (1986), and several honorary degrees. Despite all this, these tales of Cro-Magnon life are essentially romances, which even include a blonde 'bombshell' as a character!

Desmond Bagley

b. 1923   d. 1983

The Snow Tiger (1975)
and many others

A British writer of crime novels and action and adventure thrillers, Bagley began his writing career in South Africa, where his first novel

The Golden Keel (1963) was set. His most popular works were published during the 1960s and 1970s by Doubleday. His fast-moving stories, embellished with much local 'colour' and devoid of cynicism, have been compared to those of his contemporary Hammond Innes (see entry). However, Bagley's interests were much more widely spread and he was less concerned with heroes and villains than with more technical, scientific issues or natural disasters.

Bagley wrote a total of sixteen novels, of which three were filmed. He also left two unfinished manuscripts which were later completed and published by his wife Joan.

Iain (Menzies) Banks

b. 1954

PSEUDONYM: Iain M. Banks

The Wasp Factory (1984)
The Bridge (1986)
Consider Plebus (1987)
Canal Dreams (1989)
The Crow Road (1992)
Complicity (1993)

Iain Banks is a Scottish novelist, born in Fife, Scotland, in 1954. After attending Gourock and Greenock High Schools, he graduated from the University of Stirling in 1975. In 1977 Banks worked as a non-destructive testing technician in Glasgow, Scotland, and then as an expediter–analyser in 1978 for IBM in Greenock, Scotland. Until publishing his first novel in 1984, he worked as a clerk to a London solicitor.

Banks has produced work described as thrilling, fantastical, horrifying, and perverse, exhibiting elements of fantasy and science fiction. His first novel, *The Wasp Factory* (1984), is the story of a teenage boy's psychotic actions towards animals and other characters in the book. Many of the novels confront issues of insanity, murder, sexuality and the grotesque and sinister sides of human nature. Other novels include *The Bridge* (1986), where Banks develops a fictitious community segregated by railroads.

Under his pseudonym, Iain M. Banks, he has become the leading voice in British science fiction, revitalising and subverting the 'space opera'. With one exception, his contribution to the genre is set in 'the Culture', a far distant anarcho-socialist society whose wealth and stability rest on unlimited energy, unlimited resources, long life and the presence of intelligent computers who enjoy 'human' sentience. Death, imperialism and the determinants of human nature are all themes in his work but he is pre-eminently concerned with choice and its context.

Maeve Binchy

b. 1940

Light a Penny Candle (1982)
The Glass Lake (1994)
A Circle of Friends (1991)

Maeve Binchy was born just outside Dublin, graduated from University College, Dublin, in 1960, and subsequently became a teacher. She began her writing career by submitting articles on travel and teaching to the *Irish Times*, where she was made Women's Editor in 1968. In addition to her novels Binchy has also written collections of short stories, and several plays for stage and television. In 1995 her novel *A Circle of Friends*, which is set in University College, Dublin, and concerns the lives of three young women and their developing relationships, was made into a film starring Minnie Driver and Chris O'Donnell, and successfully boosted her already high book sales. She has consistently been a best-selling author since the publication of her first novel, *Light a Penny Candle* (1982).

Binchy's novels are set in Ireland and draw on her own experience there. She is particularly noted for writing about young women and about relationships between family and friends, thus attracting a large proportion of female readers.

Barbara Taylor Bradford

b. 1933

A Woman of Substance (1979)
Voice of the Heart (1983)
Hold the Dream (1985)
Act of Will (1986)
To Be the Best (1988)
The Women in His Life (1990)
Power of a Woman (1997)
A Sudden Change of Heart (1999)

Bradford's blockbuster sagas made her one of the most popular writers of the 1980s with sales of over 30 million copies (by the end of the century this had almost doubled). She began writing at ten when her father bought her a second-hand typewriter. The story she composed on it was submitted to a children's paper and published. By her twentieth year Bradford had read Dickens and the Brontës and, with the help of her mother, set her sights on an artistic career. Having attended school in Leeds she found her first job on the *Yorkshire Evening Post* during 1948, doing shorthand but secretly writing short articles, until graduating to work on *Woman's Own*, the *London Evening News* and, briefly, as an executive editor for the *London American*. In 1963 she married Robert Bradford and moved to the United States.

In the States, Bradford edited and compiled popular books on home-making and décor that enjoyed good sales and newspaper syndication. At nearly forty, Bradford had still not written a novel and was concerned she might never be able to. Nevertheless,

> I thought long and hard. In the end, I decided that I wanted to write a saga, perhaps a family saga, but certainly a saga. I wanted to write about England, more specifically, Yorkshire. I wanted it to be one of those long, traditional, old-fashioned novels about a woman who makes it in a man's world, at a time when women weren't expected to do that. I wanted to write about a woman of substance . . . the phrase stuck.[19]

A Woman of Substance was published in the United States in 1979 and in the United Kingdom in 1980 with the first paperback run reaching

1.4 million and first-year paperback sales reaching 3.5 million. In twenty years the book sold 18 million copies.

(Dame Mary) Barbara Cartland

b. 1901   d. 2000

Jigsaw (1925)
and over 500 other titles

In the period after the First World War, Barbara Cartland was one of the 'bright young things'. She wrote a gossip column for the *Daily Express*, two plays, and her first novel, *Jigsaw*, which was published in 1925. During the 1970s she became known as the 'Queen of Romance' and was one of the most prodigious best-selling authors, having written over 500 novels between 1925 and 1999. International sales of her novels, which have been translated into 36 languages, are reputed to exceed 600 million.

Cartland's name is synonymous with a particular style of historical romantic fiction which adheres quite strictly to a recognised formula and which reflects her own very traditional moral code. Most are set between 1790 and 1890. In her writing Cartland reflects a romanticised view of the world of the English upper classes and the manners and ideals of the aristocracy.

She is also known for her links with the Royal family: she married Alexander McCorquodale in 1927, thus becoming stepmother to Raine, Countess Spencer, stepmother to the late Princess of Wales, Diana Spencer. After divorcing her first husband, she married his cousin, Hugh McCorquodale, in 1936. She has had a number of public roles, including Chief Lady Welfare Officer for Bedfordshire during World War Two, a county councillor for Hertfordshire, chairman of the St John Ambulance Brigade and founder and chairman of the National Association for Health. She was made a Dame of the Order of the British Empire in 1991.

A popular figure in the media, Cartland championed the causes of nurses, midwives and gypsies, and was particularly outspoken on the subject of spiritual and physical health.

As both a health pundit and an advocate of femininity, Cartland attracted the opprobrium of critics whose dislike of her self-assuredness and eccentric liking for all things pink led to vitriolic reviews and personal attacks, nowhere more so than in the following example from Kate Saunders in *The Sunday Times*, 31 July 1994.

> Barbara Cartland . . . [looks] like a cross between Nosferatu and a knitted crinolin lady perched on a lavatory roll. . . . Dame Barbara moves through the world spreading sweetness and light – Gawd bless'er! . . . Traditional, Cartland-style romantic love is a ghastly drug, which persuades women to . . . knuckle down to domestic servitude.

Tom Clancy

b. 1947

> *The Hunt for Red October* (1984)
> *Patriot Games* (1987)
> *Clear and Present Danger* (1989)

In the mid-1980s, Clancy was an insurance salesman selling policies for boats and cars; by the early 1990s he was one of the world's best-selling authors, specialising in highly detailed and accurate political and 'techno-thrillers' many of which have been made into films. The key themes and subject matter of his fiction are espionage and the military, and he has been acclaimed for his knowledge of and detailed references to the US military, the FBI, CIA and weapons/military technology.

His first novel, *The Hunt for Red October* (1984), is a fictional account of the race between US and Soviet forces to claim a defecting Russian submarine captain and his state-of-the-art vessel, and was described by President Ronald Reagan as 'non put-downable'. It was filmed in 1990, as were two subsequent novels. Their success has significantly contributed to the continued popularity of Clancy's work as a novelist. The impetus for *The Hunt for Red October* came after Clancy attended a seminar at the United States Naval Institute, read an article on a rogue Russian submarine mutiny and immersed himself in technological books and manuals. It all suggested a novel to Clancy, who describes himself as a 'technology freak'.

Clancy has also written several non-fiction books that examine different areas of the United States armed forces, such as: *Submarine*, *Armoured Warfare*, and *Fighter Wing*. Most recently, Clancy has developed an interest in computer games and has co-founded the company Red Storm Entertainment.

A collector of guns and military memorabilia, Clancy was also one of Ronald Reagan's favourite authors.

Shirley (Ida) Conran

b. 1932

Lace: A Novel (1982)
The Magic Garden (1983)
Lace II (1985)
The Legend (1985)
Savages (1987)
Crimson (1992)
Tiger Eyes (1994)

Shirley Conran was born on 21 September 1932 in London. She married the designer and entrepreneur Terence Conran in 1955, and although that marriage ended in 1962, she co-owned and became fabric designer of Conran Fabrics (1957–62). This led to the beginning of her writing career, starting first as a design consultant and part-time writer until she proceeded to full-time writer and finally editor of *Life and Style* from 1972 to 1974. Conran's first novel, *Lace* (1982), became a bestseller, pleasing readers with its extravagance and glamour. *Savages*, her second novel, was published in 1987 and, like *Lace*, it centred on rich, good-looking women. *Crimson* (1992) involves a wealthy English romance writer and her dealings with love and betrayal. A common theme in the books is sexuality and sexual relationships. Her aim, in writing her novels, was to highlight women's feelings, in contrast to male authors who, she felt, lacked such insight. Conran has also contributed to the women's self-help genre with her series of books beginning with *Superwoman* (1975).

Catherine Cookson (née McMullen)

b. 1906   d. 1998

PSEUDONYM: Catherine Marchant

Kate Hannigan (1950)
Fifteen Streets (1979)
Colour Blind (1975)
Maggie Rowan (1954)
Katie Mulholland (1967)
The Cinder Path (1978)
Tilly Trotter (1978)
The Baily Chronicles (1988)
The Harrogate Secret (1988)
The Gillyvors (1990)
Bill Bailey's Lot (1990)
Bill Bailey's Daughter (1990)
The Love Child: A Novel (1990)
'Mary Ann' series: 9 novels (1954–81)
'Mallen Novels': trilogy (1973–74)

Between her first book, *Kate Hannigan* (1950), and her death in 1998, Cookson sold over 90 million copies of her novels.* In 1998 it is estimated that a third of all popular fiction borrowed from local libraries was by Cookson and a year before her death nine of the top ten most borrowed books were Cookson novels. From the mid-1990s Cookson's books were consistently televised, she had given her name to a burgeoning tourist industry in the North-East, and had been honoured by the University of Newcastle and the Royal Society of Literature as well as gaining the DBE (Dame of the British Empire) and the OBE (Order of the British Empire).

Cookson was born into abject poverty (like Edgar Wallace; see entry) in a slum district of Tyneside, an illegitimate child of a family riven by violence and drunkenness. The denial of this origin and the repression of knowledge about her illegitimacy set up a traumatic reaction in McMullen which was brought to a crisis after her marriage to a schoolteacher, Tom Cookson, and subsequent multiple miscarriages leading to a breakdown. The importance of these years to Cookson have

---

* This figure has been challenged but the upper figure is credible.

been documented in numerous biographies and Cookson's own autobiography, *Our Kate* (1969), a book as significant as her novels in its direct appeal to the experience of millions of women.

Introduced to a love of poetry at school (although she had to leave a the age of thirteen), Cookson nevertheless took to novels, using a story background of local and personal knowledge, an approach that made her novels at once socially realistic and regionally distinct. Nevertheless, Cookson always staunchly distanced herself from mere regionalism as indeed she did from being labelled as a women's romance writer, her husband Tom linking her rather with a tradition of fire-side storytelling going back nearly two centuries.

> In these days of advertising, she is often classified as a romantic novelist, which she certainly is not; at least in the loose way in which this word romantic is today applied to novels; she is a story-teller. And one must again remember her upbringing prior to and during the First World War: no wireless – this came in the 1920s – no TV; only reading, if possible; but certainly there was the listening to tales told and retold by members of the family, detailing events which had occurred much earlier, perhaps going back even to her great-grandmother's time before the 1850s.[20]

The family saga, often a blend of historical and generational romance and featuring a central, strong female figure or a number of mothers, daughters and wives over three generations, was continually exploited during the latter half of the twentieth century. Prominent popular exponents included **Lena Kennedy** (b. 1912, d. 1986), a London East Ender who started writing aged sixty-seven (*Maggie*, 1979), **Marie Joseph**, whose tales of Lancashire mill girls in the 1930s first appeared in 1975; and **Maisie Mosco**, whose *Almonds and Raisins* (1979) charted life for a Jewish family in a Manchester slum before the First World War. Most successful of all these writers is **Josephine Cox**, who although born in poverty (into a family of ten children) in Blackburn, Lancashire, and forced to work as a vinegar bottle labeller at fourteen, has risen to become one of Britain's most popular historical saga writers with tales of Lancashire families, their struggles with poverty and the successes and tragedies that affect the strong central female protagonists.

Jilly Cooper

b. 1937

> *Riders* (1984)
> *Rivals* (1989)
> *Polo* (1992)
> *The Man who Made Husbands Jealous* (1993)
> *Pandora* (2002)
and many others

Jilly Cooper was born in Yorkshire and was initially a journalist, eventually becoming a columnist for *The Sunday Times* and the *Mail on Sunday*. Her early fiction consisted of short romantic stories for teenage magazines, which were later extended to become a series of novels (*Emily*, *Bella*, *Imogen*, *Prudence*, *Harriet* and *Octavia*), published in the mid- to late 1970s.

Cooper writes fast-paced romances which are littered with glamorous, celebrity-style characters such as the promiscuous upper-class cad Rupert Campbell-Black, who appears in several novels. Much of her fiction is set in the Home Counties, and her themes have been described succinctly as 'sex and horses'.

Bernard Cornwell

b. 1944

PSEUDONYM: Susannah Kells

Series: 'Sharpe'
> *Sharpe's Eagle* (1981)
and many others

Cornwell graduated from the University of London in 1967 and became a television producer for the BBC in London from 1969 to 1976. He was later the head of current affairs for the BBC in Belfast from 1976 to 1979. From Belfast he went to Thames Television in London as a news editor from 1979 to 1980.

As a historical action novelist and the creator of the 'Sharpe' series, Cornwell explores not only the Napoleonic Wars but also the era of King

Arthur. The Sharpe novels concentrate on the life of Richard Sharpe, a military officer serving under Wellington during the Peninsular Campaign and after. Each book concerns a different battle, with the Battle of Waterloo the last, completing the series.

Cornwell acknowledges that Sharpe's character was inspired by C. S. Forester's 'Hornblower' (see entry). Sharpe's viewpoint highlights Cornwell's painstaking attention to detail, from the uniforms that the soldiers wore to the type of weapons used in battle.

Patricia (Daniels) Cornwell

b. 1956

Postmortem (1990)
Body of Evidence (1991)
From Potter's Field (1995)
and many others

Patricia Cornwell has seen many of her novels reach the bestseller list. Since 1990, her combination of close detail and complex mystery surrounding the life of Dr Kay Scarpetta have made her extremely popular. Cornwell's time in the Office of the Chief Medical Examiner in Richmond, Virginia, where she worked as a computer analyst and as a volunteer police officer provided her with plenty of background to construct the cases facing Scarpetta, a medical examiner. In *Postmortem* (1990), Scarpetta accepts the challenge of finding a serial rapist in Richmond, displaying forensic and technological skills. In her later novels Cornwell created Temple Gault, another serial killer, as an intellectual match for Scarpetta.

Cornwell was born on 9 June 1956 in Miami, Florida, and graduated from Davidson College in North Carolina with a degree in English Literature. She is a member of the International Crime Writers Club, the International Association of Chiefs of Police, and the National Association of Medical Examiners.

In 2000 she became the highest paid female author of all time with an estimated £20 million advance on three books. With this she overtook Barbara Taylor Bradford (see entry), who had been the best paid woman writer since 1979. In Great Britain, this position is currently held by J. K. Rowling (see entry).

Michael Crichton

b. 1942

PSEUDONYMS: John Lange (8 novels, 1966–72); Jeffrey Hudson; Michael Douglas

The Andromeda Strain (1969)
Jurassic Park (1990)

Born in Chicago, Crichton attended Harvard Medical School. One of the novels he wrote to subsidise his post-graduate studies, *The Andromeda Strain* (1969), had already become a bestseller and had been sold to Hollywood before he graduated.

Each of Crichton's novels displays his detailed knowledge of particular and very specialised subjects, including genetics, biophysics, primatology and international economics, and he is known as the creator of the 'techno-thriller'.

Crichton has directed six films, including *Coma*, *Westworld*, and *The Great Train Robbery* (from his novel), and he created the enormously successful television series *ER*. He has also collaborated as writer, co-writer or co-producer on numerous other films. The adaptation of his novel *Jurassic Park* (1990) was one of the most successful films ever made, enjoying two sequels. In addition to his work with film and as a writer, Crichton runs a software company and designs computer games.

Clive Cussler

b. 1931

Raise the Titanic (1976)
Requiem for a Princess (1988)

Cussler was born in Aurora, Illinois, and attended Pasadena City College, Orange Coast College, and California State University. From 1961 to 1965 Cussler owned Bestgen & Cussler Advertising in Newport Beach, California, but after the success of his novels featuring Dirk Pitt he devoted himself to writing underwater adventures. As the founder of the National Underwater and Marine Agency he is responsible for the discovery of many shipwrecks including that of the Confederate submarine *Hunley* and the U-20, the German submarine that sank the *Lusitania*.

Dirk Pitt, hero of Cussler's adventures and the Special Projects Director of the fictional version of the National Underwater and Marine Agency (NUMA), is a character straight out of comic books, with a tanned face, opaline green eyes, broad shoulders, a love for classic cars, shipwrecks, tequilla with lime, and beautiful women. A superficial resemblance to the tradition of international espionage thriller writers masks a debt to pulp fiction, television and B-movies. Indeed Pitt's actions are very similar to those of International Rescue in *Thunderbirds*, with an almost tongue-in-cheek pulp writing style:

> The stranger pushed a handgun with silencer into a pocket, knelt down to eye level, and nodded at the blood spreading through the material of Koplin's parka. 'I'd better get you to where I can take a look at that.' Then he picked Koplin up as one might a child and began trudging down the mountain toward the sea.
>
> 'Who are you?' Koplin muttered.
>
> 'My name is Pitt. Dirk Pitt.'
>
> 'I don't understand . . . where did you come from?'
>
> Koplin never heard the answer. At that moment, the black cover of unconsciousness abruptly lifted up, and he fell gratefully under it.
>
> (*Raise the Titanic*, ch. 2)

The recycling of such clichés highlights affinities with other media, especially television 'space opera'. The following dialogue (aboard a ship about to sink in stormy waters during 1948) could just have easily been scripted between engineer 'Scotty' and 'Captain Kirk' on board the Starship *Enterprise*. The formula has sold over 70 million copies of Dirk Pitt's adventures so far.

> Li Po answered. 'Bridge'.
>
> 'Put the captain on!' Gallagher snapped.
>
> A second's pause, and then, 'This is the captain.'
>
> 'Sir, we've got a hell of a crack in the engine room, and it's getting worse by the minute.'
>
> Hunt was stunned. He had hoped against hope that they could make port before the damage turned critical. 'Are we taking on water?'

'The pumps are fighting a losing battle.'

'Thank you, Mr Gallagher. Can you keep the engines turning until we reach land?'

'What time frame do you have in mind?'

'Another hour should put us in calmer waters.'

'Doubtful,' said Gallagher. 'I give her ten minutes, no more.'

'Thank you, Chief,' Hunt said heavily. 'You'd better leave the engine room while you still can.'

(Requiem for a Princess, ch. 1)

Cussler's work makes explicit the *interchangeable* nature of dialogues and series shared between popular genres, making them both *hybrid* and *formulaic*. Such scenes, re-enacted in the above dialogues, are reworked and usually recycled in genres with tangential relationships (in this case where ships – or star ships – are in peril). Cussler's style is reminiscent of much popular adolescent television viewing of the later 1960s and early 1970s, recycled now as text.

Colin Dexter

b. 1930

Series: 'Inspector Morse'
  Last Bus to Woodstock (1975)
  Last Seen Wearing (1976)
  The Silent World of Nicholas Quinn (1977)
  Service of All the Dead (1979)
  The Dead of Jericho (1981)
  The Riddle of the Third Mile (1983)
  The Secret of Annexe 3 (1986)
  The Wench is Dead (1989)
  The Jewel that was Ours (1991)
  The Way through the Woods (1992)
  Morse's Greatest Mystery (1993)
  The Daughters of Cain (1994)
  Death is Now My Neighbour (1996)

Colin Dexter's major literary contribution is the 'Inspector Morse' detective series, which has established Dexter as a pivotal figure in modern English detective fiction. Detective Chief Inspector Morse of the Thames

Valley Constabulary is a petulant character, fond of beer and tobacco, but still held in high esteem by his associate detective, Sergeant Lewis. An obvious parallel can be seen between this pair and that of Doyle's Holmes and Watson (see entry). Dexter adapts and updates Sir Arthur Conan Doyle's technique of reader mystification. Indeed, Dexter is a master of the ability to mislead the reader in identifying the culprit. In the style of the classic mystery novelist, Dexter presents all of the clues available to the detective, but in such a way that the reader fails to identify the criminal until after the detective accuses the guilty party. Dexter creates an intricate puzzle using misleading clues and false trails. Ultimately, Dexter's ability to take the reader on a single-minded quest for the truth enables him to contribute to the preservation of a slowly dying genre. The *Inspector Morse* television series is one of the most successful of all time and enjoys enormous audiences both in Britain and across the world.

Nicholas Evans

b. 1950

The Horse Whisperer (1995)

Nicholas Evans suddenly became internationally famous when he sold his novel *The Horse Whisperer* (1995) for 8.15 million dollars (for North American book rights, foreign rights and film rights) – before it was even completed. The film rights were sold for 3 million dollars, the largest sum ever for a first novel, and the subsequent film was directed by and starred Robert Redford, with Kirsten Scott Thomas. Set in Montana, the novel portrays a romance between a British magazine editor and a man who communicates with and cures horses.

Before he began writing novels, Evans trained as a journalist and later became a screenwriter and filmmaker, and produced a documentary on the director David Lean. Evans's second novel, *The Loop*, was published in 2000.

Colin Forbes (Raymond Harold Sawkins)

b. 1923

PSEUDONYMS: Jay Bernard; Richard Raine

The Stone Leopard (1975)
Avalanche Express (1977)
The Janus Man (1988)

Sawkins served in the British Army from 1942 to 1946 and as with many writers who served in the war the experience fed into his work. *Tramp in Armour* (1969) is a novel that concerns five soldiers who get trapped behind enemy lines in their tank. Their adventure has them trying to get back to their division, though on the way, they almost sink in quicksand and almost get burned to death. Another novel, *The Stone Leopard*, was published 1975. This novel features a hunt for a leader of the French Resistance who is trying to overthrow the government in France.

Sawkins also created works in the same genre under his other pseudonyms, whilst as Forbes he unites the plot structure of Agatha Christie (see entry) with the exotic locations of Ian Fleming (see entry) and the political detail of Frederick Forsyth (see entry) in order to create high-adventure thrillers.

Dick Francis (Richard Stanley Francis)

b. 1920

Dead Cert (1962)
Nerve (1964)
For Kicks (1965)
Odds Against (1965)
Flying Finish (1966)
Blood Sport (1967)
Forfeit (1969)
Enquiry (1969)
Rat Race (1970)
Bonecrack (1971)
Smokescreen (1972)
Slay-Ride (1973)
and many others

Richard (Dick) Francis was born in Tenby in Pembrokeshire, Wales, but was educated in Maidenhead. As a steeplechase jockey he had a successful career both as an amateur (1946) and as a professional (from 1948), winning the Steeplechase Jockey Championship in 1954. His horse 'Devon Lock' mysteriously fell fifty yards from the winning post of the Grand National in 1956. He retired as a jockey in 1957 and in 1962 published his first tale of racing and mystery, *Dead Cert*.

Francis's tales of the turf are in the direct tradition of Nat Gould (see entry), realistic and full of the subculture of the track. During the late twentieth century Francis was extraordinarily popular, especially as a writer borrowed from local libraries: *Wild Horses* (1995), for instance, sold almost 600,000 copies in paperback.

George MacDonald Fraser

b. 1925

'Flashman Papers' series:
  Flashman (1969)
  Royal Flash (1970)
  Flash for Freedom (1971)
  Flashman at the Charge (1973)
  Flashman in the Great Game (1975)
  Flashman's Lady (1977)
  Flashman and the Redskins (1982)
  Flashman and the Dragon (1986)
  Flashman and the Mountain of Light (1990)
and others

George MacDonald Fraser was born on 2 April 1925 in Carlisle, England. He is an author and a journalist who was appointed deputy editor of the *Glasgow Herald* newspaper from 1964 to 1969 before becoming a full-time author after the success of *Flashman* (1969), which revivified Thomas Hughes's bully from *Tom Brown's Schooldays* and put him in a series of comic–heroic Victorian adventures. Flashman is a rogue, a cad, a coward and a bully, not to mention a womaniser who uses cunning and grovelling to wheedle his way around the significant events and historical characters of the nineteenth century.

Fraser was involved with scriptwriting the *Three Musketeers* films with

Richard Lester as well as scriptwriting *Octopussy*, a James Bond film. His love of historical romance also provided the impetus for a pastiche of the 'swashbuckling' high seas adventures of Rafael Sabatini (see entry), Jeffrey Farnol (see entry) and C. S. Forester (see entry), called the *Pyrates* (1983) – a work he called 'an historical pantomine'. Fraser's slogan, like Charles Read's before him, is 'Make 'em laugh, make 'em cry, make 'em wait.'

Alexander (Fergus) Fullerton

b. 1924

PSEUDONYM: Anthony Fox

Series: 'Everard' including:
   The Blooding of the Guns (1976)

Fullerton attended the Royal Naval College from 1938 until 1941. From 1942 to 1949 he served as a Russian interpreter for the Navy, and eventually became a lieutenant in the submarine squadron. This became a logical source of material for Fullerton's novels. His first book, *Surface!*, published in 1953, deals with submarines.

Fullerton created a series of World War One and World War Two naval adventure novels known as the 'Everard' series. Two of the books from this series are *The Blooding of the Gun*, published in 1976, and *The Torch Bearers*, published in 1983. Most of these stories deal with an individual having to call upon his courage (or lack thereof) when faced with danger and all are full of technical and historical detail.

Alex Garland

b. 1970

   The Beach (1996)

Garland was born in London and spent his later teenage years travelling in Southeast Asia, especially the Philippines. In 1992, he received a degree from Manchester University. Before completing *The Beach*, Garland entertained hopes of becoming a comic-book or comic-strip illustrator, following in the footsteps of his cartoonist father, Nick Garland. 'Everything I know about writing, I learned through drawing comic strips', Garland admits, and this seems apposite for the most significant writer to emerge in Britain from the 'blank' generation: 'twenty somethings weaned on video games, TV and a decade's worth of pop' (Dwight Garner, *www.salon.com/Feb* 97). 'That video culture is my culture', Garland claims, an enthusiasm transferred to the book itself. *The Beach*, with its mixture of tourist brochure, *Lord of the Flies*, *Heart of Darkness* and backpacker nightmare, is a book aimed at a lost generation in search of meaning. Garland sees the book, in which a backpacker finds himself in the clutches of a cult group in Thailand, as a rejection of the blandishments of New Ageism. Nevertheless, *The Beach* may be the first work of bestselling fiction in Britain to have transferred the visual world of pop culture into an *un-ironic* textual narrative.

John Grisham

b. 1955

> *A Time to Kill* (1989)
> *The Firm* (1991)
> *The Pelican Brief* (1992)
> *The Client* (1993)
> *The Chamber* (1994)
> *The Rainmaker* (1995)
> *The Runaway Jury* (1996)
> *The Partner* (1997)
> *The Street Lawyer* (1998)

John Grisham is an American novelist, born in Jonesboro, Arkansas, in 1955. After moving to various southern towns because of his father's job in construction work, his family eventually settled in Southaven, Mississippi, where he still lives. He attended Mississippi State University, received his law degree from the University of Mississippi, and was admitted to the bar in Mississippi in 1981. He established a criminal law practice in Southaven in 1981, and soon switched his concentration to civil law. Hoping to improve Mississippi's educational system, Grisham decided to enter the political realm and was elected for two terms as a representative to the Mississippi State Legislature. He served from

1984 to 1990 when he resigned, disillusioned by his inability to make a significant impact, but continued his legal practice.

After witnessing a courtroom scene of a young rape victim confronting her violator, Grisham was motivated to write a story of a young black girl whose white rapist is killed by her father. This became his first novel, *A Time to Kill* (1989). Although it was not an instant success his first novel has become one of his most famous. Grisham's plots, settings, and characters draw from his legal and political experience and from his Southern heritage.

Amongst the many authors who occupy themselves with courtroom drama and the legal themes found in the work of John Grisham is (L.) Scott Turow (b. 1949) whose books, *Presumed Innocent* (1987) and *Burden of Proof* (1990), found success with much the same readership.

Thomas Harris

b. 1940

Black Sunday (1975)
Red Dragon (1981)
The Silence of the Lambs (1988)
Hannibal (1999)

Thomas Harris was born in Mississippi, Missouri, in 1940. Before working as a writer, Harris spent some time working as a news reporter and editor for the Associated Press in New York City. All four of Harris's novels have been made into motion pictures. Each of these novels concerns similar themes, dealing with crime and detection. Harris is the creator of Hannibal Lecter, a *grand guignol* villain set in a gothic world of psychopathic violence. Harris is one of the few authors to be able to sell between 600,000 and 700,000 harbacks in Britain.

Sarah Harrison

b. 1946

The Flowers of the Field (1980)
A Flower That's Free (1984)
Hot Breath (1985)
An Imperfect Lady (1988)

Cold Feet (1989)
Forests of the Night (1991)
Foreign Parts (1992)
Be an Angel (1993)

Sarah Martyn was born in Devon on 7 August 1946. Having gained a degree at the University of London she married Jeremy Harrison in 1969, working as a journalist and raising a family.

Harrison's work combines family sagas with comic tales of the historical novelist 'Harriet Blair'. Harrison's first two books were set across nearly fifty years of the twentieth century, encompassing the First World War, the Suffragettes, etc., and detailing the lives of three generations caught up in the turbulence of the period. She returned to historical sagas with *An Imperfect Lady* (1988). *Forests of the Night* (1991) departed from both Harrison's earlier areas of interest to deal with male relationships and male sexual identity.

James Herbert

b. 1943

The Rats (1974)
The Fog (1975)
The Survivor (1976)
Fluke (1977)
The Spear (1978)
Lair (1979)
Shrine (1983)
Domain (1984)
The Magic Cottage (1986)
Sepulchre (1987)
Creed (1990)
The Ghosts of Sleath (1994)
and many collections of short stories

Along with Stephen King (*Carrie*, 1974), James Herbert helped re-invent the literary horror genre in the 1970s with his first book, *The Rats* (1974). This tale of a plague of mutant black rats drew heavily on old American nuclear disaster B-movies, horror comics and science-fiction television series such as *Quatermass*. The story is violent and erotic and mixes pastiche with a real horror sensibility. Stephen King (see entry) jokingly named the style that he and Herbert invented 'splatterpunk', but both rejected such easy thrills after their first book.

Herbert then turned to supernatural thrillers and may be considered a successor to Dennis Wheatley. Total sales neared forty million books by the late 1990s, but unlike the books of Stephen King few have been filmed.

Jack Higgins (Harry Patterson)

b. 1929

PSEUDONYMS: Martin Fallon; James Graham; Hugh Marlow

> *The Eagle has Landed* (1975)
> *Exocet* (1983)
> *Edge of Danger* (2001)
and many others

Patterson is one of the great World War Two espionage adventure writers. *The Eagle has Landed* (1975) centred on *Wehrmacht* commandoes attempting to kidnap Churchill. The plot also topically included the Irish Republican Army and thereby successfully updated the war novel by rewriting it as a 'terrorist' style tale, with a nod towards both current IRA activity in the United Kingdom and such daring raids as that by the Israeli army on Entebbe. It was during this period that the activities of secret anti-terror groups such as Mossad and the SAS became popular with the general public.* By 1979, *The Eagle has Landed* had sold 18 million copies in forty-two languages. The cliff-hanger thriller, combining excitement and swift moving action, proved one of the most endurable genres of the twentieth century.

Peter Hoeg

b. 1957

> *Miss Smilla's Feeling for Snow* (1993)

Hoeg is a Danish author with previous careers as an actor, dancer, drama teacher and a sailor, and whose first book, *Forstilling om det tyvende*

---

* *The Eagle has Landed* pre-dates the SAS assault on the Iranian Embassy in 1980.

arhundrede (1983) (translated as *The History of Danish Dreams*, 1995), tells the story of four families through dreams, spoof fairy-tales and contemporary documentary. The tale's experimental style mirrors the exploration of alienation and emptiness felt by the characters. Hoeg, himself, lives a reclusive life, allegedly without car, television or telephone.

From a first book, originally produced in only seven copies, Hoeg continued to write until *Froken Smillas fornemmelse for sne* (1993) was translated into English and became a surprise bestseller during 1995 (with continuous sales thereafter) in both Britain and the United States. Hoeg topped *The Observer* bestseller list during the same year with over 140,000 sales in the UK.

Marketed as a murder thriller amongst the small set of Scandinavia, the work is also concerned with the 'terror of modern life' set in an unforgiving landscape of snow and ice. The plot concerns Smilla Qaavigaaq Jaspersen, a 'half Inuit, half Danish glaciologist' who stumbles upon a mystery surrounding the death of a neighbour's child. Much of the novel also contains descriptions of Greenland allowing Smilla to be both detective and adventurer. The complexity of plotting, nature of the thematic concerns and seriousness of purpose may make *Miss Smilla* one of many bestsellers bought but never fully read.

Sheila Holland (Charlotte Lamb)

b. 1938   d. 2000

Follow a Stranger (1973)
and 159 others

Without doubt, Holland remains one of Britain's most successful and least known or regarded literary figures. Her writing is to popular contemporary romance what Catherine Cookson's is to the historical saga (see entry). Born in the East End of London and convent educated, Holland found work at the age of sixteen in the Bank of England. Later, she worked as a secretary at the BBC, her appetite for lunch-time romance-reading fuelling her own desire to participate in the genre. Using a variety of pen names to produce the type of romance she herself enjoyed, Holland finally wrote her first Mills and Boon novel, *Follow a Stranger* in 1973.

Significantly, writing as Charlotte Lamb allowed Holland to produce work that explored taboo areas such as child abuse and rape. Such concerns reflected the changes in women's social position and interests as well as providing entertainment for a generation who were more sexually aware and yet who still desired a certain conventionality. Holland's extraordinary output of 160 novels is not untypical of the professional writers who write for the romance industry. What remains of interest is that as Charlotte Lamb, Holland was able to find a voice as an independent writer and not just as an anonymous name amongst many others. By the time of her death she was the most famous and successful 'modern' romance writer of the second half of the twentieth century, with sales of 70 million and library borrowing in the hundreds of million.

Nick Hornby

b. 1957

Fever Pitch (1992)
High Fidelity (1995)
About a Boy (1999)

Hornby rose rapidly to fame on his autobiographical 'novel' about his memoirs of childhood, his love of football and the symbiotic relationship of the two. *Fever Pitch* (1992) was an extraordinary *coup*, summing up a world of memories and football enthusiasm shared by a whole generation of men between their early thirties and middle age, appealing to a spirit of new 'laddishness' and answering to a need for a male-centred sensibility outside the realm of feminism. Although not strictly fiction the book could be read as a novel of nostalgia. Hornby's film adaptation converted the book to a fictional narrative. *High Fidelity* (1995) was also filmed, but this time by Hollywood; the film of *About a Boy* appeared in 2002.

P(hyllis) D(orothy) James (White)

b. 1920

PSEUDONYM: P. D. James

Cover her Face (1962)
Shroud for a Nightingale (1971)
Death of an Expert Witness (1972)
And many others

James served as a nurse during the Second World War, after which she entered the National Health Service as an administrator for psychiatric units and thence became a Senior Civil Servant in the Home Office, where she worked for much of the rest of her life, rising to considerable seniority. She wrote her first novel in her thirties having cared for her invalid husband.

Cover her Face (1962) established James as a writer in the same tradition as Agatha Christie (see entry) and Dorothy L. Sayers – her own detective, Adam Dalgliesh, being both tragic and introspective. Her stories, such as *Shroud for a Nightingale* (1971), are often as much about institutions, bureaucracy and organisations as about detection; nevertheless, James has, alongside Colin Dexter (see entry), kept the traditional and conservative British detective genre alive into the twenty-first century.

Penny Jordan

b. 1946

Falcon's Prey (1981)
and over 100 other titles

Penny Jordan is one of a number of authors who work for Mills and Boon and who regularly outsell more conventional writers who nevertheless 'show' in bestseller lists. Working on novelettes of little more than 55,000 words, Jordan expects to finish a 'novel' every four to six weeks – a rate to be compared to novelists of the pre-World War One period or the 'anonymous' hack authors of the mushroom publishers just after World War Two.

Having married, worked in mundane jobs in insurance, two firms of solicitors and a bank, Jordan took up writing in 1976, publishing with Mills and Boon in 1981. Using 'only one plot' Jordan's romances are 'brand' bestsellers with over fifty million books sold.

Jordan is one of a number of romance writers to have found success through association with Mills and Boon. Such writers include **Mary Burchell** (Ida Cook, d. 1987) from the 1930s, **Denise Robins** (b. 1897, d. 1985), Sara Seale, Charlotte Lamb (Sheila Holland, see entry), Jane Fraser (Rosamunde Pilcher; see entry) and **Vanessa James** (Sally Beauman), who 'graduated' in order to be able to pursue less restrictive individual careers.

M(ary) M(argaret) Kaye

b. 1908

> *Shadow of the Moon* (1956)
> *The Far Pavilions* (1978)
> and detective novels including:
> *Death in Berlin* (1955)

Mary Kaye was born in Simla, India, on 21 August 1908. Educated in Somerset, she married Geoffrey Hamilton in 1942 and has two daughters. Kaye became a Fellow of the Royal Society of Literature.

Kaye's best known work centres on the conflict of identity suffered by those born in India and torn between two cultures, but they are also love stories and romance sagas set against exotic locations.

Leo Kessler

b. 1926

> 'Cossacks' series (1977–9)
> 'Otto Stahl' series (1981–4)
> 'Rommel' series (1979–81)
> 'Sea Wolves' series (1982)
> 'Storm Troop' series (1983–6)
> 'Stuka Squadron' series (1983–4)
> 'Wotan/Panzer Division' series (1975–86)

Although German by birth, Kessler came to Britain before World War Two and joined the army as a volunteer in 1943. Having studied in Britain and Germany he took up university positions in England and America, also acting as German correspondent for *The Times Educational Supplement*. In 1973 he became a full-time author.

Kessler's forte are war adventures written from the point of view of the German *Wehrmacht*, *Kriegsmarine* and *Luftwaffe*. These novels (published, like J. T. Edson's books and Mills and Boon, in popular paperback editions) created a vogue for stories about the war told by unwilling 'ordinary' soldiers caught up in the machinations of Nazi world domination. The stories were especially popular during the 1970s and 1980s and often concentrated on the SS or stormtroopers fighting against overwhelming odds. Kessler's work complemented the success enjoyed by writers such as **Sven Hassel** (Sven Pederson, b. 1917), whose *Wheels of Terror* (1959) documented the lives of soldiers in a German penal regiment.

Stephen King

b. 1947

PSEUDONYM: Richard Bachman

> *Carrie* (1974)
> *Salem's Lot* (1975)
> *The Shining* (1977)
> *Cujo* (1981)
> *Christine* (1983)
> *Pet Sematary* (1983)
> *Skeleton Crew* (1985)
> *It* (1986)
> *Misery* (1987)
> *The Tommyknockers* (1987)
> *The Dark Half* (1989)
> *Needful Things* (1992)
> *The Green Mile* (serial, 1996)

and many others

Stephen King was born in Portland, Maine, in 1947. Graduating with a qualification to teach in high school, he was unable to find work and produced short stories for men's magazines whilst taking casual employment. Once settled as a teacher, King continued writing and sold *Carrie* (1974) to Doubleday.

Alongside James Herbert (see entry), King reinvented the horror genre with his book *Carrie* (1974) and the subsequent Brian de Palma film adaptation (1976). King is without doubt the most significant horror writer since **H. P. Lovecraft** (d. 1937) and the most famous since Edgar Allan Poe (1809–49). Yet he is much more than that, for he is the best-selling American author of all time, a writer not only of novels and short stories, but also of comic-book scripts, films, television screenplays and Internet 'publications'. During the 1980s he enjoyed phenomenal success, becoming almost a one-man publishing industry in a way not seen since the first quarter of the century.

King has said of his own (early) works that they were often wilfully 'derivative', exercises in rewriting classic tales or scenarios. King is also insightful (and realistic) regarding the significance and limits of the horror genre formula as he pursues it.

> But horror fiction is really as Republican as a banker in a three-piece suit. The story is always the same in terms of its development. . . . I said that horror fiction was conservative and that it appeals to teenagers – the two things go together because teenagers are the most conservative people.[21]

This conservative position has been challenged by more radical horror writers such as **Clive Barker** (b. 1952), whose own writing might not have found such acceptance without King's ground-breaking work.

Judith Krantz (Judith Tarcher)

b. 1928
   Scruples (1978)
   Princess Daisy (1980)
   Mistral's Daughter (1983)
   I'll Take Manhattan (1986)
and others

Judith Krantz found fame with *Scruples* (1978) when she swapped from writing articles for magazines to novel writing. She is the queen of the 'sex and shopping' novel (also known as the 'shopping and fucking' novel) but she herself has remained happily married – 'a nice Jewish girl' as she calls herself.

> Shopping is a form of sex. . . . For many years if I was prevented from shopping for enough time . . . say a month . . . I got a yearning, itchy, jumping feeling. Even a short bout of good shopping can cure more ills than penicillin. *Scruples* was about the world's best boutique, and when it appeared, many people told me that owning a boutique was their dream and I'd unconsciously tapped into it.
>   In many ways owning clothes was a form of magical thinking. The sad fact is that I believed profoundly, from third grade on, that if I only had absolutely the right clothes and enough of them, all my problems of growing up would be solved. And a little part of me still thinks that, even though I realize it's not true.[22]

Krantz is one of a number of American writers including Stephen King (see entry) and Danielle Steel (see entry) who also have fan-oriented websites.

Some critics here recognised that Krantz's chosen genre may be more than the crude and valueless entertainment it seems to be.

> Certainly the derogatory label 'shopping and fucking novels' (S & F) does not suggest that the genre has any great weight. Yet there is value in both elements of the label.
>
> Shopping is relevant because the Krantz characters move in a designer milieu; the brand names, the shop names and the locations are important to establish that the characters move in circles which are themselves the stuff of fantasy, evidenced by the popular success of magazines which purport to lay bare the lifestyles of the rich and famous, to purvey a fantasy vision of what life is really like for the chosen few. Yet it is ultimately an egalitarian vision in a way – success is not dependent on unachievable imponderables, birth, family, history or even merit. Entry to the chosen few depends simply on wealth. . . .
>
> This kind of fantasy is the equivalent of the techno thrills in some adventure stories, the snobbish insistence on the right way to mix Bond's martini, and is surely neither more nor less reprehensible or trivial but rather a way of asserting control over an apparently hostile area of society. The traditional woman's role of shopper, selector of the products to be consumed by the rest of the family, burdened with this never-ending chore – this task is transformed in a Krantz novel into the ultimate consumer delight, where unlimited wealth offers unlimited opportunity to select indulgences in opulence and splendor. It is no accident that *Scruples*, Krantz's first and most successful book, is about a shop, the apotheosis of shops, the consumer's earthly paradise.
>
> The second half of the insulting 'S & F' label is also significant. Male fiction has described female sexuality and told us how we ought to feel, Krantz's sex scenes are idealized from a woman's viewpoint – aspirational rather than coercive, portraying what we might want for ourselves rather than what men think we ought to want.[23]

John le Carré (David Cornwell)

b. 1931

The Spy who Came in from the Cold (1963)
The Looking-Glass War (1965)

A Small Town in Germany (1968)
Smiley's People (1980)
The Honourable Schoolboy (1982)
The Little Drummer Girl (1983)
A Perfect Spy (1986)
The Russia House (1989)

Le Carré is, alongside Len Deighton (see entry), the most famous writer of contemporary British spy fiction, inheritor of the work of Buchan, Le Queux and Edgar Wallace (see entries) despite his more modern anti-heroic style. Although receiving numerous literary awards, le Carré has never been quite accepted as a writer of 'literature' by literary critics. This may come from his extraordinary success, especially with his third book *The Spy who Came in from the Cold* (1963), which had sold twenty million copies by the end of the twentieth century.

Robert Ludlum

b. 1927   d. 2000

The Scarlatti Inheritance (1971)
The Osterman Weekend (1972)
The Chancellor Manuscript (1977)
The Matarese Circle (1979)
The Bourne Identity (1980)
The Holcroft Covenant (1985)
The Bourne Supremacy (1986)
The Matarese Countdown (1997)

Prior to becoming a writer in 1971, Ludlum was a Broadway and television actor. His espionage tales have proved highly successful, some filmed and others being turned into television mini-series. One character, Jason Bourne, appears in a number of novels.

In many ways Ludlum inherits elements of both Ian Fleming (see entry) and Alistair MacLean (see entry), with comparisons made to John le Carré (see entry) and even Graham Greene. The interesting difference is that Ludlum's books have consistently reminded critics of films rather than novels, incorporating visual elements 'like watching a James Bond movie' (*Entertainment Weekly*). The complexity of plotting, the fast pace and erotic action as well as the obligatory exotic location and technical details helped Ludlum sell over 210 million books.

Colleen McCullough

b. 1937

Tim (1974)
The Thorn Birds (1977)
An Indecent Obsession (1981)

Colleen McCullough was born in 1937 in Wellington, New South Wales, Australia. McCullough spent much of her early adulthood in the Australian Outback working in a variety of jobs, such as a teacher, a library worker and a bus driver. Eventually she obtained a position as a medical technician and became an associate in neurological research at Yale (1967–76), all the while writing in the evenings. From 1976, she committed herself to writing full-time.

McCullough is best known for *The Thorn Birds* (1977). Common to her novels, plots touch on taboo subjects, like the mentally challenged in *Tim* (1974) and a priest's sexual desires in *The Thorn Birds*. Her strengths lie in turning cliché storylines into fresh plots. She often highlights the rebirth of dull or ordinary women into animated and extrovert people; however, her novels' themes are not particularly feminist. McCullough takes criticisms in her stride, commenting that as time passes, if her novels endure, then they can be deemed to be good literature.

Patrick O'Brian (Geoffrey Jenkins)

b. 1914   d. 2000

Master and Commander (1969)
Post Captain (1972)
HMS Surprise (1973)
The Mauritius Command (1977)
Desolation Island (1978)
Fortune of War (1979)
The Surgeon's Mate (1980)
The Ionian Mission (1982)
Treason's Harbour (1983)
The Far Side of the World (1985)
Reverse of the Medal (1986)
Letter of Marque (1988)
The Thirteen Gun Salute (1989)

When O'Brian died he was the focus of intense journalistic interest; a popular and unheralded teller of tales of Nelson's navy he seemed to exemplify intelligence in a genre not considered critically significant. He also had a personal background that intrigued the media. His fictional hero is Jack Aubrey.

Edith Pargeter (Ellis Peters)

b. 1913   d. 1995

> *A Morbid Taste for Bones* (1977)
> *A Leper of St Giles* (1981)
> *The Potter's Field* (1989)
and 17 others

Edith Pargeter remains one of the most successful of the classic 'queens' of crime, alongside P. D. James (see entry), Agatha Christie (see entry), Dorothy L. Sayers, Margery Allingham and Ruth Rendell (see entry). Despite the acclaim of the Cadfael series she was also the writer of contemporary crime fiction (Inspector Felse), historical novels and translations. Indeed, her translations from Czech won her the gold medal of the Czechoslovak Society for Foreign Relations, an award to be prized alongside those from the British Crime Writers' Association and the Mystery Writers of America (who awarded her an 'Edgar').

Pargeter is best known as Ellis Peters, creator of the medieval monk detective, Brother Cadfael. Cadfael lives in twelfth-century Shrewsbury. After a life of battle and adventure he has settled into the life of a monk (and expert herbalist) using his knowledge to act the detective in a way that combines contemporary interest in detective fiction with a taste for historically accurate medieval romance. It is hard to see how Peter's love of the medieval could have failed to influence the extraordinarily successful *Name of the Rose* (1983) by Umberto Eco.

Rosamunde Pilcher

b. 1924

PSEUDONYM: Jane Fraser

The Shell Seekers (1988)
and many others

Rosamunde Pilcher was born on 22 September 1924 in Lelant, Cornwall, England. She attended public schools in England and Wales. From 1942 to 1946 she was in the Women's Royal Naval Service. In 1946 she married a company director, Graham Hope Pilcher, and moved to Scotland.

Pilcher began her career with romantic novels, which she wrote under the pseudonym of Jane Fraser. These first novels provided the basis for Pilcher to write more complex historical romances and family sagas. In 1987 she finished what was considered her first serious novel, *The Shell Seekers*, about a woman looking back at her life. The novel was an immediate bestseller. *September* (1990), Pilcher's next novel, was centred on a family celebration in the Highlands of Scotland, told from the perspective of an older female member of the family. The book confirmed Pilcher's bestseller status in Britain and the United States. Her work was considered more serious and literary by ordinary readers who disdained sagas and romances.

Pilcher's books concentrate on older women coming to terms with loss or bereavement and ageing. They often end ambiguously rather than merely 'happily ever after'.

Dudley Pope (Bernard Egerton)

b. 1925   d. 1997

'Lord Nicholas Ramage' series:
  Ramage (1965)
  Ramage and the Drum Beat (1967)
  Ramage and the Freebooters (1969)
  Governor Ramage R.N. (1973)
  Ramage's Prize (1975)
  Ramage and the Guillotine (1975)
  Ramage at Trafalgar (1986)
and others

'Yorke' series:
 Buccaneer (1981)
and others

Egerton served in World War Two and was torpedoed during the Battle of the Atlantic. He was thus invalided out in 1943 to become instead Naval Defence correspondent for the *Evening News*. He left this job only in 1959 to become a full-time writer.

The Napoleonic era has proved to be the male equivalent of the Regency period for women's historical romance. It provides excitement, glamour, adventure, and nostalgia whilst avoiding the overt jingoism of imperialist romance. Despite the use of 'realistic' dialogue and period details the books are designed as escapist yarns whose feel is essentially contemporary. Pope combines detail, action and battles.

His series of buccaneering tales centring on Ned Yorke keeps alive the minor subgenre of pirate tales that includes Robert Louis Stevenson's *Treasure Island* (1883), J. Meade Falkner's *Moonfleet* (1898), Rafael Sabatini's *Captain Blood* (1922) and F. Tennyson Jesse's *Moonraker* (1927).

Terry Pratchett

b. 1948

The 'Discworld' series (27 books to date)
'Bromeliad' trilogy
Many science fiction titles

Terry Pratchett, born 28 April 1948 in Beaconsfield, England, is one of Britain's most recognisable, and most read, authors. Pratchett began his career working as a journalist in Buckinghamshire, Bristol, and Bath. He then worked for the Central Electricity Board in the Western Region from 1980 until 1987, though his true passion has always been writing novels. Pratchett wrote his first full-length work of fiction when he was seventeen and published it as *The Carpet People* in 1971. He received the British Book Award citation in 1993 as Fantasy and Science Fiction Author of the Year. However, Pratchett is best known for his popular Discworld series, which won him the British Science Fiction Award in 1989.

Discworld is a humorous fantasy series that depicts a world that rests on a turtle's back. Discworld, as well as most of Pratchett's other works, often parodies writers such as J. R. R. Tolkien (see entry) and Larry Niven. His novels spoof modern trends and New Age philosophy. J. K.

Rowling follows Pratchett's penchant for coining new and absurd words to create an alien parallel universe. The result in both cases is strikingly intimate novels as the reader feels connected to the author through a common understanding of a singular language.

It has been reported that Terry Pratchett is the most shop-lifted author at W. H. Smith's.

Claire Rayner

b. 1931

The 'Performers' series:
  12 novels (1973–87)

The 'Poppy Chronicles' series:
  6 novels (1987–91)

One of Britain's best loved and most remembered 'agony aunts', Rayner began her career as a nurse before turning to journalism. As with so many popular women's writers she began to write gothic romance before turning to the saga.

Douglas Reeman

b. 1924

PSEUDONYM: Alexander Kent

As Alexander Kent:
  Richard Bolitho – Midshipman (1966)
and others

As Douglas Reeman:
  A Prayer for the Ship (1958)
and others

A writer fascinated by the sea, Reeman joined the Royal Navy and saw action in World War Two in the Battle of the Atlantic, and the Mediterranean and Normandy campaigns. A keen sailor like Dudley Pope (see entry), Reeman is fascinated by the details of naval life and maritime history. As Alexander Kent he is the author of the 'Richard

Bolitho' series set during the Napoleonic War, and as Douglas Reeman he writes of the First and Second World Wars. His works are action adventures and he is probably the most popular latter day exponent of the naval saga.

Ruth Rendell

b. 1930

PSEUDONYM: Barbara Vine
'Inspector Wexford' series:
  From Doon with Death (1964)
  A New Lease of Death (1967)
  Wolf to the Slaughter (1968)
  The Best Man to Die (1969)
  A Guilty Thing Surprised (1970)
  No More Dying Then (1971)
  Murder being Once Done (1972)
  Some Lie and Some Die (1973)
and others

A very private individual, Rendell is nevertheless, probably the most famous British female crime writer after Agatha Christie (see entry). Her books use psychological insight, a greater level of realism, and police procedural style to create intimate and disturbing tales. As Barbara Vine she writes gothic tales as well as being the author of books whose central characters are psychologically motivated, a theme popular since Robert Bloch's *Psycho* (1959). Her 'Inspector Wexford' books have been regularly adapted for television.

J(oanna) K(athleen) Rowling

b. 1966

Harry Potter and the Philosopher's Stone (1997)
Harry Potter and the Chamber of Secrets (1998)
Harry Potter and the Prisoner of Azkaban (1999)
Harry Potter and the Goblet of Fire (2000)

Born in Chepstow, Rowling studied French and Classics at university before beginning her career as a teacher of English Language in Portugal where she met and married Jorge Arantes with whom she had a daughter. After her divorce, Rowling returned to Britain where she lived in Edinburgh, taught French and finished an adventure book for children featuring the orphan Harry Potter. Published in 1997, the book was intended as the first of seven, charting Potter's life and magical adventures. To obscure the fact that the author was a woman, Rowling's publishers persuaded her to use initials like J. R. R. Tolkien (see entry). The almost immediate success of the books and Rowling's extraordinary rise in fame and fortune is well documented. With the film version of the first book, Rowling rose to become Britain's highest paid author, surrounded by a whole Harry Potter industry.

The stories themselves are curiously conservative and traditional with their public school backgrounds reminiscent of Billy Bunter, Jennings or Mallory Towers and their wizardry suggestive of Tolkien and C. S. Lewis (two authors Rowling says she has no interest in, and both representative of a genre she consciously avoids). Even boarding-school life is also, curiously, a *bête noire* for the author. Nevertheless, with its magic railway, school adventures, fantasy and invented works, Rowling has been able to capture both a children's and an adult market with the books repackaged for 'grown up' readers. Unlike Tolkien, whose *Lord of the Rings* was an *adult* rethinking of *The Hobbit*, Rowling is the first author of children's work to be simultaneously read as an author for adults.

Salman Rushdie

b. 1947

Midnight's Children (1981)
The Satanic Verses (1988)

Educated at Cathedral School in Bombay and then King's College, Cambridge, Rushdie graduated in 1968 with a Masters degree in history. For a time he was an actor before becoming a freelance copy-editor in London between 1970 and 1980. The publication of *Midnight's Children* (1981) brought Rushdie to the wider public attention that his first book, *Grimus* (1979), lacked. Prizes, including Booker (1981), English Speaking Union Award (1981), James Tait Black Memorial Prize (1982) and many others followed for Rushdie's complex tales of Anglo-India told in a magic-realist style. *The Satanic Verses* (1988) was also short-listed for the Booker and the Whitbread Prize but was banned in India and South Africa. Nevertheless, this confirmed him as Britain's leading novelist.

> Rushdie's background seems to incline him naturally towards characters who inhabit the Borderline. One thinks of Omar Khayyam in *Shame*, 'a peripheral man': or that novel's narrator who, like Rushdie himself is 'an emigrant from one country' and 'a newcomer in two'; of Adam Aziz in *Midnight's Children*; and above all, of Saleem Sinai, born at the stroke of midnight on 15 August 1947, an Anglo-Indian, a changeling. In each of these novels, however, by centering the Borderline character as the 'I' narrator, the perspective is remade and Borderline territory is transformed into 'a strange middle country', a position of vantage from which the narrator tells his story, or, more accurately, his 'so many stories'.[24]

The publication of *The Satanic Verses* brought extraordinary (and extra literary) attention. In the book a rather infantile (but calculated) attack on the fundamentalism of one character overly reminiscent of the Ayatollah Khomeini brought the wrath of devout Muslims all the way from Pakistan to Bradford and the Iranian government pronounced a *fatwah* (or death sentence) on Rushdie and broke off diplomatic relations with Britain. Rioting caused the death of demonstrators in India and the book's Japanese translator was assassinated. Penguin Books and a syndicate of other publishers nevertheless published the paperback and Rushdie was given a bodyguard of Special Branch officers and went into hiding.

The cult status of *The Satanic Verses* meant that large numbers of ordinary readers purchased the book in order to see what the fuss was about. Few read much of it and it remained one of the great *unread* but heavily purchased books of the century.

Rushdie has long considered himself undervalued in Britain and a scathing attack on London life led him to relocate to New York. His high profile as a personality as well as a writer means that he lives the life of a socialite whose celebrity status is a guarantee of media publicity. Thus he has recently been seen as an 'extra' in the film version of *Bridget Jones's Diary* (2000).

Dora (Jessie) Saint (Miss Read)

b. 1913

Village School (1955)
Village Diary (1957)
Hobby Horse Cottage (1958)
Storm in the Village (1958)
Thrush Green (1959)
Fresh from the Country (1960)
Winter in Thrush Green (1961)
Village Affairs (1978)
Return to Thrush Green (1979)
Village Centenary (1981)

Dora Saint worked for many years as a primary school teacher turning first to short humorous articles about the profession, which she published with *Punch* before writing for *The Times Education Supplement* and later the BBC Schools Department. An article for the *Observer* caught the eye of publisher Robert Lusty of Michael Joseph, who suggested that she write a novel about life as a school teacher in the manner of the *Punch* articles. The subsequent book, *Village School* (1955), began a long-running saga of village life based on the fictional villages of Thrush Green and Fairacre and the gentle goings-on of the inhabitants. By the late 1990s more than 50 novels had appeared and Saint (to whom Lusty had suggested the rather prim Jane Austen-like name 'Miss Read') became one of the most borrowed authors in the library system. Written to evoke happy, nostalgic and traditional thoughts, Saint's books have created an entire country 'universe' similar to that of the long-running BBC serial *The Archers*.

A curious bonus in her work is the inclusion of illustrations by John Strickland Goodall, continuing an almost lost tradition of combining adult fiction with pictures.

Tom Sharpe

b. 1928

'Wilt' series:
> *Wilt* (1976)
> *The Wilt Alternative* (1979)
> *Wilt on High* (1984)

Also:
> *Riotous Assembly* (1971)
> *Indecent Exposure* (1973)
> *Porterhouse Blue* (1974)
> *Blott on the Landscape* (1975)
> *Vintage Stuff* (1982)

and others

Tom Sharpe was educated at Lancing College and at Pembroke College, Cambridge, before doing National Service and then emigrating to South Africa as a social worker and teacher. Deported from South Africa he took up lecturing at the Cambridge College of Arts and Technology.

Sharpe's amusing tales of college teaching were recorded in *Wilt* (1976), filmed using Middlesex University premises. His books, many of which have been made into television series, sum up a type of farcical awfulness amid slapstick belly laughs.

Sarah Shears

b. 1910(?)   d. 2001
'Courage' series (1973–7)
'Louise' series (1975–7)
'Annie Parsons' series (1978–80)
'The Neighbours' series (1982–6)
'The Village' series (1984–6)
   The Landlady (1980)
   Deborah Hammond (1981)
   The Apprentice (1981)
   The Old Woman (1987)
   The Sisters (1988)

Born in Kent at the start of the century, Shears was forced to leave school at fourteen and was then apprenticed as a post-office clerk before drifting between numerous other jobs as a nanny, gardener, housekeeper and housemaid. Whilst working, she wrote children's books and magazine articles but continued to find her main income first from a job in sales and then as a warden of an old people's home. Her writing took over on her retirement and her tales of country life and ordinary family events make her popular with older women readers who dislike the 'racier' women's romances.

Sidney Sheldon

b. 1917

   The Other Side of Midnight (1974)
   Bloodline (1977)
   Rage of Angels (1980)
   If Tomorrow Comes (1985)
   Memories of Midnight (1990)
   The Stars Shine Down (1992)
   The Sky is falling (2001)
and many others

Sheldon was a writer/producer of such television programmes as 'I Dream of Jeannie' and 'Hart to Hart' before becoming a novelist at the age of 53. His first novel, *The Naked Face* (1970), immediately won Best

First Mystery Novel of the Year but sold few copies, whereas his second attempt, in the glamour-novel style and featuring a strong, resourceful and beautiful heroine, sold 7 million paperbacks – it was called *The Other Side of Midnight* (1974). By 1991, Sheldon was in competition for the title of most read author in the world with stories that were essentially implausible but exciting melodramas.

Danielle Steel

b. 1947

> *Going Home* (1973)
> *The Promise* (1978)
> *The Ring* (1980)
> *Loving* (1980)
> *To Love Again* (1980)
> *A Perfect Stranger* (1982)
> *Once in a Lifetime* (1982)
> *Secrets* (1985)
> *Fine Things* (1987)
> *Star* (1989)
> *Daddy* (1989)
> *Heartbeat* (1991)
> *The Long Road Home* (1998)
> *Mirror Image* (1998)

Born in New York and educated at New York University and in Europe, Steel began her working life in public relations before turning to full-time authorship in 1973.

> She is undoubtedly the most popular writer in the [glamour] genre, and the most prolific. Her stories are about rich and privileged women, whose characters are explored in some depth. However, they invariably tire of life in high society, and long for fulfillment in the creative arts. All suffer some dramatic experience of tragedy which changes their lifestyle and strengthens their character. Danielle Steel uses the same plot over and over again, changing the locations and the characters, but still manages to retain credibility. After Catherine Cookson, Steel is the most borrowed woman writer in the British library system.[24]

Jessica Stirling (Peggy Coughlan and Hugh C. Rae)

Series:
'The Stalker Family Trilogy'
'Holly Beckman Trilogy'
'The Patterson Family Trilogy'

'Jessica Sterling' is the name used by Peggy Coghlan (b. 1920) and Hugh C. Rae (b. 1935), two Glasgow writers who produced popular family sagas centred on Scotland and the East End of London.

Craig Thomas

b. 1942

Rat Trap (1976)
Firefox (1977)
Wolfsbane (1978)
Snow Falcon (1979)
Firefox Down (1983)
and many more

Born in Cardiff, Thomas graduated from University College in 1967 to become a teacher. Like other writers of technological thrillers, Thomas's work deals with international plots, exciting settings and adventure.

Rat Trap (1976), Thomas's first novel, is an 'aircraft hijack' thriller using a cast of Middle Eastern terrorists. As with Tom Clancy (see entry) or Michael Crichton (see entry), Thomas utilises current politics and technological fears (in this case 1970s terrorism) in order to make his narrative sufficiently plausible and relevant. *Firefox* (1977) established Thomas as a techno-thriller writer but fans consider his work more subtly nuanced with greater care paid to characterisation and narrative. The story of *Firefox* dealt with the 'theft' of a MIG-31 Firefox during the height of late 1970s Cold War concerns. A film staring Clint Eastwood followed and the narrative is taken up again in *Firefox Down* (1983). Thomas uses a number of re-occurring characters throughout his novels.

Sue Townsend

b. 1946

The Secret Diary of Adrian Mole (1985)
The Queen and I (1991)

Born and brought up in Leicester, Townsend worked in a number of jobs including in a factory, as a shop assistant and in a garage before finding success with writing. She won the Thames Television playwright's award which was followed by the first of a series of books detailing the life and loves of Adrian Mole, a self-knowing but troubled teenager. *The Queen and I* (1991), a comic novel in which the Royal Family end up in a Leicester Council estate, was also made into a play whilst the Adrian Mole stories formed the basis of a successful television series. Townsend's use of comic 'diaries' forms a link to the success of Helen Fielding's *Bridget Jones's Diary* (1996), and her ability to find a simultaneous readership of both younger and older readers presaged the later success of J. K. Rowling (see entry).

Joanna Trollope (Joanna Potter)

b. 1943

PSEUDONYM: Caroline Harvey

Eliza Stanhope (1978)
Parson Harding's Daughter (1979)
The Choir (1988)
A Village Affair (1989)
A Passionate Man (1990)
The Rector's Wife (1991)
Legacy of Love (1992)
and many others

Trollope began her working life as a teacher, having graduated from St Hugh's College, Oxford. A winner of the Romantic Novelists' Association Major Award in 1980, her historical and contemporary romances are identified with the 'Aga saga' style: intrigue, sexual dalliance and hidden family secrets behind the curtains, all in apparently idyllic rural settings.

Alice Walker

b. 1944

> *The Third Life of Grange Copeland* (1970)
> *Meridian* (1976)
> *The Color Purple* (1982)

Walker was born in Eatonton, Georgia, the last of eight children born to sharecropping parents. The poverty created by this new 'slavery' deeply affected her outlook on life. Injured by a chance BB gun pellet hitting her eye (a problem later corrected), Walker was nevertheless able to go to Spelman College on a disabled student bursary, whence she transferred to Sarah Lawrence College. Here her writing talent was discovered but pregnancy and facial disfigurement left her lonely and suicidal. A coincidental trip to Africa led to her first collection of poems (*Once*, 1968). Several more volumes of poetry followed.

The Third Life of Grange Copeland (1970) was her first novel and dealt with the humiliation of the black exploited population of the South – a theme that crystallised around the fate of black women. *Meridian* (1976) chronicled civil rights protests but it was with *The Color Purple* (1982), a story of violence, abusive relationships and the hostility of black men towards their wives and daughters, that she found world-wide bestsellerdom. Her heroine Celie, a victim of incest and abuse, finds not only new hope by the book's end but also lesbian love. Promoted as an insight into the black American psyche the book was promoted on chat shows, especially as the choice of the highly influential television presenter Oprah Winfrey, and made into a film by Steven Spielberg. To date over half a million copies have been bought in the United Kingdom alone. A writer, academic and activist, Walker is also the recipient of numerous international awards, mostly for *The Color Purple*.

Irvine Welsh

b. 1961

> *Trainspotting* (1993)
> *The Acid House* (short stories) (1994)
> *Marabou Stork Nightmares* (1995)
> *Ecstasy* (1996)
> *Filth* (1998)
> *Glue* (2002)

Irvine Welsh was part of an incredible revival of Scottish national literature at the end of the twentieth century leading up to devolution. Like the novelist James Kelman and the playwright Liz Lochhead he has no use for the romanticism of the Highlands, preferring instead the hard realist tones of working-class slang and drug-culture aggression. *Trainspotting* (1993), although originally a series of short stories/ sketches, became one of the greatest cult books of the last decade of the twentieth century with a new poetics brought from the violent language of Edinburgh's heroin-addicted underclass.

> He pierces her flesh and injects a wee bit slowly, before sucking blood back intae the chamber. Her lips are quivering as she gazes pleadingly at him for a second or two. Sick Boy's face looks ugly, leering and reptilian, before he slams the cocktail toward her brain.
>
> She pulls back her heid, shuts her eyes and opens her mooth, givin oot an orgasmic groan. Sick Boy's eyes are now innocent and full ay wonder, his expression like a bairn thit's come through oan Christmas morning tae a pile ay gift-wrapped presents stacked under the tree. They baith look strangely beautiful and pure in the flickering candlelight.
>
> – That beats any meat injection . . . that beats any fuckin cock in the world . . . Ali gasps, completely serious. It unnerves us tae the extent that ah feel ma ain genitals through ma troosers tae see if they're still their. Touchin masel like that makes us feel queasy though.
>
> *(Trainspotting*: 'the Skag Boys')

Mary Wesley

b. 1912

PSEUDONYM: Mary Aline Farmer

The Camomile Lawn (1984)
Harnessing Peacocks (1985)
The Vacillations of Polly Carew (1986)
Not That Sort of Girl (1988)
Second Fiddle (1988)
A Sensible Life (1990)
A Dubious Legacy (1992)
An Imaginative Experience (1994)
Part of the Furniture (1997)

Wesley was born in Surrey, England, the daughter of Violet and Colonel Harold Mynors. After an education with numerous governesses, she was able to secure a place at Queen's College, London (1928 to 1930) and then at the London School of Economics (1931 to 1932), going on later to have a career in the Civil Service. After her divorce from Charles Eady (Lord Swinfen) she married another writer, Eric Siepmann, in 1952, although he died in 1971.

Her books included works for children such as *The Sixth Seal* (1969) before she turned to adult fiction, combining in novels of manners quirky plots and darkly humorous incidents amongst the middle classes.

Phyllis A. Whitney

b. 1903

Red is for Murder (1943) and many others

Born in Yokohama of American parents, Whitney was fifteen years old when she moved to the United States. After graduating, she began writing stories for pulp magazines and worked as a children's librarian in Chicago. She combined a dual career as a highly popular mystery writer for young people as well as a short-story writer and novelist for adults.

Gothic settings are favoured by Whitney, who combines such elements with the thriller to produce atmospheric women's romances. The combination proved irresistible and put her in the top 100 writers regularly borrowed from British libraries during the 1980s – a matter of significance because her work was first published in America and she had to wait some years to find popularity in Great Britain. Her first book, *The Red Carnelian* [*Red is for Murder*] (published first in 1943) had to wait until 1976 to be published in the United Kingdom once her popularity had been established. From the late 1960s onwards her work was published on both sides of the Atlantic and made her the 'reigning queen of gothic' (*New York Times*), President of the Mystery Writers of America, and helped sell 50 million copies of her books.

Appendix 1
Number of individuals out of every 1000 who could not sign their name on a marriage register: 1896–1907

	Male	Female	Total
1896–1900	32	37	69
1901–1905	20	24	44
1905–1907	27	27	54

Appendix 2
Extract from Beatrice Harraden, 'What Our Soldiers Read', *Cornhill Magazine*, vol. XLI (Nov. 1916)

Turning aside from technical subjects to literature in general, I would like to say that although we have not ever attempted to force good books on our soldiers, we have of course taken great care to place them within their reach. And it is not an illusion to say that when the men once begin on a better class of book, they do not as a rule return to the old stuff which formerly constituted their whole range of reading. My own impression is that they read rubbish because they have had no one to tell them what to read. Stevenson, for instance, has lifted many a young soldier in our hospital on to a higher plane of reading whence he has looked down with something like scorn – which is really very funny – on his former favourites. For that group of readers, 'Treasure Island' has been a discovery in more senses than one, and to the librarians a boon unspeakable.

We have had, however, a large number of men who in any case care for good literature, and indeed would read nothing else. Needless to say, we have had special pleasure in trying to find them some book which they would be sure to like and which was already in our collection, or else in buying it, and thus adding to our stock. The publishers, too, have been most generous in sending us any current book which has aroused public interest and on which we have set our hearts. For we have tried to acquire not only standard works, but books of the moment bearing on the war, and other subjects too.

The following are items from two or three of our order books. The order books have been chosen at random, but the items are consecutive; and the list will give some idea of the nature of our pilgrimages from one bedside to another bedside, and from one ward to another.

One of Nat Gould's novels; Regiments at the Front; Burns's Poems; A book on bird life; 'The Last Days of Pompeii', *Strand Magazine*; *Wide World Magazine*; *The Spectator*; A scientific book; *Review of Reviews*; 'By the Wish of a Woman' (Marchmont); one of Rider Haggard's; Marie Corelli [sic]; Nat Gould; Rider Haggard; Nat Gould; Nat Gould; Nat Gould; Good detective story; Something to make you laugh; *Strand Magazine*; Adventure story; 'Tale of Two Cities'; 'Gil Blas'; Browning's Poems; Tolstoy's 'Resurrection'; Sexton Blake; 'Scarlet Pimpernel', Nat Gould; *Wide World Magazine*; *Pearson's Magazine*; 'Arabian Nights'; Jack London Shakespeare; Nat Gould; 'The Encyclopedia'; Rex Beach; Wm. Le Queux; *Strand Magazine*; Nat Gould; Something in the murder line; *Country Life*; *The Story Teller Magazine*; one of Oppenheim's novels; 'The Crown of Wild Olive'; 'Kidnapped'; Nat Gould; Shakespeare; Nat Gould; Silas Hocking; Oppenheim; Le Queux; Nat Gould; Nat Gould; Jack London; 'Handy Andy'; 'Kidnapped'; 'Treasure Island'; Book about rose growing; 'Montezuma's Daughter' (Rider Haggard); 'Prisoner of Zenda'; Macaulay's Essays; 'The Magnetic North' (Elizabeth Robins); Nat Gould;

Sexton Blake; Modern High Explosives; 'Dawn' (Rider Haggard); 'Wild Animals'; Book on horse-breaking; 'Radiography'; 'Freckles' (by Gene Stratton-Porter); 'The Blue Lagoon'; 'Caged Birds'; 'The Corsican Brothers'; 'Sherlock Holmes'; French Dictionary; Kipling; 'Mysticism'; Nat Gould; 'Pilgrim's Progress'; 'Mystery of Cloomber' (Conan Doyle); and so on.

These are, of course, only a few items. I should say that on the whole, and leaving out entirely books on technical and special subjects, the authors most frequently asked for are: Nat Gould, Charles Garvice, Wm. Le Queux, Rider Haggard, Guy Boothby, Oppenheim, Rex Beach, Conan Doyle, Marie Corelli, Joseph and Silas Hocking, Jack London, Dickens, Mrs. Henry Wood, Kipling (whose 'Barrack Room Ballads' they learnt by heart), Dumas, Ian Hay, Baroness Orczy, and Hornung's Raffles.

And very favourite books are those dealing with wild animals and their habits, with ferrets, rats, and birds, and all stories of adventure and travel, and of course detective stories.

Appendix 3
Booksellers from whose returns the *Bookseller* compiled its bestseller list during the 1930s and 1940s under the title 'What the Other Fellow is Selling'

London, W1: J. & E. Bumpus, Ltd
London, EC4: A. & F. Denny, Ltd
London, WC2: W. & G. Foyle, Ltd
London, EC4: Jones and Evans
 Bookshop, Ltd
London, SW7: Lamley & Co.
London, SWI: Hugh Rees, Ltd
London, W1: Selfridge's Book Dept
London, WC2: W. H. Smith & Son,
 Ltd.
London, W1: Times Book Club
London, W1: F. J. Ward
London, W2: Wm Whitely, Ltd
London, EC3: Alfred Wilson, Ltd
Belfast, W. Erskine Mayne
Bristol: Wm George's Sons, Ltd
Cambridge: Bowes & Bowes
Cambridge: Deighton Bell & Co., Ltd
Cambridge. W. Heffer & Sons, Ltd
Cheltenham Spa: Banks of
 Cheltenham, Ltd
Chester: Philipson & Golder
Dublin: Eason & Son, Ltd
Durham: House of Andrews
Edinburgh: Andrew Elliot
Exeter: A. Wheaton & Co., Ltd

Glasgow: John Smith & Son
 (Glasgow), Ltd
Glasgow: W. & R. Holmes
Glasgow: Jackson, Son & Co.
Guildford: Biddles, Ltd
Hanley: Webberley, Ltd
Hove: Combridges
Hull: A. Brown & Sons
Ipswich: W. E. Harrison & Sons
Liverpool: Philip, Son & Nephew
Liverpool: Henry Young & Sons, Ltd
Manchester: W. H. Willshaw
Newcastle-on-Tyne. Mawson, Swan &
 M., Ltd.
Norwich: Jarrold & Sons, Ltd
Nottingham: Henry B. Saxton
Oldham: J. A. Bardsley, Ltd
Oxford: Basil Blackwell, Ltd
Oxford: Slatter & Rose, Ltd
Ramsgate: Blinko & Sons, Ltd
Rugby: George Over, Ltd
St Andrews: W. C. Henderson & Son,
 Ltd
Seaford: Ronald Gibson
Sheffield: A. B. Ward
Swansea: Morgan & Higgs, Ltd

Appendix 4
From the Mass Observation
Archive (ref. FR 2537): 'Reading in
Tottenham, November 1947'

Lists of fiction subjects were shown to all those questioned (as with non-fiction subjects) and their comments were invited. Some of these are:

On love stories:

'I like old fashioned novels. Love and happy endings I suppose – by big writers.'
'I remember queuing up after the last war to get two books, one called 'This Freedom'; and 'If Winter Comes'. There's been nothing like them since, only 'Gone with the Wind'. I liked that, but there's no *big* books by *big* writers, is there?' (Housewife, aged over 41, elementary education)

'I don't like modern books at all, especially love stories – they're too trashy and they're unpleasant and they've got no story in them – they're not a patch on the old ones that kept you interested – something happening all the way through.' (Housekeeper, aged over 41, single)

On horror stories:

'I love them horror stories. Sort of make yer creep they do, and those detective stories. Real clever some of them are. The men as write them must have brains, some of 'em. 'Cos, some of them aren't worth the paper they're written on. It gets yer out of yerself as you might say when you read a good one and it makes yer think.' (Woman, sugar boiler, aged over 41, elementary education.)

On adventure:

'I buy those westerns and thrillers they sell in the shops, you know, about a bob apiece.' (Youth, 16–20 yrs, engineering worker, elementary education)

On fiction in general:

'Like books on philosophical problems – horror stories bore me to tears. I like reading books about men who have created changes – when you read books like that you pick up such a lot of facts.' (Man, aged over 41, local govt official, secondary ed.)

'I read mystery stories for amusement. . . . I've read several American stories about white men and niggers [*sic*].' (Man, aged 21–40, photographic block-maker, secondary education)

'I don't like my love stories too sloppy, though like some books are, and I like to be able to guess who committed the murder and sometimes I look at the end. I know I shouldn't but I often do.' (Woman, aged 21–40, elementary education)

'I like a good mystery story and I like adventure stories very much. I've had some very good books from the library round here. I've belonged to it so long that I've read nearly all the books. I like a good book like 'Gone with the Wind' and other picture novels but they're hard to find really. They say, like everything else, a good book's hard to find.' (Man, corporation worker, aged 21–40, secondary ed.)

Favourite fiction subject

When asked to give their favourite fiction subject (as opposed to saying which were of interest) the largest proportion plumped for 'Detective and mystery' – three people in every ten. It will be remembered that 'Travel and adventure', the most popular non-fiction subject, was the favourite of less than one in ten, and was *of interest* only to three in ten. The second most popular fiction subject is 'Love': this is just half as popular as 'Detection and mystery', but then it appeals only to the female half of the population. Historical stories are the next most popular, and then short stories. It is interesting to compare subjects of interest with subjects preferred: subjects were mentioned in the following order, the percentage mentioning them is given in brackets after:

Of Interest	*Preferred*
Detection (60%)	Detection (30%)
Short stories (35%)	Love (15%)
Love (34%)	Historical (10%)
Adventure (31%)	Short stories (9%)
Funny (30%)	Adventure (7%)
Historical (27%)	Funny (6%)
Horror (21%)	
Others mentioned by less than one in five	Others mentioned by less than one in twenty

Although the percentages of people in any social group preferring any subject is necessarily small, some interesting facts emerge. For instance, those people who are married without young children are very much more interested in love stories than the single people – but love stories are more frequently mentioned as their favourite subject by the single group; that is, though fewer single people like love stories, those who do are more vehement in their affection. Those with young children seldom say they like love stories best and are very much more interested in detection.

Favourite subjects show many of the same variations as subjects of interest – interest in detection, love and adventure decreases with class and education: interest in history and humour increases. Why humorous books should be so much the prerogative of the middle-class is hard to explain.

The feminine interest in love stories is even more marked when it comes to making the choice of one favourite – they are the favourite of more than a quarter of the women, and of only one man in a hundred. They are more popular with women at home than those in jobs, but since women in jobs care little for detective stories, love stories are still their favourite form of fiction. Women in jobs show an extremely high degree of interest in historical stories – possible they think of the romantic historical novel of the 'Gone with the Wind' or 'Forever Amber' type.

Enthusiasm for detective stories, love and adventure declines slightly with distance from the library – perhaps this is fortuitous, perhaps it is a revolt against the books in the 2d. library on which an increasing proportion depend.

There is considerable discrepancy between the favourite subjects of those who read mainly non-fiction and the rest. Among non-fiction readers, detective stories are still the most popular, but by a very short head, and they are chosen by less than two in ten. Short stories are next in importance, then historical subjects, then funny or satirical books; no other subject is mentioned more than once in ten replies. Love stories come very low on the list – they are mentioned only by one person in a hundred. The biggest difference between the two groups is the drop in the interest in detective and love stories among the non-fiction readers, which is compensated for by a slight increase in interest in almost all other subjects.

Library members show little peculiarity in their fiction tastes – they are a little less interested in detection, love and short stories and rather more interested in adventure stories and historical subjects, but the differences are small. The greatest interest in adventure stories is a little unexpected, but the numbers of detective and love stories in 2d. libraries probably explains why these are read more often by those outside the Public Library.

Those least interested in detective stories are the book-buyers, but they are mainly middle-class people. . . . Love stories are also popular with those who favour indoor activities and hobbies – perhaps these are the quiet and unadventurous people, looking for restful light reading. Historical novels are popular with cinema-goers – the influence of the costume drama – and short stories with those who like gardening and sport, and those who have no spare time.

Fiction authors

The names quoted were very scattered, and no one author was mentioned by as many as one person in ten. The name most frequently given was that of Edgar Wallace, mentioned by not quite one in ten: this, of course, is due to the popularity of detective and mystery stories. Since Wallace has been dead for some years it is interesting that he is still the favourite in spite of a flood of similar stories since his death. The next most popular detective story writer is Agatha Christie, who comes sixth on the list of authors, and who is mentioned by about 3%. She represents the more modern type of writer, but she is only slightly more popular than the old-fashioned – Conan Doyle – ninth on the list and mentioned by 2%. Leslie Charteris, author of the 'Saint' books is equally popular. The author second most frequently mentioned is Charles Dickens, but third and fourth come the representatives of the good old-fashioned love story – Ethel M. Dell and Ruby N. Ayres [*sic*]. Naomi Jacob, whose stories are more of a family type, comes next, although this kind of book is considerably less popular.

Between Christie and Conan Doyle come Zane Grey and P. G. Wodehouse, then Charteris and W. W. Jacobs. After this came the more 'highbrow' names, in this order – Shaw, Priestley, Wells, A. J. Cronin, Dumas, Edgar Allen Poe [*sic*], Scott, Hugh Walpole, G. K. Chesterton, John Galsworthy, Dorothy Sayers and Shakespeare. Three less 'highbrow' names are mentioned equally frequently – Sax Rohmer, Rafael Sabatini and Warwick Deeping. All other authors were mentioned by less than 1%.

The numbers are too small to make class, age or other breakdowns reliable.

Appendix 5
From Mills and Boon, 'A FINE ROMANCE . . . is hard to find!'

Every Mills & Boon reader and every aspiring Mills & Boon writer has a very clear picture of what makes our books so successful. . . .

We believe that the so-called formula is only the beginning, that originality, imagination and individuality are the most important qualities in a romance writer. . . .

Each of our authors must possess an individual touch, her own particular way of telling a story, and this quality is vital. . . . The story doesn't necessarily have to be complicated – in fact, a simple tale introducing only a few characters besides the hero and heroine is often very successful. Make sure, however, that the characters are convincing. . . . A would-be writer should be aware all the time of everyday patterns of speech, and should try to make the characters as true to life as possible. . . .

All Mills & Boon authors spend a good deal of time checking the material used in their books, because they realise how quickly the recognition of a fault or inaccuracy can spoil the reader's enjoyment of a scene. . . .

When attempting a Mills & Boon novel, concentrate on writing a good book rather than a saleable proposition. A good book sells itself and is good indefinitely, while a 'saleable proposition' tends to be based on what is saleable at the time of writing – even if a publisher snaps it up, the world will have moved on by at least nine months by the time it finally appears. Think of what you, as a reader, would like to read. . . .

Appendix 6
British Library loans, 1987–8, showing the top 100 authors as recorded by the *Bookseller* (13 July 1990)

Top 10 adult fiction authors (by alphabetical order)

Agatha Christie	Ed McBain
Catherine Cookson	Alistair MacLean
Dick Francis	Ruth Rendell
Jack Higgins	Wilbur Smith
Victoria Holt	Danielle Steel

Top 100 adult fiction authors (by alphabetical order)

Ted Allbeury	J. T. Edson	Alexander Kent
Charlotte Vale Allen	Elizabeth Ferrars	Stephen King
Margery Allingham	Colin Forbes	Louis L'Amour
Lucilla Andrews	Helen Forrester	Charlotte Lamb
Virginia Andrews	Frederick Forsyth	Norah Lofts
Evelyn Anthony	Dick Francis	Robert Ludlum
Jeffrey Archer	Alexander Fullerton	Helen MacInnes
Desmond Bagley	John Gardner	Alistair MacLean
Barbara Taylor Bradford	Catherine Gaskin	Ngaio Marsh
Iris Bromige	Michael Gilbert	Graham Masterson
Elizabeth Cadell	Winston Graham	Anne Mather
Victor Canning	Graham Greene	Daphne du Maurier
Philippa Carr	John Harris	Ed McBain
John le Carré	James Herbert	Philip McCutchan
Barbara Cartland	Georgette Heyer	Carole Mortimer
James Hadley Chase	Jack Higgins	Maisie Mosco
Agatha Christie	Patricia Highsmith	Betty Neels
Jon Cleary	Jane Aitken Hodge	Christopher Nicole
Virginia Coffman	Victoria Holt	Pamela Oldfield
Jackie Collins	Hammond Innes	Ellis Peters
Catherine Cookson	Michael Innes	Jean Plaidy
Jilly Cooper	Brenda Jagger	Dudley Pope
Sara Craven	P. D. James	Anthony Price
Janet Dailey	Penny Jordan	Claire Rayner
Len Deighton	Marie Joseph	Miss Read
R. F. Delderfield	M. M. Kaye	Douglas Reeman
Dorothy Eden	Lena Kennedy	Ruth Rendell

Harold Robbins
Denise Robins
Tom Sharpe
Sarah Shears
Sidney Sheldon
Nevil Shute
Helen Van Slyke

Wilbur Smith
Danielle Steel
Jessica Steel
Mary Stewart
Jessica Sterling
Leslie Thomas
E. V. Thompson

John Wainwright
Phyllis A. Whitney
Kate Williams
Sara Woods
Margaret Yorke

Appendix 7
Comparative library loans between 1988 and 1998 by genre

Registered Loans by Category (%)

	1988–89	1997–98
Adult Fiction		
General Fiction	17.8	22.1
Historical	3.5	2.9
Mystery and Detection	12.8	12.8
Horror	0.7	0.4
Science Fiction	0.8	0.8
War	1.8	1.3
Humour	0.7	0.2
Light Romance	14.1	10.6
Westerns	1.2	0.7
Short Stories	0.5	0.2
Total	53.9	52.0

Source: Public Lending Right, 1999.

Appendix 8
Waterstone's and Channel 4's survey to discover the greatest books of the twentieth century (1996): the following are the top works of fiction

1. *Lord of the Rings* (J. R. R. Tolkien)
2. *Nineteen Eighty-Four* (George Orwell)
3. *Animal Farm* (George Orwell)
4. *Ulysses* (James Joyce)
5. *Catch-22* (Joseph Heller)
6. *The Catcher in the Rye* (J. D. Salinger)
7. *To Kill a Mockingbird* (Harper Lee)
8. *One Hundred Years of Solitude* (Gabriel García Márquez)
9. *The Grapes of Wrath* (John Steinbeck)
10. *Trainspotting* (Irving Welsh)
11. *The Wild Swans* (Jung Chang)
12. *The Great Gatsby* (F. Scott Fitzgerald)
13. *Lord of the Flies* (William Golding)
14. *On the Road* (Jack Kerouac)
15. *Brave New World* (Aldous Huxley)
16. *The Wind in the Willows* (Kenneth Grahame)
17. *The Color Purple* (Alice Walker)
18. *The Hobbit* (J. R. R. Tolkien)
19. *The Outsider* (Albert Camus)
20. *The Trial* (Franz Kafka)
21. *Gone with the Wind* (Margaret Mitchell)
22. *The Hitch Hiker's Guide to the Galaxy* (Douglas Adams)
23. *Midnight's Children* (Salman Rushdie)
24. *A Clockwork Orange* (Anthony Burgess)
25. *Sons and Lovers* (D. H. Lawrence)
26. *To the Lighthouse* (Virginia Woolf)
27. *If This is a Man* (Primo Levi)
28. *Lolita* (Vladimir Nabokov)
29. *The Wasp Factory* (Iain Banks)
30. *Remembrance of Things Past* (Marcel Proust)
31. *Of Mice and Men* (John Steinbeck)
32. *Beloved* (Toni Morrison)
33. *Possession* (A. S. Byatt)
34. *Heart of Darkness* (Joseph Conrad)
35. *A Passage to India* (E. M. Forster)

36. *Watership Down* (Richard Adams)
37. *Sophie's World* (Jostein Gaarder)
38. *The Name of the Rose* (Umberto Eco)
39. *Love in the Time of Cholera* (Gabriel García Márquez)
40. *Rebecca* (Daphne du Maurier)
41. *The Remains of the Day* (Kazuo Ishiguro)
42. *The Unbearable Lightness of Being* (Milan Kundera)
43. *Birdsong* (Sebastian Faulks)
44. *Howard's End* (E. M. Forster)
45. *Brideshead Revisited* (Evelyn Waugh)
46. *A Suitable Boy* (Vikram Seth)
47. *Dune* (Frank Herbert)
48. *A Prayer for Owen Meany* (John Irving)
49. *Perfume* (Patrick Suskind)
50. *Doctor Zhivago* (Boris Pasternak)
51. *Gormenghast Trilogy* (Mervyn Peake)
52. *Cider with Rosie* (Laurie Lee)
53. *The Bell Jar* (Sylvia Plath)
54. *The Handmaid's Tale* (Margaret Atwood)
55. *The Magus* (John Fowles)
56. *Brighton Rock* (Graham Greene)
57. *The Ragged-Trousered Philanthropists* (Robert Tressell)
58. *The Master and Margarita* (Mikhail Bulgakov)
59. *Tales of the City* (Armistead Maupin)
60. *The French Lieutenant's Woman* (John Fowles)
61. *Captain Corelli's Mandolin* (Louis de Bernières)
62. *Slaughterhouse 5* (Kurt Vonnegut)
63. *A Room with a View* (E. M. Forster)
64. *Lucky Jim* (Kingsley Amis)
65. *It* (Stephen King)
66. *The Power and the Glory* (Graham Greene)
67. *The Stand* (Stephen King)
68. *All Quiet on the Western Front* (Erich Maria Remarque)
69. *Paddy Clarke Ha Ha Ha* (Roddy Doyle)
70. *American Psycho* (Bret Easton Ellis)
71. *Lady Chatterley's Lover* (D. H. Lawrence)
72. *The Bonfire of the Vanities* (Tom Wolfe)
73. *The Rainbow* (D. H. Lawrence)
74. *2001: A Space Odyssey* (Arthur C. Clarke)
75. *The Tin Drum* (Günter Grass)
76. *One Day in the Life of Ivan Denisovich* (Alexander Solzhenitsyn)
77. *Jurassic Park* (Michael Crichton)
78. *The Alexandria Quartet* (Lawrence Durrell)
79. *Cry the Beloved Country* (Alan Paton)
80. *High Fidelity* (Nick Hornby)
81. *The Van* (Roddy Doyle)
82. *Earthly Powers* (Anthony Burgess)
83. *I, Claudius* (Robert Graves)
84. *The Horse Whisperer* (Nicholas Evans)

Appendix 9
Which companies owned what imprints at the end of the twentieth century

Company	Imprint
Reed Elsevier	Butterworth
	Heinemann
	Charles Knight Publishing
	Ginn
	Mitchell Beazley
	Tolley
	Elsevier Science
Pearson	Penguin
	Viking
	Frederick Warne
	Simon & Schuster
	Meridian
	Michael Joseph
	Longman
	Addison Wesley Longman
News Corporation	HarperCollins
	Collins
	Flamingo
Thomson	Thomson Nelson
Bertelsman	Secker & Warburg
	Vintage
	Transworld
	Corgi
	Anchor
	Bantam
	Black Swan
	Random House
	Bodley Head
	Chatto & Windus
	Jonathan Cape
	Doubleday
	Mandarin

(Continued)

Company	Imprint
	Methuen
	Hutchinson
Holtzbrinck	Macmillan
	Macmillan Heinemann ELT
	Sidgwick & Jackson
	Picador
	Pan
Orion	Weidenfeld & Nicolson
	Orion
	Phoenix
	Cassell
Hodder Headline	Hodder & Stoughton
	New English Library
	Headline

Source: Key Note, 1999.

Appendix 10
Helena Blakemore, 'Gender Bias in Publishing and Reviewing'*

The first survey into gender bias in reviewing was carried out in 1985 by Women in Publishing, a group dedicated to 'promoting the status . . . of women in the industry'. Their findings clearly indicated that only about 30 per cent of general reviewing was undertaken by women for the top twenty-one publications aimed at a broad readership. A second, but much smaller study was carried out in 1992 on behalf of Women in Management in Publishing [WiMP], with the specific aim of updating the earlier survey and discovering if bias against women writers was still apparent in the book pages of the national press. The study monitored seventeen national daily, Sunday and mid-market newspapers from 1 September to 15 December 1991, and books published by twenty-one major trade publishers. The resulting report was produced in February 1992. The three main points raised in the report can be summarised as follows:

1. Sex of reviewer: 65% male
                                      23% female
                                      12% unknown

2. Sex of author: 73% male
                                      24% female
                                      3% unknown

3. In nearly half the newspapers monitored, less than 20% of the reviews were written by women.

The trends revealed by the research carried out for WiMP reinforced this view. It was found, for example, that in general men were nearly three times more likely to review male fiction and nearly five times more likely to review male non-fiction than were women. There was also a distinct tendency for women to review female authors, and even where there was a relatively high proportion of reviews of books by women authors (such as 31 per cent in *The Sunday Times*), only 14 per cent of the reviews were by women.

Perhaps all that can be surmised from this is that women as both authors and reviewers were under-represented in the media: Liz Calder (Publishing Director, Bloomsbury Publishing Ltd and member of WiMP) commented that, 'the report

* Information compiled from the following sources: Quentin Oates, *Bookseller*, 22 May 1992; Women in Publishing (eds), *Reviewing the Reviewers: A Woman's Place in the Book Pages* (London: Journeyman Press, 1987); Joanna Luke and Dianne Stratton, 'Investigation into the Representation of Women Authors and Reviewers on the Book Pages of Quality and Mid-market Newspapers' (unpublished paper).

seems to confirm one's gut instinct that what appeared to be paranoia isn't. In this respect, the findings might make people act a little more carefully.' However, seen in the context of a professional world where the 'rules' were not fixed but were the result of a chiefly uncontested and unexamined concurrence of standards, these results do display evidence that the precepts and criteria being used could be prejudiced. By extension, they also suggest what the possible consequences might be: if book reviews, as a component of marketing and publicity, did in fact lead either directly (via the reader) or indirectly (via the bookseller) to book sales, then certain groups of writers were significantly under-represented and accordingly, in commercial terms, they were failing to secure – or were being denied the opportunity to achieve – their proportionate share of the market.

Not surprisingly, there were strong reactions to these reports. Quentin Oates in the *Bookseller*, for example, referring to an article by David Sexton in the *Daily Telegraph*, remarked that, 'it is a pretty nonsensical aspect of "political correctness" to worry about the sex of a reviewer. Surely, the only criterion should be the best person for the job.' Whilst it would be utterly untrue to suggest that qualified female critics did not exist, it was rarely disputed that there were fewer of them and that a more concerted effort was therefore required to seek them out. Undoubtedly, however, there were those with vested interests in maintaining existing standards by denying the need to change them and hence to make that effort. Suggesting that 'the only criterion should be the best person for the job' implied that the current system was inherently fair and meritocratic – it could only be so if the system was equally accessible to everyone, which it was not.

Appendix 11
From the *Bookseller* (Web page: 20 Dec. 1999)

It was only a matter of time before Internet booksellers began giving books away free. Last week's offer of free books from Bol.com was only the latest wheeze in an Internet price war that is as gripping as it is alarming. In the space of just two hours www.uk.bol.com gave away 20,000 books at a cost of more than £100,000. In return, it got 40,000 book buyers to register their e-mail addresses, and lengthy articles in at least two national newspapers. In terms of marketing spend it was a cheap deal.

The genesis of this latest battle for market share on the Internet can be dated back to May this year, when US Internet bookseller Amazon.com pushed the discounts it offered on *New York Times* bestsellers up from 40% to 50%. The move was immediately followed by Barnesandnoble.com and Borders.com as a tidal wave of escalating discounts swept across the US.

According to Rick Latham, managing director of W. H. Smith, WHS Online (which includes the Internet Bookshop), Amazon.com's move was not 'mould-breaking', the Internet Bookshop had discounted Terry Pratchett's *Carpe Jugulum* (Doubleday) at 50% last Christmas and Alphabetstreet.com started discounting bestsellers at 50% in March. But if Amazon.com did not break the mould, it certainly swept away the pieces, and it did not take long for UK Internet booksellers to follow the lead set by their cousins across the pond.

WHS Online (which relaunched officially in April) and its subsidiary the Internet Bookshop were the first to move, boosting the discount on bestselling hardbacks from 40% to 50% at the beginning of June, two weeks after Amazon.com's increase.

Barely a week later both Amazon.co.uk and Bol.com announced similar strategies as the pricing war hit UK based Internet sites. One week on and Bol.com trumped everyone when it announced a summer promotion with paperback bestsellers such as Lisa Jewell's *Ralph's Party* (Penguin) and Ian McEwan's Booker winning *Amsterdam* (Vintage) priced at £2, or, in some cases, a discount of 70%. WHS Online retaliated in mid-July with an offer of an extra 10% discount on all of its 1.4 million titles until 11th August. This pushed the discount on its bestselling hardbacks and summer reading titles to 60%.

Publisher reaction to this has, so far, been minimal. As managing director of Amazon.com Simon Murdoch points out, it is the Internet booksellers that are taking the hit, with publishers enjoying increased sales and, in some cases, increased publicity as a result of the booksellers' sacrifice.

But the furore which erupted around Thomas Harris's novel *Hannibal* (W. M. Heinemann), which was heavily discounted both online and offline, has raised fears about the sense and long-term viability of such pricing strategies, even if they are limited to a small selection of bestselling or specially promoted titles.

Internet booksellers argue that these short-term promotions on a minority of titles are about buying market share and encouraging book buyers to use the Internet. But as the size of the market grows so will its influence on the traditional book trade, with discounting likely to become a serious issue faced by all booksellers.

The Internet book market was thought to be worth about £30 million in 1998 (roughly the size of two Foyles bookshops or one small chain), but with increasing numbers using the Web, and growing confidence in virtual shopping, predictions that over the next five years the Internet will account for between 15% and 20% of the book market do not seem that far fetched. The fact is that nobody knows how fast it is going to grow, but estimates that suggest Internet book sales could be worth as much as £600m by 2003 are probably not far off the mark.

If this proves true, then, as Sridhar Gowda, owner of the small independent bookshop Country Bookstore, which operates its own Website (countrybookstore.co.uk), argues, traditional booksellers will need to be active on the Net. If they are not, they will risk seeing their market share eroded, as has already happened in the face of competition from supermarkets and book superstores.

There are suggestions that this is already happening. According to Whitaker BookTrack, the general retail market (which includes high street booksellers, independents and supermarkets) has fallen marginally in the first half of this year when compared to last year, with sales in the first six months of 1991 of £331.7m against £333.5m last year. It is difficult to imagine that the Internet is not a factor in this.

But if traditional booksellers do decide to compete in this arena, what strategy can they employ? The challenge they must face is at what level they will need to discount to compete with Internet booksellers. How will this affect pricing in their offline store? How should the traditional retailers react when bestsellers are used as loss-leaders by retailers who are more interested in market share than profit, and who have deeper pockets than most bricks and mortar booksellers?

Publishers face a completely different set of questions. As Internet bookselling grows, so too will its influence on publishers' trade terms. There has already been some resistance to Amazon.co.uk's efforts to move to direct supply, but in the long term it is inevitable. With WHS Online backed by W. H. Smith, the UK's largest bookseller, and Bol.com part of Bertelsmann, one of the largest media groups in the world, it will be difficult for publishers to hold firm on terms.

It is inevitable that Internet booksellers will not want to continue funding their discounts alone. Special promotions on the high street already receive special terms from publishers and this model could easily transfer to the Internet.

It could be said that a sustainable business model for selling books on the Internet has not yet been discovered and, ultimately, discounts will be clawed back, although no one spoken to in relation to this article seemed to imagine that this was a possibility in the short term.

If the business model for Internet bookselling retains its current form then it may only be a matter of time before the whole industry starts taking the hit for the unprofitable discounts that the consumer has now been educated to expect. If this is the case, it is almost exactly what the industry feared would happen after the demise of the Net Book Agreement. More books may be being sold but at cheaper prices meaning, inevitably, less investment in the future for new authors and ultimately less range.

On the other hand, the Internet and Internet booksellers have helped to create a 'buzz' about books that is unparalleled in recent publishing history. A bookseller, Amazon.com, is the leading e-commerce company in the world. Rather than being pushed into the background by new technologies, the written word has emerged as central to the e-revolution. The industry, authors, booksellers, publishers, ignore this at their peril.

Appendix 12
Comparative paperback bestseller lists showing relative change over the last decade of the twentieth century

1992
1. Jilly Cooper (Br)
2. Jeffrey Archer (Br)
3. Wilbur Smith (SA)
4. Frederick Forsyth (Br)
5. Barbara Taylor Bradford (Br)
6. Catherine Cookson (Br)
7. Catherine Cookson (Br)
8. Dick Francis (Br)
9. Stephen King (US)
10. Tom Clancy (US)
11. Danielle Steel (US)
12. Sidney Sheldon (US)
13. Danielle Steel (US)
14. Judith Krantz (US)
15. Len Deighton (Br)
16. John Grisham (US)
17. Jean Auel (US)
18. Stephen Fry (Br)
19. Ken Follett (Br)
20. Ben Elton (Br)
21. Jack Higgins (Br)
22. Joanna Trollope (Br)
23. Rosamunde Pilcher (Br)

1999
1. Maeve Binchy (IR)
2. John Grisham (US)
3. Patricia Cornwell (US)
4. Nick Hornby (Br)
5. Tom Clancy (US)
6. Danielle Steel (US)
7. Danielle Steel (US)
8. Jeffrey Archer (Br)
9. Catherine Cookson (Br)
10. Robert Harris (Br)
11. Stephen King (US)
12. Nicholas Evans (Br)
13. Danielle Steel (US)
14. Sidney Sheldon (US)
15. Sebastian Faulks (Br)
16. James Patterson (US)
17. Dick Francis (Br)
18. Terry Pratchett (Br)
19. Catherine Cookson (Br)
20. Patricia Cornwell (US)

Source: Writers' and Artists' Yearbook, 2001.

Joanna Trollope, Josephine Cox, Ruth Rendell and P. D. James all narrowly missed top-twenty status. Removing authors who entered the list for one book or for special reasons (after the award of a literary prize) leaves a remarkably conservative result. Readers' tastes and publishers' instincts remain static for long periods.

Appendix 13
World Book Day 2000 Poll to find Britain's favourite writers

World Book Day 2000 was part of a continuing UNESCO project to foster reading awareness amongst children. It was sponsored in the United Kingdom by Harper-Collins and carried out by public relations company Coleman Getty on behalf of Book Marketing Ltd. Over 4,000 bookshops and libraries were polled to find Britain's favourite writers. It is not surprising that Roald Dahl and J. K. Rowling (both children's writers) headed the list, nor that they were followed by Terry Pratchett (who appeals to both younger and older readers). Discounting these writers (as well as Jane Austen who polled seventh, Dickens who polled thirteenth and Shakespeare who came in at number 50 on the original list), the following authors represented the most famous fiction writers for adults at the Millennium.

1. Catherine Cookson	18. Iain Banks
2. Maeve Binchy	19. Jack Higgins
3. Dick Francis	20. Mary Higgins Clark
4. Stephen King	21. Anne McCaffrey
5. Danielle Steel	22. Ellis Peters
6. J. R. R. Tolkien	23. Ian Rankin
7. Wilbur Smith	24. Sebastian Faulks
8. Patricia Cornwell	25. Tom Clancy
9. John Grisham	26. Barbara Erskine
10. Josephine Cox	27. Margaret Forster
11. Rosamunde Pilcher	28. Dean Koontz
12. Bernard Cornwell	29. George Orwell
13. Agatha Christie	30. Graham Greene
14. Joanna Trollope	31. James Patterson
15. Patrick O'Brian	32. Colin Forbes
16. Georgette Heyer	33. P. G. Wodehouse
17. Ruth Rendell	34. Colin Dexter

Notes

Notes to Chapter 1: Origins, Problems and Philosophy of the Bestseller

1. Bram Stoker, quoted in Richard Dolby, 'Hall Caine', *The Bram Stoker Society Journal*, no. 11 (1999), p. 24.
2. Thomas F. G. Coates and R. S. Warren-Bell, *Marie Corelli: The Writer and the Women* (London: Hutchinson, 1903), p. 264.
3. Robert Calasso, *The Ruin of Kasch*, tr. William Weaver and Stephen Sartarelli (London: Vintage, 1994), p. 16.
4. Ibid.
5. Ibid.
6. Ibid.
7. Ibid.
8. Ibid., p. 40.
9. George MacDonald Fraser, quoted in *Million*, no. 2 (Mar.–Apr. 1991), pp. 6–7.

Notes to Chapter 2: How the British Read

1. Augustus D. Webb, *The New Dictionary of Statistics* (London: Routledge and Sons, 1911).
2. Charles Jeffries, *Illiteracy. A World Problem* (London: Pall Mall, 1967), p. 6.
3. Cyril Burt, 'The Education of Illiterate Adults', in *British Journal of Educational Psychology*, vol. 15 (1945), p. 21.
4. See David Barton and Mary E. Hamilton, *Researching Literacy in Industrialised Countries: Trends and Prospects* (Lancaster: Lancaster University/UNESCO, 1990).
5. See Anon., *A Right to Read: Action for a Literate Britain* (London: British Association for Settlements, 1974).
6. Greg Brooks, 'What national surveys tell us about performance in reading', on the National Library Trust Database website (Oct. 1999).
7. Information from 'Reading Habits in the UK', on the National Literacy Trust Database website (Oct. 1999); Anon., *Adult Literacy in Britain* (London: The Stationery Office, 1997); and Anon., *Literacy Skills for the Knowledge Society: Further Results from the International Adult Library Survey* (Paris: Organisation for Economic Co-operation and Development, 1997), quoted in Jennifer Wellman, unpublished research paper (South Bend: University of Notre Dame, 1999).
8. Ibid., p. 21.
9. Information from 'Most Borrowed Authors and Books', on the Public Lending Right Database website (Oct. 1999).
10. See Anon., *Attitudes towards Reading: A Report* (London: National Literacy Trust, 1998), p. 19. These figures are obviously contradicted by the sugges-

tion in the *Moser Report* (1999) that at least 23 per cent of Britons may be illiterate, a suggestion repeated in the *Daily Telegraph* two years later (10 Feb. 2001). The *Evening Standard* (25 Mar. 1999) claimed that '7 million adults can't read'. The ability to read *at all* is different from a low level of reading capability, at which level many such people operate (there is, of course, no absolute measure of competence). The extreme variations of measurement suggest difficulties inherent in testing and monitoring and in experimental expectations.

11. John Conston, quoted in Joseph McAleer, *Popular Reading and Publishing in Britain, 1914–1950* (Oxford: Clarendon Press, 1992), p. 87.
12. Clive Bloom (ed.), *Literature and Culture in Modern Britain, 1900 to 1929* (Harlow: Longman, 1996), p. 123.
13. McAleer, *Popular Reading and Publishing*, p. 64.
14. Edith Thompson and her lover Frederick Bywaters were convicted during 1922 for the murder of her husband. Despite pleas for clemency Edith was hanged. The case became one of the most celebrated and notorious in British criminal history, not least because of the erotic and romantic nature of Edith's diaries, her 'novelistic' imagination and the combination of these with her lower middle-class origins.
15. Bloom, *Literature and Culture, 1900 to 1929*, p. 134.
16. Clive Bloom, *Literature, Politics and Cultural Confusion in Britain Today* (Basingstoke: Palgrave Macmillan, 2000), p. 201.
17. Clive Bloom and Gary Day (eds), *Literature and Culture in Modern Britain, 1956 to 1999* (Harlow: Addison Wesley/Longman, 1999), p. 126.
18. Kristina Zurcher, unpublished research paper (South Bend: University of Notre Dame, 1999).
19. *Bookseller*, Jan. 1951.
20. Ibid., Feb. 1953.
21. Zurcher, unpublished paper.
22. *Bookseller*, Aug. 1957.
23. Ibid., Oct. 1961.
24. Ibid., Aug. 1961.
25. Amy Cruse, *The Victorians and Their Books* (London: Allen and Unwin, 1935), p. 315.
26. See 'Reading Habits in the UK' (National Library Trust, Oct. 1955).
27. See 'Most Borrowed Authors and Books' (Public Lending Right, Oct. 1999).
28. Mass Observation Archive, no. 782 'US13' (26/4/1940), p. 124.
29. Ibid., p. 125.
30. Ibid., p. 125.
31. Ibid., pp. 125–6.
32. Ibid., p. 127.
33. Ibid., p. 128.
34. Ibid., p. 129.
35. Chris Smith, quoted in the *Evening Standard*, 3 Feb. 2000.
36. John Feather, *A History of British Publishing* (London: Routledge, 1988), p. 137.
37. J. A. Sutherland, *Fiction and the Fiction Industry* (London: Athlone Press, 1978), p. xxi.

38. Ibid., p. xxi.
39. Elyce Deeb, quoted in Clive Bloom, *Literature, Politics and Cultural Confusion in Britain Today*, p. 73.
40. Christina Foyle, quoted in the *Bookseller*, May 1953.
41. S. H. Steinberg, *Five Hundred Years of Printing* (Harmondsworth: Penguin, 1955), p. 255.
42. Ibid., p. 256.
43. *Bookseller*, March 1920.
44. Ibid., [no month] 1923.
45. Ibid., March 1940.
46. Sutherland, *Fiction and the Fiction Industry*, p. 5.
47. Christina Foyle, quoted in the *Bookseller*, March 1940.
48. Sutherland, *Fiction and the Fiction Industry*, p. x.
49. Ibid., p. xi.
50. Michael Grant, *Penguin's Progress* (Harmondsworth: Penguin, 1960), p. 20.
51. *Bookseller*, Dec. 1957.
52. Ibid., Oct. 1969.
53. Ibid., July 1969.
54. Ibid.
55. *Guardian*, 31 Jan. 1976, in Sutherland, *Fiction and the Fiction Industry*, pp. 12–13.
56. *Bookseller*, March 1994.
57. Ibid.
58. Ibid.
59. *Guardian*, 7 March 1992.
60. As early as April 1968 the *Bookseller* had noted the importance of computerisation to book trade work, first used by the Greater London Council when ordering using IBM computers.
61. *Key Note*, p. 47.
62. In 1994 only Dillons and Hammicks opposed the NBA (see *Bookseller*, Sept. 1974).
63. *Bookseller*, Dec. 1998.
64. *Key Note*, p. 6.
65. Ibid.

Notes to Chapter 3: Genre: History and Form

1. Anon., *The Life of Florence L. Barclay: A Study in Personality* (London: G. P. Putnam's Sons, 1921), p. 240.
2. Ibid., pp. 242–3.
3. Ibid., p. 24.
4. Ibid., p. 310.
5. Robert Graves and Alan Hodge, *The Long Week-End: A Social History of Great Britain, 1918–1939* (London: Hutchinson, [1940] 1985).
6. For an explicit commentary on European fascism, see Rex Warner, *The Aerodrome* (1941). The first novelistic reference to fascism in Britain seems to be in Bruce Graeme, *Blackshirt* (1925).
7. *Bookseller*, June 1955.

8. Martin J. Wiener, *English Culture and the Decline of the Industrial Spirit, 1850–1950* (Cambridge: Cambridge University Press, 1981), p. 102.
9. Joseph McAleer, 'Scenes from Love and Marriage: Mills and Boon and the Popular Publishing Industry in Britain, 1908–1950', in *Twentieth Century British History*, vol. 1, no. 3 (1990), p. 267.
10. Ibid., p. 270.
11. Ibid., p. 272.
12. George Paizis, 'Love and the Novel: The Poetics and Politics of Romantic Love' (unpublished manuscript), p. 17.
13. Ibid., p. 1.
14. Ibid.

Chapter 4: The Best-Selling Authors of the Twentieth Century

1. Anon., *Life of Florence L. Barclay: A Study in Personality* (London: G. P. Putnam's Sons, 1921), p. 240.
2. David Pringle, *Imaginary People* (Aldershot: Scolar Press, 1996), p. 105.
3. Rosemary Herbert, *Oxford Companion to Crime and Mystery Writers* (New York: Oxford University Press, 2000), p. 1113.
4. Vivien Allen, 'Hall Caine: Prince of Romantic Novelists', *Million*, no. 8 (March–April 1992), p. 44.
5. John Lucas, in Lesley Henderson, *Twentieth Century Romantic and Historical Writers* (London: St James, 1990), p. 283.
6. Brian Stableford, 'Yesterday's Bestsellers: Robert Hichens and *The Garden of Allah*', *Million*, no. 3 (May–June 1992), pp. 50–1.
7. Pringle, *Imaginary People*, p. 213.
8. Penelope Dell, *Nettie and Sissie: A Biography of Bestselling Novelist Ethel M. Dell and her Sister Ella* (London: Hamish Hamilton, 1977), pp. xiii–xiv.
9. Henderson, *Twentieth Century Romantic and Historical Writers*, p. 365.
10. Mary Hicken and Ray Prytherch, *Now Read On: A Guide to Contemporary Popular Fiction* (Aldershot: Gower, 1990).
11. *Times Literary Supplement*, 18 January 1957.
12. Christopher Wordsworth, quoted in *Million*, no. 7 (Jan.–Feb. 1992), p. 9.
13. Karen Lorenz and Annie Thompson, research paper (unpublished).
14. *Times Literary Supplement*, September 1957.
15. Herbert, *Oxford Companion to Crime and Mystery Writers*, p. 978.
16. Pringle *Imaginary People*, pp. 63–4.
17. Jackie Collins, quoted on Web page: www.romwell.com.
18. D. L. Kirkpatrick (ed.), *Contemporary Novelists* (London: St James, 1972), p. 585.
19. Quoted in Richard Joseph, *Bestsellers: Top Writers Tell How* (Chichester: Summersdale, 1998), p. 152.
20. Catherine Cookson, *Catherine Cookson Country: Her Pictorial Memory* (London: Heinemann, 1986), p. 30.
21. Quoted in Clive Bloom, *Gothic Horror: A Guide from Poe to Stephen King* (Basingstoke: Palgrave Macmillan, 1998), pp. 96–7.

22. Judith Krantz, Internet home page.
23. Wendy Bradley, 'Judith Krantz', *Million*, no, 2 (March–April 1991), p. 31.
24. Shirley Chew, in D. L. Kirkpatrick, *Contemporary Novelists* (London and Chicago: St James, 1986) p. 728.
25. Hicken and Prytherch, *Now Read On*, p. 26.

Bibliography

Anon., *An Almanac for the Year of Our Lord 1963* (London: J. Whitaker and Sons, 1963).

——, *A Right to Read: Action for a Literate Britain* (London: British Association of Settlements, 1974).

——, *Attitudes towards Reading: A Report* (London: MORI Social Research, 1998).

——, *Books and the Consumer, 1989–1997* (London: Book Marketing Ltd, 1997).

——, *Book Sales Yearbook* (London: Whitaker Business Publishing, 1999).

——, *Borrowing Books*, BNBRF Report 59 (London: Book Marketing Ltd, 1992).

——, *British Businessman Readership Survey* (London: MIL Research Ltd, 1971).

——, 'Children's Books: PLR Estimates of Public Library Borrowing, 1985–1996', *Register of Public Lending Right* (Stockton-on-Tees: S. D. Print).

——, *Getting to Know Britain* (London: HMSO, 1998).

——, *Heavy Book Borrowers: A Report of the Leisure Habits of Key Library Users* (London: Book Marketing Ltd, 1996).

——, *The Hulton Readership Survey, 1948–1955* (London: Hulton Press).

——, *Key Note Market Report: Book Publishing* (London: Key Note, 1999).

——, *The Library User*, BNBRF Report 68 (London: Book Marketing Ltd, 1994).

——, *Life of Florence L. Barclay: A Study in Personality* (London: G. P. Putnam's Sons, 1921).

——, *LISU Annual Library Statistics* (Loughborough: Loughborough University Press, 1997).

——, *Literacy Skills for the Knowledge Society: Further Results from the International Adult Literacy Survey* (Paris: Organisation for Economic Co-operation and Development, 1997).

——, *Mintel Marketing Intelligence: Books* (May 1999).

——, 'Most Borrowed Authors in UK Public Libraries, 1983–1996', *Register of Public Lending Right* (Stockton-on-Tees: S. D. Print).

——, 'Most Borrowed Non-Fiction, 1991–1996', *Register of Public Lending Right* (Stockton-on-Tees: S. D. Print).

——, *Penguin's Progress, 1935–1960* (Harmondsworth: Penguin, 1960).

——, *Public and Specialist Libraries*, BLRDD Report 6203 (London: Book Marketing Ltd, 1995).

——, 'Registered Loans by Category, 1988/89–1995/96', *Register of Public Lending Right* (Stockton-on-Tees: S. D. Print).

——, *Sixpenny Wonders* (London: Chatto and Windus/Hogarth Press, 1985).

——, *Story of W. H. Smith and Sons* (London: W. H. Smith and Sons, 1955).

——, 'Trends in Library Borrowing, 1995–1996', *Register of Public Lending Right* (Stockton-on-Tees: S. D. Print).

——, *Yearbook for the Scottish Newsagent, Bookseller and Stationer* (1954).

——, *Writers' and Artists' Year Book* (London: A. & C. Black, 2001).

Athenaeum, 10/6/11.

Bainbridge, Cyril and Roy Stockdill, *The News of the World Story: 150 Years: 1843–1993* (London: HarperCollins, 1993).

Barker, Martin, *A Haunt of Fears: The Strange History of the British Horror Comics Campaign* (London: Pluto, 1984).

Barton, David and Mary E. Hamilton, *Researching Literacy in Industrialised Countries: Trends and Prospects* (Lancaster: University of Lancaster Press/UNESCO Institute for Education, 1990).

Binyon, T. J., *Murder will Out: The Detective in Fiction* (Oxford: Oxford University Press, 1989).

Blackwell, Basil, *The Nemesis of the Net Book Agreement* (London: Society of Bookmen, 1933).

Blair, Virginia, Patricia Clements and Isobel Grundy (eds), *The Feminist Companion to Literature in England* (London: Batsford, 1990).

Bloom, Clive, *Cult Fiction* (Basingstoke: Palgrave Macmillan, 1996).

——, *Gothic Horror: A Reader's Guide from Poe to King and Beyond* (Basingstoke: Palgrave Macmillan, 1998).

——, *Literature, Politics and Intellectual Crisis in Britain Today* (Basingstoke: Palgrave Macmillan, 2001).

The Bookseller, 1911–1999 inclusive.

Boyle, Thomas, *Black Swine in the Sewers of Hampstead* (London: Hodder and Stoughton, 1990).

Bram Stoker Society Journal, no. 11, 1999.

Brooks, Greg, *What National Surveys Tell us about Performance in Reading* (National Literacy Trust: Web database, 1999).

Burt, Cyril, 'The Education of Illiterate Adults', in *British Journal of Educational Psychology*, vol. 15 (1945).

Butler, Lawrence and Harriet Jones (eds), *Britain in the Twentieth Century, 1900–1939* (Oxford: Heinemann, 1994).

Calasso, Roberto, *The Ruin of Kasch* (London: Vintage, 1995).

Cawelti, John G., *Adventure, Mystery and Romance* (Chicago: University of Chicago Press, 1976).

Chapell, Warren, *A Short History of the Printed Word* (London: André Deutsch 1972).

Chevalier, Tracey (ed.), *Twentieth-Century Children's Writers*, 3rd edition (London: St James Press, 1989).

Christie, Agatha, *Agatha Christie: An Autobiography* (London: Fontana, 1978).

Church, Jenny (ed.), *Social Trends*, vols 23–7 (London: The Stationery Office, 1993–7).

Clure, Maggie, Gary Day and Chris Maguire, 'Decline or Fall? The Course of the Novel', in Gary Day (ed.), *Literature and Culture in Modern Britain, 1930–1955* (Harlow: Addison Wesley/Longman, 1997).

Coates, T. E. G. and R. S. Warren-Bell, *Marie Corelli: The Writer and the Woman* (London: Hutchinson and Co., 1903).

Cockburn, Claud, *Bestseller: The Books that Everyone Read, 1900–1939* (London: Sidgwick and Jackson, 1972).

Cook, Lez, 'British Cinema: Class, Culture and Consensus, 1935–55', in Gary Day (ed.), *Literature and Culture in Modern Britain* (Harlow: Longman, 1998).

Cookson, Catherine, *Our Kate* (London: McDonald and Co., [1969] 1982).

Curren, Peter J., *The UK Publishing Industry* (Oxford: Pergamon Press, 1981).

David, Hugh, *The Fitzrovians: A Portrait of Bohemian Society, 1900–1955* (London: Sceptre, 1988).

Dell, Penelope, *Nettie and Cissie: A Biography of Bestselling Novelist Ethel M. Dell and her Sister Ella* (London: Hamish Hamilton, 1977).

Dent, J. M., *The Memoirs of J. M. Dent, 1849–1926* (London: Dent, 1928).

Doran, George H., *Chronicles of Barabas, 1884–1934* (London: Methuen, 1935).

Dudgen, Piers, *The Girl from Leam Lane: The Life and Writings of Catherine Cookson* (London: Headline, 1997).

Eliot, Andrew George, *Who's Who and What's What in Publishing* (Liverpool: C. Tinling, 1960).

Emery, Charles D., *Buyers and Borrowers: The Application of Consumer Theory to the Study of Library Use* (New York: Haworth Press, 1993).

England, Len, *The Library User: The Reading Habits and Attitudes of Public Library Users in Great Britain*, BNBRF Report 68 (London: Book Marketing Ltd, 1994).

——, and John Sumsion, *Perspectives of Public Library Use* (Loughborough: Loughborough University Press, 1997).

Evans, Hilary and Dik Evans, *Beyond the Gaslight* (London: Muller, 1976).

Faber, Gilbert, *The Romance of a Bookshop, 1904–1934* (private publication, 1938).

Feather, John, *A History of British Publishing* (London: Routledge, 1988).

Flanagan, Maurice, *British Gangster and Exploitation Paperbacks of the Postwar Years*, vol. 2 (Westbury: Zardoz Books, 1997).

Fountain, Nigel, *Underground: The London Alternative Press, 1966–1974* (London: Routledge, 1988).

Goodwin, Cliff, *To Be a Lady: A Biography of Catherine Cookson* (London: Century, 1994).

Graham, Judith (ed.), *Current Biography Year Book* (New York: H. W. Wilson, 1994).

Graves, Robert and Alan Hodge, *The Long Week-End: A Social History of Great Britain, 1918–1939* (London: Hutchinson, [1940] 1985).

Gross, Gerald (ed.), *Publishers on Publishing* (London: Secker and Warburg, 1961).

The Guardian, 20/8/90; 15/12/90; 1/1/91; 10/1/91; 12/1/91; 16/4/91; 15/5/91; 30/5/91; 13/6/91; 17/8/91; 15/10/91; 19/12/91; 4/1/92; 9/1/92; 17/1/92; 10/11/92; 29/3/94; 5/7/94; 20/8/94; 19/11/94; 10/1/95; 29/4/95; 19/5/95; 22/7/95; 22/9/95; 2/11/95; 22/4/96; 3/10/97; 25/10/99; 28/10/99.

Hackett, Alice Payne, *Sixty Years of Best Sellers, 1895–1955* (New York: R. R. Bowker, 1956).

——, and James Henry Burke, *80 Years of Bestsellers, 1895–1975* (New York: R. R. Bowker, 1977).

Haining, Peter, *The Penny Dreadful* (London: Gollancz, 1975).

——, *Murder at the Races* (London: Orion Books, 1996).

Hampden, John, *The Book World Today* (London: George Allen and Unwin, 1957).

Hare, Steve (ed.), *Penguin Portrait: Allen Lane and the Penguin Editors, 1935–1970* (Harmondsworth: Penguin, 1995).

Harraden, Beatrice, 'What Our Soldiers Read', *Cornhill Magazine*, vol. XLI (Nov. 1916).

Harrison, Stanley, *Poor Men's Guardians: A Survey of the Struggle for a Democratic Newspaper Press, 1763–1973* (London: Lawrence and Wishart, 1974).

Harrisson, Tom and Charles Madge, *Books and the Public* (Mass Observation, Feb. 1944, no. 2018).

——, *Reading in Tottenham* (Mass Observation, Nov. 1947, no. 2537).

——, *A Report on Penguin World* (Mass Observation, Dec. 1944, no. 2545).

Hart, James D., *The Popular Book* (Oxford: Oxford University Press, 1950).

Haycraft, Howard and Stanley J. Kunitz (eds), *Twentieth-Century Authors: A Biographical Dictionary* (New York: H. W. Wilson, 1992).

Henderson, Lesley (ed.), *Contemporary Novelists* (London: St James Press, 1991).

—— (ed.), *Twentieth-Century Romance and Historical Writers* (London: St James Press, 1990; 2nd edition, 1990; 3rd edition, 1991).

—— (ed.), *Twentieth Century Crime and Mystery Writers*, 3rd edition (Chicago: St James Press, 1991).

Herbert, Rosemary, *Oxford Companion to Crime and Mystery Writing* (New York: Oxford University Press, 1999).

Hicken, Mandy and Ray Prytherch, *Now Read On: A Guide to Contemporary Popular Fiction* (Aldershot: Gower, 1990).

Hodges, Sheila, *The Story of a Publishing House, 1928–1978* (London: Victor Gollancz, 1978).

Hoggart, Richard, *The Way We Live Now* (London: Chatto and Windus, 1995).

Holland, Steve, *The Mushroom Jungle: A History of Postwar Paperback Publishing* (Westbury: Zardoz Books, 1993).

Hollis, Patricia, *The Pauper Press: A Study in Working-Class Radicalism of the 1830s* (Oxford: Oxford University Press, 1970).

Hughes, Helen, *The Historical Romance* (London: Verso, 1987).

The Idler, vol. 4 (Aug. 1893–Jan. 1894).

The Independent, 28/3/90; 20/9/90; 18/2/91; 17/10/91; 6/10/91; 21/12/91; 31/12/91; 28/10/99; 8/12/99.

The Independent on Sunday, 17/11/91.

Isaac, Peter (ed.), *Six Centuries of the Provincial Book Trade in Britain* (Winchester: St Paul's Bibliographies, 1990).

Jeffries, Charles, *Illiteracy: A World Problem* (London: Pall Mall, 1967).

Jenkins, Henry, *Textual Poachers* (London: Routledge, 1992).

Johnson, Paul, *20th-Century Britain: Economic, Social and Cultural Change* (Harlow: Longman, 1994).

Jones, Stephen (ed.), *James Herbert – By Horror Haunted* (London: New English Library, nd).

—— and Kim Newman (eds), *Horror: 100 Best Books* (London: Hodder and Stoughton, 1992).

Joseph, Richard, *Bestsellers: Top Writers Tell How* (Chichester: Summersdale, 1998).

Keating, Peter, *The Haunted Study: A Social History of the English Novel, 1875–1914* (London: Secker and Warburg, 1989).

Kendall, Maurice (ed.), *The Source and Nature of Statistics of the United Kingdom* (London: Oliver and Boyd, 1952).

Kinnell, Margaret, *Managing Fiction in Libraries* (London: Library Association, 1991).

Kirkpatrick, D. L. (ed.), *Contemporary Novelists* (Chicago: St James Press, [1986] 1988).

Lee, Alan J., *The Origins of the Popular Press in England, 1855–1914* (London: Croom Helm, 1977).

Linklater, Andro, *Compton Mackenzie: A Life* (London: Chatto and Windus, 1987).

Livling, Edward, *Adventures in Publishing: The House of Ward Lock, 1854–1954* (London: Ward Lock, 1954).

Lowenthal, Leo, *Literature and Mass Culture* (New Brunswick: Transaction Books, 1984).

Macadam, Ivison (ed.), *The Annual Register of World Events: A Review of the Year 1961* (London: Longman, Green and Co., 1962).

——, *Review of the Year 1964.*

Matthews, John D., *Censored* (London: Chatto & Windus, 1994).

McAleer, Joseph, *Popular Reading and Publishing in Britain, 1914–1950* (Oxford: Clarendon Press, 1992).

——, 'Scenes from Love and Marriage: Mills and Boon and the Popular Publishing Industry in Britain, 1908–1950', in *Twentieth-Century British History*, vol. 1, no. 3 (1990).

Miss Read, *The World of Thrush Green* (London: Michael Joseph, 1988).

Monk, L. A., *Britain, 1945–1970* (London: G. Bell and Sons, 1976).

Morpurgo, J. E., *Allen Lane, King Penguin: A Biography* (London: Hutchinson, 1979).

Munfow, W. A., *Penny Rate: Aspects of British Public Library History, 1850–1950* (London: Library Association, 1951).

The Nation, 9/8/19.

New York Times, 12/8/90; 19/8/90; 3/9/90; 30/9/90; 14/10/90; 30/12/90; 30/12/90; 15/4/91; 1/5/91; 6/5/91; 26/5/91; 27/5/91; 6/10/93; 26/5/94; 1/8/94; 25/9/94; 2/10/94; 19/10/94; 19/2/95; 15/3/95; 6/4/95; 20/4/95; 4/9/95; 5/9/95; 8/10/95; 10/10/95; 16/10/95; 16/10/95; 17/4/96; 23/1/97; 28/2/97; 6/4/97; 15/4/97; 30/7/97; 20/10/97.

Nissel, Muriel, *Facts about the Arts: A Summary of Available Statistics* (London: Policy Studies Institute, 1983).

O'Brien, Geoffrey, *Hardboiled America: The Lurid Years of Paperbacks* (New York: Van Nostrand Reinhold, 1981).

The Obscene Publications Act (1964).

The Observer, 26/3/95; 2/4/95; 29/10/95; 31/12/95; 18/8/96; 24/10/97.

Ousby, Ian, *The Cambridge Guide to Literature in English* (Cambridge: Cambridge University Press, [1988] 1993).

Owen, Peter (ed.), *Publishing Now* (London: Peter Owen, 1993).

Paizis, George, 'Love and the Novel: The Poetics and Politics of Romantic Love' (unpublished manuscript).

Palmer, Jerry, *Potboilers: Methods, Concepts and Case Studies in Popular Fiction* (London: Routledge, 1992).

Pearson, John, *The Life of Ian Fleming, Creator of James Bond* (London: Jonathan Cape, 1966).

Peel, Gillian, *Governing the UK* (Oxford: Basil Blackwell, 1995).

Plant, Marjorie, *The English Book Trade: An Economic History of the Making and Sale of Books* (London: Allen Unwin, [1939] 1965).

Pringle, David, *Imaginary People*, 2nd edition (Aldershot: Scolar Press, 1996).

Radford, Jean (ed.), *The Progress of Romance* (London: Routledge and Kegan Paul, 1986).

Radway, Janice, *Reading the Romance* (London: Verso, 1987).

Raphael, Frederic, *Somerset Maughan* (London: Cardinal, 1989).

Reilly, John M. (ed.), *Twentieth Century Crime and Mystery Writers* (London: St James Press, 1985).

Richards, Jeffrey and Dorothy Sheridan, *Mass-Observation at the Movies* (London: Routledge, 1987).

Robyns, Gwen, *Barbara Cartland* (Poole, Dorset: Javelin Press, 1987).

Rolph, C. H., *The Trial of Lady Chatterley* (Harmondsworth: Penguin, 1990).

Rubin, Joan Shelley, *The Making of Middlebrow Culture* (Carolina: University of Carolina Press, 1992).

Ryan, A. P., *Lord Northcliffe* (London: Collins, 1953).

Sabin, Roger, *Adult Comics* (London: Routledge, 1994).

St John, John, *William Heinemann: A Century of Publishing* (London: Heinemann, 1990).

Sandler, Geoff (ed.), *Twentieth-Century Western Writers* (Chicago: St James Press, 1991).

Seymour-Smith, Martin (ed.), *Novels and Novelists: A Guide to the World of Fiction* (New York: Windward Press, 1980).

——, *16 Victorian Novelettes* (London: Wolfe, 1965).

Scott-Kilvert, Ian, *British Writers: Supplement 1* (New York: Scribner's, 1987).

Smith, Anthony, *The Newspapers: An International History* (London: Thames and Hudson, 1979).

Snoddy, Raymond, *The Good, the Bad and the Unacceptable: The Hard Facts about British Publishing* (London: Faber and Faber, 1992).

Steinberg, S. H., *Five Hundred Years of Printing* (Harmondsworth: Penguin, 1955).

Strand Magazine, Aug. 1906.

Street, Brian V., *Literacy in Theory and Practice* (Cambridge: Cambridge University Press, 1984).

Stubbs, Patricia, *Writers and their Work* (Harlow: Longman, 1973).

The Sunday Times, 1/1/53 to 1/1/54 inclusive; 1/9/63 to 30/12/63 inclusive; 30/11/69; 16/12/69.

Sutherland, John, *Bestsellers* (London: Routledge and Kegan Paul, 1981).

——, *Fiction and the Fiction Industry* (London: Athlone Press, 1978).

——, *Offensive Literature: Censorship in Britain, 1960–1982* (London: Junction Books, 1982).

Taylor, A. J. P., *English History, 1914–1945* (Harmondsworth: Penguin, 1965).

Taylor, D. J., *After the War: The Novel and England since 1945* (London: Flamingo, 1993).

Taylor, S. J., *Shock! Horror!* (London: Bantam Books, 1991).

Terry, R. C., *Victorian Popular Fiction, 1860–80* (London: Macmillan, 1983).

The Times, 29/7/19; 1/1/53 to 20/1/54 inclusive; 26/3/69 to 25/7/69 inclusive; 1/1/73 to 25/12/73 inclusive.

The Times Literary Supplement, 7/9/51; 4/11/51; 7/12/51; 4/1/74.

Todd, Janet (ed.), *Dictionary of British Women Writers* (London: Routledge, 1989).

Todd, Richard, *Consuming Fictions: The Booker Prize and Fiction in Britain Today* (London: Bloomsbury, 1996).

The Trade Circular, 9/7/38; 5/11/49.

Trotter, David, *The English Novel in History, 1895–1920* (London: Routledge, 1993).

Truman, Myron, *Word Perfect: Literacy in the Computer Age* (London: Palmer Press, 1992).

Truth, 22/1/13.

Turner, E. S., *Boys Will be Boys* (Harmondsworth: Penguin, 1976).

Unwin, Philip, *The Publishing Unwins* (London: Heinemann, 1972).

——, *The Book in the Making* (London: Allen and Unwin, 1931).

Unwin, Stanley, *The Truth about Publishing* (London: Allen and Unwin, 1926).

Usborne, Richard, *Clubland Heroes* (London: Hutchinson, 1983).

Van Ash, Cay and Elizabeth Sax Rohmer, *Master of Villainy* (Bowling Green, Ohio: Popular Press, 1972).

Vasudevan, Aruna (ed.), *Twentieth-Century Romance and Historical Writers* (Chicago: St James Press, 1994).

Vincent, David, 'Reading in the Working-Class Home', in John K. Walton and James Walvin, *Leisure in Britain, 1780–1939* (Manchester: Manchester University Press, 1983).

Vinson, James (ed.), *Great Writers of the English Language* (Basingstoke: Macmillan, 1979).

Wakeman, John (ed.), *World Authors, 1950–1970* (New York: H. M. Wilson, 1979).

Warburg, Frederic, *An Occupation for Gentlemen* (London: Hutchinson, 1979).

Waters, Chris, *British Socialists and the Politics of Popular Culture, 1884–1914* (Manchester: Manchester University Press, 1990).

Waterstone's Booksellers, *Catalogue* (1999).

Watson, Colin, *Snobbery with Violence* (London: Methuen, 1987).

Waugh, Arthur, *A Hundred Years of Publishing: Being the Story of Chapman and Hall* (London: Chapman and Hall, 1930).

Webb, Augustus D., *The New Dictionary of Statistics: A Complement to the Fourth Edition of Mulhall's 'Dictionary of Statistics'* (London: George Routledge, 1911).

Wellman, Jennifer, 'Contemporary Literacy' (unpublished research paper).

Wiener, Martin J., *English Culture and the Decline of the Industrial Spirit, 1850–1980* (Cambridge: Cambridge University Press, 1981).

Williams, W. E., *Allen Lane: A Personal Portrait* (London: Bodley Head, 1973).

Winks, Robin W. (ed.), *Detective Fiction* (Englewood Cliffs, NJ: Prentice-Hall, 1980).

Wisniewski, Daniel (ed.), *Annual Abstract of Statistics* (London: Government Statistics Session, 1997).

Name Index

Page references in **bold** denote major reference

Subject Index

Title Index